YOUR CHINESE
HOROSCOPE 2004

NEIL SOMERVILLE

What the Year of the Monkey holds in store for you

TO ROS, RICHARD AND EMILY

Element
An Imprint of HarperCollins*Publishers*
77–85 Fulham Palace Road
Hammersmith, London W6 8JB

The website address is: www.thorsonselement.com

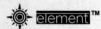 *element*™

and *Element* are trademarks of
HarperCollins*Publishers* Limited

Published by Element 2003

10 9 8 7 6 5 4 3 2 1

A catalogue record for this book
is available from the British Library

ISBN 0 00 714397 4

Printed and bound in Great Britain by
Clays Ltd, St Ives plc

CONTENTS

———◆·◆———

ABOUT THE AUTHOR

Neil Somerville is one of the leading writers in the West on Chinese horoscopes. He has been interested in Eastern forms of divination for many years and believes that much can be learned from the ancient wisdom of the East. His annual book on Chinese horoscopes has built up an international following and he is also the author of *What's Your Chinese Love Sign?* (Thorsons, 2000) and *Chinese Success Signs* (Thorsons, 2001).

Neil Somerville was born in the Year of the Water Snake. His wife was born under the sign of the Monkey, his son is an Ox and daughter a Horse.

ACKNOWLEDGEMENTS

———◆———

In writing *Your Chinese Horoscope 2004* I am grateful for
the assistance and support that those around me have
given.

I wish to acknowledge Theodora Lau's *The Handbook of
Chinese Horoscopes* (Harper & Row, 1979; Arrow, 1981),
which was particularly useful to me in my research.

In addition to Ms Lau's work, I commend the following
books to those who wish to find out more about Chinese
horoscopes: Kristyna Arcarti, *Chinese Horoscopes for
Beginners* (Headway, 1995); Catherine Aubier, *Chinese
Zodiac Signs* (Arrow, 1984), series of 12 books; E. A.
Crawford and Teresa Kennedy, *Chinese Elemental
Astrology* (Piatkus Books, 1992); Paula Delsol, *Chinese
Horoscopes* (Pan, 1973); Barry Fantoni, *Barry Fantoni's
Chinese Horoscopes* (Warner, 1994); Bridget Giles and the
Diagram Group, *Chinese Astrology* (Collins Gem,
HarperCollins*Publishers*, 1996); Kwok Man-Ho, *Authentic
Chinese Horoscopes* (Arrow, 1987), series of 12 books; Lori
Reid, *The Complete Book of Chinese Horoscopes* (Element
Books, 1997); Paul Rigby and Harvey Bean, *Chinese
Astrologics* (Publications Division, South China Morning
Post Ltd, 1981); Ruth Q. Sun, *The Asian Animal Zodiac*
(Charles E. Tuttle Company, Inc., 1996); Derek Walters,
Ming Shu (Pagoda Books, 1987) and *The Chinese*

Astrology Workbook (The Aquarian Press, 1988); Suzanne White, *Suzanne White's Book of Chinese Chance* (Fontana/Collins, 1978), *The New Astrology* (Pan, 1987) and *The New Chinese Astrology* (Pan, 1994).

———◆◆◆———

As we march into a new year
we each have our hopes, our ambitions and our dreams.

Sometimes fate and circumstance will assist us,
sometimes we will struggle and despair,
but march we must.

For it is those who keep going,
and who keep their aspirations alive,
who stand the greatest chance of securing what they want.

March determinedly,
and your determination will, in some way, be rewarded.

Neil Somerville

———◆◆◆———

INTRODUCTION

———•◦•———

The origins of Chinese horoscopes have been lost in the mists of time. It is known that Oriental astrologers practised their art many thousands of years ago and even today Chinese astrology continues to fascinate and intrigue.

In Chinese astrology there are 12 signs named after 12 different animals. No one quite knows how the signs acquired their names, but there is one legend that offers an explanation.

According to this legend, one Chinese New Year the Buddha invited all the animals in his kingdom to come before him. Unfortunately, for reasons best known to the animals, only 12 turned up. The first to arrive was the Rat, followed by the Ox, Tiger, Rabbit, Dragon, Snake, Horse, Goat, Monkey, Rooster, Dog and finally Pig.

In gratitude, the Buddha decided to name a year after each of the animals and that those born during that year would inherit some of the personality of that animal. Therefore those born in the Year of the Ox would be hardworking, resolute and stubborn, just like the Ox, while those born in the Year of the Dog would be loyal and faithful, just like the Dog. While not everyone can possibly share all the characteristics of a sign, it is incredible what similarities do occur and this is partly where the fascination of Chinese horoscopes lies.

In addition to the 12 signs of the Chinese zodiac there are also five elements, and these have a strengthening or moderating influence upon the sign. Details about the effects of the elements are given in each of the chapters on the 12 signs.

To find out which sign you were born under, refer to the tables on the following pages. As the Chinese year is based on the lunar year and does not start until late January or early February, it is particularly important for anyone born in those two months to check carefully the dates of the Chinese year in which they were born.

Also included, in the appendices, are two charts showing the compatibility between the signs for personal and business relationships, and details about the signs ruling the different hours of the day. From this it is possible to locate your ascendant and, as in Western astrology, this has a significant influence on your personality.

In writing this book, I have taken the unusual step of combining the intriguing nature of Chinese horoscopes with the Western desire to know what the future holds and have based my interpretations upon various factors relating to each of the signs. I have been pleased that over the years in which *Your Chinese Horoscope* has been published so many have found the sections on the forth-coming year of interest, and hope that the horoscope has been constructive and useful. Remember, though, that at all times you are the master of your own destiny. I sincerely hope that *Your Chinese Horoscope 2004* will prove interesting and helpful for the year ahead.

THE CHINESE YEARS

———◆————

Rabbit	29 January	1903	to	15 February	1904
Dragon	16 February	1904	to	3 February	1905
Snake	4 February	1905	to	24 January	1906
Horse	25 January	1906	to	12 February	1907
Goat	13 February	1907	to	1 February	1908
Monkey	2 February	1908	to	21 January	1909
Rooster	22 January	1909	to	9 February	1910
Dog	10 February	1910	to	29 January	1911
Pig	30 January	1911	to	17 February	1912
Rat	18 February	1912	to	5 February	1913
Ox	6 February	1913	to	25 January	1914
Tiger	26 January	1914	to	13 February	1915
Rabbit	14 February	1915	to	2 February	1916
Dragon	3 February	1916	to	22 January	1917
Snake	23 January	1917	to	10 February	1918
Horse	11 February	1918	to	31 January	1919
Goat	1 February	1919	to	19 February	1920
Monkey	20 February	1920	to	7 February	1921
Rooster	8 February	1921	to	27 January	1922
Dog	28 January	1922	to	15 February	1923
Pig	16 February	1923	to	4 February	1924
Rat	5 February	1924	to	23 January	1925
Ox	24 January	1925	to	12 February	1926
Tiger	13 February	1926	to	1 February	1927

Rabbit	2 February	1927	to	22 January	1928
Dragon	23 January	1928	to	9 February	1929
Snake	10 February	1929	to	29 January	1930
Horse	30 January	1930	to	16 February	1931
Goat	17 February	1931	to	5 February	1932
Monkey	6 February	1932	to	25 January	1933
Rooster	26 January	1933	to	13 February	1934
Dog	14 February	1934	to	3 February	1935
Pig	4 February	1935	to	23 January	1936
Rat	24 January	1936	to	10 February	1937
Ox	11 February	1937	to	30 January	1938
Tiger	31 January	1938	to	18 February	1939
Rabbit	19 February	1939	to	7 February	1940
Dragon	8 February	1940	to	26 January	1941
Snake	27 January	1941	to	14 February	1942
Horse	15 February	1942	to	4 February	1943
Goat	5 February	1943	to	24 January	1944
Monkey	25 January	1944	to	12 February	1945
Rooster	13 February	1945	to	1 February	1946
Dog	2 February	1946	to	21 January	1947
Pig	22 January	1947	to	9 February	1948
Rat	10 February	1948	to	28 January	1949
Ox	29 January	1949	to	16 February	1950
Tiger	17 February	1950	to	5 February	1951
Rabbit	6 February	1951	to	26 January	1952
Dragon	27 January	1952	to	13 February	1953
Snake	14 February	1953	to	2 February	1954
Horse	3 February	1954	to	23 January	1955
Goat	24 January	1955	to	11 February	1956
Monkey	12 February	1956	to	30 January	1957
Rooster	31 January	1957	to	17 February	1958

Dog	18 February	1958	to	7 February	1959
Pig	8 February	1959	to	27 January	1960
Rat	28 January	1960	to	14 February	1961
Ox	15 February	1961	to	4 February	1962
Tiger	5 February	1962	to	24 January	1963
Rabbit	25 January	1963	to	12 February	1964
Dragon	13 February	1964	to	1 February	1965
Snake	2 February	1965	to	20 January	1966
Horse	21 January	1966	to	8 February	1967
Goat	9 February	1967	to	29 January	1968
Monkey	30 January	1968	to	16 February	1969
Rooster	17 February	1969	to	5 February	1970
Dog	6 February	1970	to	26 January	1971
Pig	27 January	1971	to	14 February	1972
Rat	15 February	1972	to	2 February	1973
Ox	3 February	1973	to	22 January	1974
Tiger	23 January	1974	to	10 February	1975
Rabbit	11 February	1975	to	30 January	1976
Dragon	31 January	1976	to	17 February	1977
Snake	18 February	1977	to	6 February	1978
Horse	7 February	1978	to	27 January	1979
Goat	28 January	1979	to	15 February	1980
Monkey	16 February	1980	to	4 February	1981
Rooster	5 February	1981	to	24 January	1982
Dog	25 January	1982	to	12 February	1983
Pig	13 February	1983	to	1 February	1984
Rat	2 February	1984	to	19 February	1985
Ox	20 February	1985	to	8 February	1986
Tiger	9 February	1986	to	28 January	1987
Rabbit	29 January	1987	to	16 February	1988
Dragon	17 February	1988	to	5 February	1989

YOUR CHINESE HOROSCOPE 2004

Snake	6 February	1989	to	26 January	1990
Horse	27 January	1990	to	14 February	1991
Goat	15 February	1991	to	3 February	1992
Monkey	4 February	1992	to	22 January	1993
Rooster	23 January	1993	to	9 February	1994
Dog	10 February	1994	to	30 January	1995
Pig	31 January	1995	to	18 February	1996
Rat	19 February	1996	to	6 February	1997
Ox	7 February	1997	to	27 January	1998
Tiger	28 January	1998	to	15 February	1999
Rabbit	16 February	1999	to	4 February	2000
Dragon	5 February	2000	to	23 January	2001
Snake	24 January	2001	to	11 February	2002
Horse	12 February	2002	to	31 January	2003
Goat	1 February	2003	to	21 January	2004
Monkey	22 January	2004	to	8 February	2005

Note: The names of the signs in the Chinese zodiac occasionally differ in the various books on Chinese astrology, although the characteristics of the signs remain the same. In some books the Ox is referred to as the Buffalo or Bull, the Rabbit as the Hare or Cat, the Goat as the Sheep and the Pig as the Boar.

For the sake of convenience, the male gender is used throughout this book. Unless otherwise stated, the characteristics of the signs apply to both sexes.

WELCOME TO THE
YEAR OF THE MONKEY

Whether leaping from branch to branch, playing chase or sitting immersed in his own thoughts, there is something very compelling about the Monkey. He is entertaining to watch and keeps himself occupied. You never quite know what he is going to do next, and as the Chinese have so often said, anything can happen in a Monkey year. This one will certainly see some dramatic events.

The year will have its successes, and innovation and enterprise will be to the fore, but unfortunately there are more ominous aspects as well. Monkey years are notorious for their flash points and 2004 is unlikely to be an exception. The Hungarian revolution occurred in a Monkey year, as did the Suez crisis, the student riots in Paris, the escalation of the troubles in Northern Ireland and, in the last Monkey year, the Los Angeles riots and fighting in the Balkans. There will be tensions too in 2004 when certain factions and nationalities will rise up in protest about their situation. As a result, there will be times of political uncertainty, with peace-keeping organizations such as the United Nations often playing a pivotal role. Some of the year's events will have far-reaching implications. The Polish Solidarity movement which was to have such a marked effect on events in Eastern Europe was formed in a Monkey year, and 12 years ago South Africa held its historic referendum in favour of the ending of apartheid. The last Monkey year also saw the inauguration of the single European market and 2004 will bring a further expansion of the European Community, an event which is likely to be highly significant in the history of Europe.

The volatility of the year will have an effect on stock markets around the world, with dramatic swings being experienced. While at times the market will rally, investors will need to keep their wits about them and base their decisions on fact rather than emotion. Monkey years can cost the unwary dear. Investors, be careful.

It is also likely that the currency markets will be highly volatile, with certain currencies coming under pressure. In the last Monkey year the British pound sank to an all-time low and Black Wednesday occurred, a day that will be forever marked in the annals of British fiscal history.

Another grim feature of Monkey years is the number of assassinations that have taken place during them. These have included President Doumer of France, Martin Luther King, John Lennon, Senator Robert Kennedy, Archbishop Romero and, in the last Monkey year, the President of Algeria. While it is hoped that 2004 will be free from similar acts, the indications are not promising.

While some of the foregoing may have made sombre reading, the Monkey year does have its more promising aspects and 2004 will be marked by some major achievements. The Monkey year is very much one that pushes the boundaries in many different fields. In medicine it was in a Monkey year that the World Health Organization announced the eradication of smallpox, and further advances in the treatment of disease will be made in 2004.

Similarly, in science, technology and communication, new research and inventions will have far-reaching effects. A previous Monkey year saw the launch of the first of the Intelsat satellites, with its great communication capacity. In other Monkey years the Bell Telephone Company began to develop the 'visual telephone' and, many years before, Marconi launched the first public broadcasting system in Britain, an event which was to pave the way to so much. Further advances in communication will be made in 2004. But progress will not stop there. Monkey years have seen many great achievements, particularly feats of engineering. The Aswan Dam was completed in a Monkey year, as were the Zuider Zee drainage project, Britain's first atomic power station, Sydney Harbour Bridge and, in Switzerland, the world's largest road tunnel, running over 10 miles under the St Gotthard mountain range. This year could again see the completion of some major projects.

In the world of entertainment this is a year for experiment and will be marked by new trends and fashions as well as considerable advances in home entertainment. It is likely that new cult figures will emerge and capture the imagination with their distinctive styles. Interestingly, it was in a Monkey year that Elvis Presley first came to prominence.

This year will also see the Olympic Games return to Greece and the games in Athens will see many new records and exciting personal feats. In this area, too, the Monkey year will be one for breaking new barriers.

For the individual, the Monkey year is a time to make the most of ideas and talents. This is a year for enterprise and commitment, and for those who are prepared to take the initiative, it can often turn out to be especially rewarding.

The motto of the Boy Scout movement, founded in 1908, a Monkey year, is 'Be Prepared', and this is an apt motto for us all this year. Be prepared, be bold and be positive. The Monkey year may be dramatic, but it *is* a time of opportunity. Make the most of it and you can reap the benefits that this special Chinese year will bring.

Good luck and good fortune.

18 FEBRUARY 1912 ~ 5 FEBRUARY 1913 *Water Rat*

5 FEBRUARY 1924 ~ 23 JANUARY 1925 *Wood Rat*

24 JANUARY 1936 ~ 10 FEBRUARY 1937 *Fire Rat*

10 FEBRUARY 1948 ~ 28 JANUARY 1949 *Earth Rat*

28 JANUARY 1960 ~ 14 FEBRUARY 1961 *Metal Rat*

15 FEBRUARY 1972 ~ 2 FEBRUARY 1973 *Water Rat*

2 FEBRUARY 1984 ~ 19 FEBRUARY 1985 *Wood Rat*

19 FEBRUARY 1996 ~ 6 FEBRUARY 1997 *Fire Rat*

THE
RAT

THE PERSONALITY OF THE RAT

The secret of success in life is for a man to be ready for his opportunity when it comes.

Benjamin Disraeli, a Rat

The Rat is born under the sign of charm. He is intelligent, popular and loves attending parties and large social gatherings. He is able to establish friendships with remarkable ease and people generally feel relaxed in his company. He is a very social creature and is genuinely interested in the welfare and activities of others. He has a good understanding of human nature and his advice and opinions are often sought.

The Rat is a hard and diligent worker. He is also very imaginative and is never short of ideas. However, he does sometimes lack the confidence to promote his ideas and this can often prevent him from securing the recognition he deserves.

The Rat is very observant and many Rats have made excellent writers and journalists. The Rat also excels at personnel and PR work and any job which brings him into contact with people and the media. His skills are particularly appreciated in times of crisis, for the Rat has an incredibly strong sense of self-preservation. When it comes to finding a way out of an awkward situation, the Rat is certain to be the one who comes up with a solution.

The Rat loves to be where there is a lot of action, but should he ever find himself in a very bureaucratic or restrictive environment he can become a stickler for discipline and routine.

He is also something of an opportunist and is constantly on the look-out for ways in which he can improve his wealth and lifestyle. He rarely lets an opportunity go by and can become involved in so many plans and schemes that he sometimes squanders his energies and achieves very little as a result. He is also rather gullible and can be taken in by those less scrupulous than himself.

Another characteristic of the Rat is his attitude to money. He is very thrifty and to some he may appear a little mean. The reason for this is purely that he likes to keep his money within his family. He can be most generous to his partner, his children and close friends and relatives. He can also be generous to himself, for he often finds it impossible to deprive himself of any luxury or object he fancies. The Rat is very acquisitive and can be a notorious hoarder. He hates waste and is rarely prepared to throw anything away. He can also be rather greedy and will rarely refuse an invitation for a free meal or a complimentary ticket to some lavish function.

The Rat is a good conversationalist, although he can occasionally be a little indiscreet. He can be highly critical of others – for an honest and unbiased opinion, the Rat is a superb critic – and sometimes will use confidential information to his own advantage. However, as the Rat has such a bright and irresistible nature, most are prepared to forgive him his slight indiscretions.

Throughout his long and eventful life the Rat will make many friends and will find that he is especially well suited to those born under his own sign and those of the Ox, Dragon and Monkey. He can also get on well with those born under the signs of the Tiger, Snake, Rooster, Dog and

Pig, but the rather sensitive Rabbit and Goat will find the Rat a little too critical and blunt for their liking. The Horse and Rat will also find it difficult to get on with each other – the Rat craves security and will find the Horse's changeable moods and rather independent nature a little unsettling.

The Rat is very family-orientated and will do anything to please his nearest and dearest. He is exceptionally loyal to his parents and can himself be a very caring and loving parent. He will take an interest in all his children's activities and will see that they want for nothing. The Rat usually has a large family.

The female Rat has a kindly, outgoing nature and involves herself in a multitude of different activities. She has a wide circle of friends, enjoys entertaining and is an attentive hostess. She is also conscientious about the upkeep of her home and has good taste in home furnishings. She is most supportive to the other members of her family and, due to her resourceful, friendly and persevering nature, can do well in practically any career.

Although the Rat is something of an extrovert, he is also a very private individual. He tends to keep his feelings to himself and while he is not averse to learning what other people are doing, he resents anyone prying too closely into his own affairs. He also does not like solitude and if he is alone for any length of time he can easily get depressed.

The Rat is undoubtedly very talented, but he does sometimes fail to capitalize on his many abilities. He has a tendency to become involved in too many schemes and chase after too many opportunities all at once. If he were to slow down and concentrate on one thing at a time, he could become very successful. If not, success and wealth could elude him. But the Rat, with his tremendous ability to charm, will rarely, if ever, be without friends.

THE FIVE DIFFERENT TYPES OF RAT

In addition to the 12 signs of the Chinese zodiac there are five elements, and these have a strengthening or moderating influence on the sign. The effects of the five elements on the Rat are described below, together with the years in which the elements were exercising their influence. Therefore all Rats born in 1960 are Metal Rats, those born in 1912 and 1972 are Water Rats, and so on.

Metal Rat: 1960
This Rat has excellent taste and certainly knows how to appreciate the finer things in life. His home is comfortable and nicely decorated and he likes to entertain and mix in fashionable circles. He has considerable financial acumen and invests his money well. On the surface the Metal Rat appears cheerful and confident, but deep down he can be troubled by worries that are quite often of his own making. He is exceptionally loyal to his family and friends.

Water Rat: 1912, 1972
The Water Rat is intelligent and very astute. He is a deep thinker and can express his thoughts clearly and persuasively. He is always eager to learn and is talented in many different areas. He is usually very popular, but his fear of

loneliness can sometimes lead him into mixing with the wrong sort of company. He is a particularly skilful writer, but he can get side-tracked very easily and should try to concentrate on just one thing at a time.

Wood Rat: 1924, 1984

The Wood Rat has a friendly, outgoing personality and is popular with his colleagues and friends. He has a quick, agile brain and likes to turn his hand to anything he thinks may be useful. His one fear is insecurity, but given his intelligence and capabilities, this fear is usually unfounded. He has a good sense of humour, enjoys travel and, due to his highly imaginative nature, can be a gifted writer or artist.

Fire Rat: 1936, 1996

The Fire Rat is rarely still and seems to have a never-ending supply of energy and enthusiasm. He loves being involved in the action – be it travel, following up new ideas or campaigning for a cause in which he fervently believes. He is an original thinker and hates being bound by petty restrictions or the dictates of others. He can be forthright in his views, but can sometimes get carried away in the excitement of the moment and commit himself to various undertakings without thinking through all the implications. Yet he has a resilient nature and with the right support can often go far in life.

Earth Rat: 1948

This Rat is astute and very level-headed. He rarely takes unnecessary chances and while he is constantly trying to improve his financial status, he is prepared to proceed slowly and leave nothing to chance. The Earth Rat is probably not as adventurous as the other types of Rat and prefers to remain in familiar territory rather than rush headlong into something he knows little about. He is talented, conscientious and caring towards his loved ones, but at the same time can be self-conscious and worry a little too much about the image he is trying to project.

PROSPECTS FOR THE RAT IN 2004

The Chinese New Year starts on 22 January 2004. Until then, the old year, the Year of the Goat, is still making its presence felt.

The Rat's resourceful nature and ability to spot opportunities and latch on to ideas will have served him well in the Goat year (1 February 2003 to 21 January 2004), and in the closing months the aspects remain encouraging.

Rats who are keen to advance their career at this time or are seeking work should remain alert for opportunities and actively follow up any openings that interest them. October to December 2003 could bring some interesting developments. What is accomplished or set in motion at this time will often stand the Rat in good stead for the year ahead.

Although the Goat year will have been a reasonable one for money matters, in the closing months the Rat's outgoings will often be considerable and he needs to be careful with his spending and avoid risks.

The Rat will also find the closing months of the Goat year busy on a personal level. There will be much domestic and social activity, with the Rat enjoying time spent with loved ones and many opportunities to go out, particularly in November and December. Towards the end of 2003 some Rats could meet someone who could become important in the year ahead, either as a close personal friend or in relation to their work prospects.

Overall, the Goat year is a promising one for the Rat and by making the most of himself and his skills, he can make useful advances as well as enjoy himself. There will be ample opportunity for him to build on his achievements in the auspicious Monkey year that follows.

The Year of the Monkey starts on 22 January and will be an excellent one for the Rat. It will be a year for making progress, realizing ambitions and enjoying great personal happiness. In Monkey years the Rat comes into his own.

One area which will see important developments will be the Rat's work. In 2004 there will be some excellent opportunities for him to build on his existing position and secure promotion or to move to something more in keeping with what *he* wants to do. Any Rat who feels stale in his present work, considers himself in a rut or would like to transfer to something different should make it his resolution for the year to make some changes and improve his position.

Almost as soon as the Monkey year starts, interesting developments could occur. More senior colleagues could move on, creating opportunities, or the Rat could be offered a new opening within his current organization or see an attractive vacancy elsewhere. Whenever an opportunity arises, the Rat should act swiftly. With his skills and experience, as well as his ability to get on with others, he has a great deal in his favour, and he should make the most of it. Even if some job applications do not go his way, he should not lose heart. Events *will* work out well for him in the end, although in some cases he will need to persist. For work opportunities February, March, June and September are particularly favourable, but the aspects are so good that chances could arise at almost any time during the year.

Rats who are seeking work or wanting to change career should take advantage of any training opportunities that are available as well as carry out any background reading and research that could be useful. Keeping themselves informed and developing their skills will often help them secure a suitable position.

Also, if the Rat has creative aspirations or has a particular idea he wishes to develop, he should aim to take this further over the year. With his talents and good communication skills, he could make quite an impression. As the saying goes, 'Nothing ventured, nothing gained,' and in the Monkey year the Rat has much to gain by venturing.

The year is also favourably aspected for financial matters, with many Rats enjoying a noticeable increase in their income. Often this will arise from the advances they are able to make in their work, but some may be able to supplement this by either working on a freelance basis or by putting their skills to a different use. The year does favour enterprise and the Rat, with his ability to identify opportunities, can benefit from the prevailing trends. He should, however, still manage his money well and would find it helpful to regularly set funds aside for specific purposes as well as adding to his savings. With control and self-discipline, he will be pleased with the improvement in his financial situation.

Another excellently aspected area is the Rat's personal life. The sociable Rat always sets great store by his relationships with others and in the Monkey year these will mean a great deal to him. In his domestic life he will watch with fondness the progress of those close to him and by encouraging and supporting them and taking an interest in their affairs, he will play a valued role. Even if there are differences of opinion, as there may be in all years, by being willing to talk over any problems the Rat can do much to defuse awkward situations as well as maintain the rapport he so values. In addition, the year could bring some notable family occasions, including a possible wedding, addition to his family or celebration of a personal triumph. The Monkey year will certainly see some memorable family moments!

The Rat can also look forward to a pleasing social life, with invitations to a variety of parties and events. Being such a sociable person, he will revel in the activity and the chance to meet others. Also, if he is able to meet up with colleagues or work associates on a social basis, he could find himself forging valuable contacts and impressing others.

For unattached Rats and those looking for more companionship this can be a splendid year, with romance, close relationships and the prospects of new friendships all wonderfully aspected. The months of March, May, July and September are particularly favourable for meeting others. On a personal level, this will be a year that the Rat will have good reason to enjoy.

In so many respects the Monkey year is a time of opportunity, but it is still important that the Rat makes sure his life has balance and sets aside time for himself. With so much happening, there is a risk that he could find some of his recreational pursuits being squeezed out. To prevent this, he should set a regular time aside for activities he enjoys. Whether he wants to carry on with existing hobbies or take up something new, he will find his interests will not only bring him pleasure but also do him good.

Overall, the Monkey year is one of the best years for the Rat and is very much a time when he should seize the initiative and move forward. He will be given every chance to put his resourcefulness and fine talents to good use and will enjoy some well-deserved and sometimes long-overdue success as a result.

The Metal Rat

As far as the different types of Rat are concerned, this will be a positive year for the Metal Rat. When opportunities are right, the Metal Rat is always willing to take a chance, and in 2004 there will be opportunities aplenty!

Work prospects are especially promising. No matter whether the Metal Rat has recently taken on new duties, is seeking work or been in the same position for some time, the Monkey year will enable him to make good headway and move his career forward. Such is the nature of the year that opportunities could arise at short notice and, by being swift in putting himself forward, the Metal Rat will find his keenness and experience a winning combination. In 2004 it will be a case of 'striking while the iron is hot'.

Over the year many Metal Rats can benefit from openings created by colleagues moving on or from internal reorganization, but there will be some who decide there are better opportunities elsewhere or, in some cases, better careers elsewhere. Again, by following up any openings they learn about (and here some of the Metal Rat's contacts could prove helpful), many Metal Rats will be successful in securing a position which will allow them to develop as well as make excellent use of their talents.

Those Metal Rats seeking work should also remain determined in their quest. Admittedly, sometimes their morale and self-esteem may be at a low ebb, but inside they know they have much to offer and they should try to draw a line under the past and move forward with *renewed* determination. By persisting, many Metal Rats will be able to secure a position with good potential for development. This is a year to advance, with the months from February to April and June and September seeing some interesting developments.

The Metal Rat will also gain over the year by developing his own skills. Whether in relation to his work, his personal interests or his general well-being, it is important that he continues to learn and improve himself.

As far as financial matters are concerned, this will be a positive year, with the Metal Rat enjoying an increase in income as well as sometimes receiving a sum of money from another source. Some Metal Rats may be able to put an idea or skill to good use and supplement their income that way. However, while money will flow into the Metal Rat's accounts, it can, unless watched, flow out again all too easily. To benefit from the financial upturn, the Metal Rat should aim to save for the longer term as well as keep a watchful eye on his outgoings. With care and control, though, this can be a good year financially.

On a personal level, too, this will be an important year for the Metal Rat and he can look forward to many happy occasions, including a family celebration. Maintaining a good family life does require time and input, and despite the many calls on his time the Metal Rat should always bear this in mind and preserve some of the day for those who matter.

On a social level too, the Metal Rat will find himself in demand. With his agreeable nature he makes popular company and over the year he will be invited to a wide range of social occasions and will greatly enjoy himself. For those Metal Rats who may be lonely or have had some personal misfortune, the Monkey year offers a much improved time. By making the most of their opportunities to go out and meet others (perhaps by taking up a new interest), these Metal Rats may well meet someone who will quickly become special and will find their lives undergoing quite a transformation. The Monkey year will support them well.

Overall, the Monkey year holds great potential for the Metal Rat and by making the most of the opportunities it will bring, he can look forward to making good progress, while his personal life promises much happiness.

TIP FOR THE YEAR
Look to advance. As an eager Metal Rat, you will have many dreams and ambitions. Now is your chance. Seize

the opportunities the year will bring and make the most of your talents. This is a time when your goals can be realized. Take the initiative and act.

The Water Rat

The Water Rat has a keen and ambitious nature, and in 2004 his faith in himself will lead him forward. This is a year of progress and in some of his activities the Water Rat will be blessed with a certain amount of good fortune too.

In his work the Water Rat can look forward to making substantial progress, although this may not always be in the way he envisaged. In recent years he will not only have gained useful experience but will also have met and impressed many. In the Monkey year, he will find his experience and contacts very useful. Some Water Rats, by virtue of their reputation, will find themselves ideally placed to take advantage of a position that has fallen vacant or an opening worth considering. By making the most of the situations that arise, the Water Rat will be able to further his career and add to his experience. Admittedly, sometimes the opportunities may not be exactly what he had in mind, but he should remember that there are many routes to the top and chance could lead him to one which will serve him equally well or perhaps be even better.

This also applies to those Water Rats currently seeking work or a new position. By following up opportunities and making the most of the chances they are given, even though these may be slightly different from what they were hoping for, they too can find their prospects suddenly improving. The Monkey year is an encouraging one for the Water Rat and often has far-reaching effects. For work opportunities, the months from February to April and June and September are especially favourable.

In addition to career progress, this is also an excellent year for the Water Rat to add to his skills, and he should take advantage of any training that is available. Some Water Rats may find the acquisition of an additional skill can open up new possibilities.

The progress that the Water Rat makes in his work will lead to an increase in his income. However, he does have many obligations and should manage his finances carefully rather than proceed on too much of an ad hoc basis. By budgeting and setting funds aside for specific purposes he will find he is often able to make better use of his resources. Also, by regularly reviewing his financial situation, he could make some improvements, including possibly moving funds to more profitable accounts or reducing some expenses that may no longer be necessary. By being careful and attending to his financial situation, he will benefit from this positive year.

As far as the Water Rat's personal life is concerned, this will be a busy and sometimes demanding year. His home life is likely to see much activity and he may find himself juggling many calls on his time. In addition to the demands of his own work he is aware of his family responsibilities, and in 2004 it is important he gives time to those who are important to him. Those Water Rats with children will find that guiding, assisting and playing with them will bring some memorable moments. Throughout the year the Water Rat should also encourage openness and dialogue between family members. As an effective communicator himself, this is something he is usually adept at doing.

On a social level, the Water Rat will also find himself in demand and will be invited to a wide range of social events. As a result, he will find his social circle widening quite considerably. For those Water Rats who would welcome more companionship, the Monkey year will mark a great improvement in their situation, with the prospects of new friendships, romance and, for some, marriage. This is a positive and encouraging time.

In so many respects the Monkey year is one that holds great potential for the Water Rat. The opportunities will be there and if there is some aspect of his life that he wants to change or improve upon, he should take steps to do so. The Water Rat has a great and promising future ahead of him and in 2004 he will be doing much to shape and secure it.

TIP FOR THE YEAR
Look to develop and advance. You have great skills and potential. Make the most of yourself and the opportunities that arise. What you learn and accomplish now can bring great rewards in the future.

The Wood Rat

This will be an exciting and significant year for the Wood Rat. In recent years events will have moved at quite a fast pace for him. Many Wood Rats will have taken important exams and some will have entered the world of work, while on a personal level, too, a great deal will have happened. The changes will continue in this, the Wood Rat's twentieth year.

Especially well aspected is the Wood Rat's personal life. For those who are unattached, the Monkey year can bring significant romance and the chance to meet someone who will quickly become important. Sometimes such a meeting will come through a fortuitous sequence of events, but however it happens, it will certainly help to make this already auspicious year all the more special. Affairs of the heart are wonderfully aspected and even those Wood Rats for whom a previous romance may have caused heartache will find that the Monkey year can bring healing, often with someone new entering their life. March, May and July to September are all favourably aspected for meeting others. For those Wood Rats who are already enjoying a close relationship, this can also be an auspicious time, with many settling down with their partner and/or marrying in the Monkey year.

This will also be a promising year socially, with the Wood Rat enjoying many opportunities to go out and meet friends. Some parts of the year could be especially busy, with the Wood Rat's social diary becoming quite full. Some Wood Rats could also gain a great deal from joining a group connected with one of their interests, which would allow them to add to their knowledge and meet other enthusiasts as well as have some fun.

Although the Wood Rat may like to keep his various activities and interests separate from other family members, he should remember that they are often willing to help and advise him. Whenever he has any concerns, or important decisions to take, he should seek the views of those close to him. He will often find family members understand his problems better than he originally thought and are supportive and constructive in the advice they offer.

Another positive aspect of the year is the Wood Rat's personal development. Those Wood Rats studying for qualifications will find that by working steadily throughout the year and making the most of the opportunities available, their efforts will be well rewarded and will enhance their future prospects. Even if the Wood Rat may sometimes despair of the amount of studying he has to face, he should keep in mind what he is working towards and the openings that qualifications will bring.

This will also be an important year for those Wood Rats who are in work, enabling them to discover where their true strengths lie and what they should be looking to build upon. For those seeking work or wanting to try something different, the months from February to April and June and September could see important developments.

The Wood Rat has an adventurous streak and there will be some who decide to travel over the year. To make the most of their time away, these Wood Rats should plan their itinerary and give some thought to what they will need. The better their preparation, the more they will enjoy their travels. The Monkey year can provide the Wood Rat with some great memories and experiences!

As far as money matters are concerned, the Wood Rat's resourcefulness will prove a useful asset over the year. With his various activities and lively personal life, he will want to do a lot on often limited resources, and may find he is spending a great deal. As far as possible he should keep track of his outgoings and control over his purse strings. The more disciplined he is, the better he will fare.

In many respects, the Monkey year holds great promise for the Wood Rat. In his work and education he can learn and accomplish a great deal, while personally, romance, friendship and a lively social life can bring him much happiness. The Wood Rat's twentieth year can be a fine and exciting one.

TIP FOR THE YEAR

Build up your experience and be willing to try things out and to make the most of your talents. As the saying goes, the world is your oyster. *Now* is the time to discover that world and to find out about the important part you can play in it.

The Fire Rat

The Fire Rat has always been one to make good use of his time and ideas, and in view of the prevailing aspects, he can look forward to a satisfying 12 months. This is a year in which he can realize plans, start new activities and enjoy himself in the way *he* wants. Throughout the Monkey year, he will also be grateful for the support he receives from both family and friends, and whenever he has ideas he would like to try out, he should not hesitate to put them forward. By being forthcoming he will gain encouragement and sometimes assistance he had not envisaged.

One area which is particularly favoured is the Fire Rat's personal interests and over the year he should aim to develop these. They will not only bring him a great deal of pleasure but will often have other benefits too, perhaps allowing him to get additional exercise, bringing him into contact with other enthusiasts or inspiring him through an interesting and worthwhile project. The more creatively inclined Fire Rats should aim to experiment with their talents over the year. Whether fond of art, writing, craftwork, drama, photography or some other form of creative expression, they will find that by experimenting they can not only push their talent further but also take greater pleasure in what they achieve.

Many Fire Rats will also find themselves spending more time in their garden over the year and being tempted to try out new stock and to add new features as well as appreciating how their garden looks during the different seasons. Gardening, and even just being out of doors, can appeal to the Fire Rat's creative instincts, although when digging or carrying out other strenuous activities, he should be careful not to over-exert himself. Without care, a pulled muscle or strain could cause him considerable discomfort. Fire Rats, take note. Digging and other heavy work does need to be conducted carefully and, if possible, with assistance from others.

There will be several opportunities for the Fire Rat to travel over the year, both to visit relatives and friends who may live some distance away and to go on holiday. If there are any places he has been yearning to see, he should mention it to others. Sometimes his dreams may be more possible than he may realize.

The Fire Rat will also fare well in financial matters, with many Fire Rats receiving an extra sum of money over the year. This could be through the fruition of a policy, as a gift or even as a stroke of luck. While the Fire Rat will be glad of any improvement, he should think carefully about what he wants do with his money and plan his more substantial purchases. As he will find, planning will often be more satisfying than succumbing to too many immediate temptations.

As always, the Fire Rat's relations with others will mean a great deal to him and he will value both his home and social life over the year. He will not only appreciate the support shown for his own activities, but will be glad to assist others with their pursuits. In addition, some joint projects to improve either home or garden will be especially satisfying, particularly as the results can be appreciated by all. The Fire Rat will also enjoy some of the more spontaneous occasions of the year, perhaps trips or events arranged at short notice, or surprise visits. The Monkey year will certainly contain its share of unexpected pleasures.

Also, for those Fire Rats who may have had some personal sadness, the Monkey year will often help the healing process. By becoming involved in new activities, meeting others (perhaps through a local club or society) and devoting more time to what they want to do, these Fire Rats will find some brightness coming back into their lives. For the unattached and lonely, the year can also bring the gift of an important friendship. However, for the Monkey year to work its magic, the Fire Rat should make the effort to go out more, get in contact with others and, if it would help, talk over any concerns with those close to him. Openness and action can be of great value.

In many respects, the Monkey year holds considerable promise for the Fire Rat and, by following through his ideas and spending time on activities he enjoys, he will find this a rewarding and pleasant time, made all the more so by the love and support he receives from those around him.

TIP FOR THE YEAR
Be forthcoming with your plans, ideas and concerns. Others can really help, but first they need to be informed. Also, aim to develop your personal interests. These can be both satisfying and beneficial.

The Earth Rat

The Earth Rat is set to do well in 2004, particularly as the year will allow him to carry out some of the plans he has been thinking about for some time. As a result, there will be change as well as some demanding moments, but the upside of this is that the changes are in line with what the Earth Rat wants, and the effects of what he undertakes will often be far-reaching.

One area which will see change will be the Earth Rat's work. Many Earth Rats who have been in the same position for some time will feel the time has now come to set themselves a new challenge. As a result, many will start to look at other ways in which they can draw on their experience and will follow up openings that appeal to them. Exploring possibilities will often lead to the chance to do something different and will give their career a new lease of life.

Some Earth Rats, though, will be content to remain in their existing role or within their current organization. However, for these too the Monkey year can hold some surprises. In view of their knowledge and skills, many will find themselves being offered the chance to take on new responsibilities or given attractive promotion opportunities. By taking advantage of these, the Earth Rat will not only advance his position but also feel more inspired by the new role and challenge before him. Work-wise, the Monkey year is an exciting and progressive time.

Those Earth Rats seeking work should remain determined in their quest. Many will find that by some almost fortuitous chance, they see or hear of an opening which proves ideal and holds interesting prospects for the future. For work opportunities, February, March, June and September could see important developments.

Some Earth Rats will, however, decide to take early retirement or opt to work fewer hours. For these Earth Rats too, the Monkey year offers exciting prospects, especially as they will now be able to give more time to their own interests.

This will also be a positive year for financial matters, and by planning and saving towards his activities and purchases, the Earth Rat will be pleased with his general situation. To get the most from his resources, though, he does need to exercise careful financial management.

Another well-aspected area concerns the Earth Rat's own personal interests. He should spend some time developing these over the year, as they will often enable him to explore his creative talents, satisfy his curiosity, take some additional exercise and/or meet fellow enthusiasts. Whether expanding existing interests or trying out new ones, the Earth Rat will find they will bring him pleasure *and* benefit.

The Earth Rat's personal life is also favourably aspected and again can see much activity. Over the year, many Earth Rats will feel drawn to practical activities and will set about home improvements with relish. Some will decide to tackle household projects they have had in mind for some while, especially redecorating and refurbishing certain rooms, while others may move altogether. In addition to the more practical aspects of home life, the Earth Rat can look forward to some notable family occasions. For some there could be the prospect of a wedding in the family or the birth of a grandchild. Family-wise, a great deal will happen and some of the events will truly delight the Earth Rat.

Despite the year's more positive aspects, however, there could be times when the Earth Rat is concerned about someone close to him. Although he may not wish to appear interfering, if he feels he can offer support in any way, he will find this will be appreciated and will do a great deal of good. As with so many of his sign, the Earth Rat is able to empathize and relate well to others, and this will prove a worthy asset during the year.

Socially, this is a promising year, with the Earth Rat enjoying going out and meeting friends. With his personal interests so well aspected, if he is able to join or contact a group of fellow enthusiasts, he will find this both useful and enjoyable, and it will lead to a widening of his social circle.

Overall, the Monkey year is a promising one for the Earth Rat, but to benefit he needs to follow through his ideas. This is a year of opportunity and he should make the most of those that come his way or that he can create.

Go after what you want, whether pursuing ambitions or launching ideas. Action taken during the Monkey year can have positive effects.

FAMOUS RATS

Ben Affleck, Alan Alda, Ursula Andress, Louis Armstrong, Charles Aznavour, Lauren Bacall, James Baldwin, Shirley Bassey, Kathy Bates, Irving Berlin, Silvio Berlusconi, Kenneth Branagh, Marlon Brando, Charlotte Brontë, Jackson Browne, Chris de Burgh, George H. Bush, Glen Campbell, David Carradine, Jimmy Carter, Maurice Chevalier, Aaron Copland, Cameron Diaz, Benjamin Disraeli, David Duchovny, T. S. Eliot, Eminem, Colin Firth, Clark Gable, Liam Gallagher, Gareth Gates, Hugh Grant, Geri Halliwell, Daryl Hannah, Thomas Hardy, Prince Harry, Vaclav Havel, Haydn, Charlton Heston, Buddy Holly, Mick Hucknall, Englebert Humperdink, Henrik Ibsen, Jeremy Irons, Samuel L. Jackson, Jean-Michel Jarre, Danny Kaye, Gene Kelly, Lawrence of Arabia, Gary Lineker, Lord Andrew Lloyd Webber, Claude Monet, Nana Mouskouri, Richard Nixon, Roy Orbison, Ozzy Osbourne, Sean Penn, Terry Pratchett, the Queen Mother, Ian Rankin, Lou Rawls, Vanessa Redgrave, Burt Reynolds, Rossini, William Shakespeare, Tommy Steele, Donna Summer, James Taylor, Leo Tolstoy, Henri Toulouse-Lautrec, Spencer Tracy, the Prince of Wales, George Washington, the Duke of York, Emile Zola.

6 FEBRUARY 1913 ∼ 25 JANUARY 1914	*Water Ox*
24 JANUARY 1925 ∼ 12 FEBRUARY 1926	*Wood Ox*
11 FEBRUARY 1937 ∼ 30 JANUARY 1938	*Fire Ox*
29 JANUARY 1949 ∼ 16 FEBRUARY 1950	*Earth Ox*
15 FEBRUARY 1961 ∼ 4 FEBRUARY 1962	*Metal Ox*
3 FEBRUARY 1973 ∼ 22 JANUARY 1974	*Water Ox*
20 FEBRUARY 1985 ∼ 8 FEBRUARY 1986	*Wood Ox*
7 FEBRUARY 1997 ∼ 27 JANUARY 1998	*Fire Ox*

THE

OX

THE PERSONALITY OF THE OX

What would life be if we had no courage to attempt anything?

Vincent van Gogh, an Ox

The Ox is born under the signs of equilibrium and tenacity. He is a hard and conscientious worker and sets about everything he does in a resolute, methodical and determined manner. He has considerable leadership qualities and is often admired for his tough and uncompromising nature. He knows what he wants to achieve in life and, as far as possible, will not be deflected from his ultimate objective.

The Ox takes his responsibilities and duties very seriously. He is decisive and quick to take advantage of any opportunity that comes his way. He is also sincere and places a great deal of trust in his friends and colleagues. He is, nevertheless, something of a loner. He is a quiet and private individual and often keeps his thoughts to himself. He also cherishes his independence and prefers to set about things in his own way rather than be bound by the dictates of others or influenced by outside pressures.

The Ox tends to have a calm and tranquil nature, but if something angers him or he feels that someone has let him down, he can have a fearsome temper. He can also be stubborn and obstinate and this can lead him into conflict with others. Usually the Ox will succeed in getting his own way, but should things go against him he is a poor loser and will take any defeat or setback extremely badly.

The Ox is often a deep thinker and rather studious. He is not particularly renowned for his sense of humour and does not take kindly to new gimmicks or anything too innovative. The Ox is too solid and traditional for that and he prefers to stick to the more conventional norm.

His home is very important to him and in some respects he treats it as a private sanctuary. His family tends to be closely knit and the Ox will make sure that each member does their fair share around the house. The Ox tends to be a hoarder, but he is always well organized and neat. He also places great importance on punctuality and there is nothing that infuriates him more than to be kept waiting, particularly if it is due to someone's inefficiency. The Ox can be a hard taskmaster!

Once settled in a job or house the Ox will quite happily remain there for many years. He does not like change and he is also not particularly keen on travel. He does, however, enjoy gardening and other outdoor pursuits and he will often spend much of his spare time out of doors. The Ox is usually an excellent gardener and whenever possible he will always make sure he has a large area of ground to maintain. He usually prefers to live in the country rather than the town.

Due to his dedicated and dependable nature, the Ox will usually do well in his chosen career, providing he is given enough freedom to act on his own initiative. He invariably does well in politics, agriculture and in careers which need specialized training. The Ox is also very gifted in the arts and many Oxen have enjoyed considerable success as musicians or composers.

The Ox is not as outgoing as some and it often takes him a long time to establish friendships and feel relaxed in another person's company. His courtships are likely to be long, but once he is settled he will remain devoted and loyal to his partner. The Ox is particularly well suited to those born under the signs of the Rat, Rabbit, Snake and Rooster. He can also establish a good relationship with the Monkey, Dog, Pig and another Ox, but he will find that he has little in common with the whimsical and sensitive Goat. He will also find it difficult to get on with the Horse, Dragon and Tiger – the Ox prefers a quiet and peaceful existence and those born under these three signs tend to be a little too lively and impulsive for his liking.

The female Ox has a kind and caring nature, and her home and family are very much her pride and joy. She always tries to do her best for her partner and can be a most conscientious and loving parent. She is an excellent organizer and also a very determined person who will often succeed in getting what she wants in life. She usually has a deep interest in the arts and is often a talented artist or musician.

The Ox is a very down-to-earth character. He is sincere, loyal and unpretentious. He can, however, be rather reserved and to some he may appear distant and aloof. He has a quiet nature, but underneath he is very strong-willed and ambitious. He has the courage of his convictions and is often prepared to stand up for what he believes to be right, regardless of the consequences. He inspires confidence and trust, and throughout his life he will rarely be short of people who are ready to support him or who admire his strong and resolute manner.

THE FIVE DIFFERENT TYPES OF OX

In addition to the 12 signs of the Chinese zodiac there are five elements, and these have a strengthening or moderating influence on the sign. The effects of the five elements on the Ox are described below, together with the years in which the elements were exercising their influence. Therefore all Oxen born in 1961 are Metal Oxen, those born in 1913 and 1973 are Water Oxen, and so on.

Metal Ox: 1961
This Ox is confident and very strong-willed. He can be blunt and forthright in his views and is not afraid of speaking his mind. He sets about his objectives with a dogged determination, but he can become so involved in his various activities that he can be oblivious to the thoughts and feelings of those around him, and this can sometimes be to his detriment. He is honest and dependable and will never promise more than he can deliver. He has a good appreciation of the arts and usually has a small circle of very good and loyal friends.

Water Ox: 1913, 1973
This Ox has a sharp and penetrating mind. He is a good organizer and sets about his work in a methodical manner. He is not as narrow-minded as some of the other types of Ox and is more willing to involve others in his plans and aspirations. He usually has very high moral standards and

is often attracted to careers in public service. He is a good judge of character and has such a friendly and persuasive manner that he usually experiences little difficulty in securing his objectives. He is popular and has an excellent way with children.

Wood Ox: 1925, 1985

The Wood Ox conducts himself with an air of dignity and authority and will often take a leading role in any enterprise in which he becomes involved. He is very self-confident and is direct in his dealings with others. He does, however, have a quick temper and has no hesitation in speaking his mind. He has tremendous drive and willpower and has an extremely good memory. The Wood Ox is particularly loyal and devoted to the members of his family and has a most caring nature.

Fire Ox: 1937, 1997

The Fire Ox has a powerful and assertive personality and is a hard and conscientious worker. He holds strong views and has very little patience when things do not go his own way. He can also get carried away in the excitement of the moment and does not always take into account the views of those around him. He nevertheless has many leadership qualities and will often reach positions of power, eminence and wealth. He usually has a small group of loyal and close friends and is very devoted to his family.

Earth Ox: 1949

This Ox sets about everything he does in a sensible and
level-headed manner. He is ambitious, but also realistic in
his aims and is often prepared to work long hours in order
to secure his objectives. He is shrewd in financial and business matters and is a very good judge of character. He has a
quiet nature and is greatly admired for his sincerity and
integrity. He is also very loyal to his family and friends
and his views and opinions are often sought.

PROSPECTS FOR THE OX IN 2004

The Chinese New Year starts on 22 January 2004. Until
then, the old year, the Year of the Goat, is still making its
presence felt.

The Year of the Goat (1 February 2003 to 21 January
2004) will not have been the easiest of years for the Ox.
The Ox likes certainty and to follow carefully laid plans, but
during some parts of 2003 he could have found himself in
muddled situations and encountered difficulties in getting
results. However, there is good reason for the Ox to take
heart. The closing months of the Goat year will see a shift
in his favour, with some of his efforts now bearing fruit.

In his work the Ox will, at last, have more chance to
demonstrate his worth and put his skills to good use. As a
result, he will be in an excellent position to make progress
during the closing stages of the year as well as boost his
prospects in the more favourable Monkey year that
follows. Similarly, those Oxen seeking work will find that a
position obtained late in 2003 could prove an excellent

stepping-stone to something greater in the next year. October could see important developments work-wise.

Although the Ox is usually careful in money matters, in the closing months of the Goat year he would be wise to watch his spending as well as be careful when entering into important transactions. This is not a time when he can let his vigilance slip.

One of the more favourably aspected areas for the Ox in the Goat year is his relations with others. Although the Ox may be a private person and does not lower his guard easily, in the last quarter of the year he will enjoy some fine domestic and social occasions, including parties and the chance to meet relations and friends he may not have seen for some time. By being forthcoming and involving those close to him in his various activities, he will gain much from the advice and encouragement he is given.

Although the Goat year will have had its difficult moments, the Ox will have gained much from it and will be able to build on this in the year ahead.

The Year of the Monkey starts on 22 January and will be an interesting one for the Ox. Although events may some-times move more swiftly than he may like – the Ox prefers a steady and planned course – they will often work in his favour. In his work good progress is indicated, while his personal life is favourably aspected.

As the year starts the Ox would do well to give some thought to recent developments and to formulate his plans for the next 12 months. In this way he will be able to iden-tify areas which he would like to improve upon as well as clarify his aims for the year ahead. Having a sense of direction will help him to channel his energies in a more purposeful way and to accomplish more as a result. The Monkey year is certainly a time when the Ox should be looking to move himself forward.

In general, the Monkey year will allow the Ox to make excellent use of his skills and experience. These are a real asset and can lead to significant advances during the year. Sometimes, as a result of his knowledge, the Ox could find himself being singled out for certain responsibilities, promotion or a new role. The Monkey year is also capable of springing some surprises and the Ox could find opportunities arising almost out of the blue. By taking advantage of them, unexpected though they may be, the Ox can improve his prospects and develop his career. The Monkey year is indeed one of positive change.

For those Oxen who are seeking work or feeling unfulfilled in their present position, the Monkey year will also bring some excellent opportunities and often set them off on a more rewarding career path. By considering different ways in which they can use their skills and widening the scope of their search, these Oxen will often secure a position which offers an interesting challenge as well as good prospects for the future. The Monkey year is capable of introducing important changes in the Ox's working life, ones which will be of benefit to him and have long-term value.

The months from March to May and August to October could see some interesting career opportunities, but generally 2004 is a rewarding year work-wise and one in which the Ox can make the most of his talents.

This is also a positive year for financial matters and in addition to seeing an increase in income, some Oxen may be able to supplement their earnings through some additional work. Again, this could sometimes arise in an unexpected way and will be a pleasant bonus for the Ox. For those Oxen with an enterprising disposition, an idea they have could bring interesting results. However, while the Ox's financial situation will show an improvement, paperwork does need close attention. To prevent problems the Ox should ensure he keeps documents and guarantees safe and policies up to date, and deals with financially-related forms promptly and carefully. The extra attention he pays to this will certainly be worth his while.

The Monkey year is favourable for self-development and the Ox would do well to further some of his interests and skills at this time, perhaps by setting himself a new challenge, taking up a different interest or enrolling on a course. Adding to his knowledge and interests in some way will not only be satisfying but also a welcome contrast to some of his more usual activities. Many Oxen have a fondness for gardening and for being out of doors, and the Ox should make sure he allows time for this and for other activities he enjoys. He works hard and it is important that he does not deny himself some well-deserved pleasures.

The Ox's relations with others are also favourably aspected in the Monkey year. For the unattached or those enjoying the early stages of romance, this can be a significant and happy time. Existing romances will often continue to flourish, with many Oxen becoming engaged or settling down with their partner, while those who may start the year in low spirits will find the Monkey year can herald a major transformation in their life. An existing friendship could suddenly develop into a meaningful romance and there will be opportunities for those who may feel lonely to build up their social life, with excellent prospects for meeting someone who will, in time, become special. It may require some Oxen to draw a line under past hurt and make a conscious effort to move their life forward, but it will be well worth it. For personal matters, April, May, August and November are favourable months.

In addition to a promising social life, the Ox's domestic life will generally go well, with some memorable high points to the year. These will include celebrating the successes and progress of family members (including some of his own). Other enjoyable occasions will include interests and activities that can be shared, spontaneous events, and holidays and trips with loved ones. As the Ox realizes, a good family life does require input, and the Ox takes his responsibilities seriously. His willingness to contribute so much *will* make a difference this year and be appreciated by many. His care and concern for others will also be valued, and even when, as with all years, problems raise their head, his advice will help. The Ox's domestic life is important to him and in 2004 it will bring both satisfaction and contentment.

Overall, the Monkey year holds good prospects for the Ox and while he may sometimes have to move swiftly to make the most of the opportunities that arise, events will often be to his advantage and long-term interest. Both professionally and personally, a great deal will work out well for him.

The Metal Ox

As far as the different types of Ox are concerned, the Monkey year holds good prospects for the Metal Ox, allowing him to build on recent developments and make useful progress.

Work aspects are especially encouraging. As the Metal Ox has so often shown, he is a conscientious and tenacious worker, and this, combined with his experience, makes him a valued member of any team. During the Monkey year he will find his reputation will place him in an excellent position to benefit when openings arise as more senior colleagues move on or he sees a more responsible position elsewhere. To make the most of his opportunities he will, though, need to be swift in making an application as well as prepare well for any interview and stress what he can bring to the role. This is not a year to undersell himself. But for those Metal Oxen keen on furthering themselves, the Monkey year will prove a successful and encouraging time.

This also applies to those seeking work or feeling dissatisfied with their present job. By following up positions that interest them, they will find their tenacity rewarded, and once they have been given a chance, they will rise to the challenge and make impressive headway. The months from March to May and October will see important work developments, but generally 2004 is a positive year for the Metal Ox and he should make the most of the chances that come his way.

The Metal Ox should also aim to further his skills over the year, especially those that can help in the performance of his duties or could be of use in the future. These might include adding to his computer knowledge or learning about another aspect of his work. Additional study, even if it has to be done in his own time, will prove helpful both now and in the future.

The Metal Ox should also make sure he allows time for activities he enjoys and which give him a break from his usual routine. Out-of-door activities are particularly well aspected over the year and those Metal Oxen who are keen on travel should take up some of the opportunities and offers that appeal to them.

As far as his finances are concerned, the Metal Ox will enjoy an increase in his income and by managing his finances well he will find his general position improving. If he is able, he would find it helpful to reduce some of his borrowings and interest payments and set some funds aside for the longer term. With care, this can be a positive financial year.

The Monkey year will also bring some memorable personal occasions, with many Metal Oxen being involved in a family celebration. This could be a graduation, wedding or the success of someone close. The Metal Ox will feel a sense of personal pride at some of the events that take place as well as help to ensure that any arrangements go well. His ability to plan and organize will prove a great asset here.

The Metal Ox will do much to assist others over the year too, offering help and advice as well as, in some cases, practical support. Again, his caring but level-headed manner will be greatly valued. Also, his practical nature will often get the better of him and many Metal Oxen will decide to launch some fairly ambitious undertakings in their home during the year. These could include redecorating and altering certain rooms or adding new features and comforts. Although what is accomplished will satisfy the Metal Ox, he could find some of the projects he starts will take longer and be more disruptive than he originally anticipated. Metal Oxen, take note and do allow for this when commencing practical projects.

The Metal Ox may not always be the most active of socializers, preferring to spend time in the company of those he knows well. However, his social life could see quite a transformation over the year. An interest of his or a change in his work could bring him into contact with a new group of people, some of whom he will strike up a good rapport with and who will, in time, become close friends. With the year holding such encouraging prospects, those Metal Oxen who may have let their social life lapse or may have had some recent personal difficulty will find some brightness being brought back into their life through new friendships and, for some, romance. April, May, August and November are particularly well aspected for personal and social matters.

In many respects, this will be a positive year for the Metal Ox and it will allow him to make good use of his talents and many fine personal qualities.

TIP FOR THE YEAR
Make the most of your ideas, experience and skills. These are real assets and can lead to considerable success over the year.

The Water Ox

The Water Ox will be keen to make much of 2004 and his determination and efforts will be well rewarded. He knows that he is capable of a great deal and this year he will be setting himself more on the course he wants.

Some Water Oxen, already established in their line of work, will decide that with the experience they now have, this is the right time to advance. Accordingly, when promotion opportunities arise or they see an opening which allows them to move their career on, they should put themselves forward. Even if an application does not go their way, they should persist. Sometimes a rejection, even though disappointing at the time, will prove to be a blessing in disguise, with something better following in its wake. Also, the Water Ox should remember that the Monkey year can bring its surprises and as far as his work and prospects are concerned, he may see some unexpected but positive developments.

Those Water Oxen considering switching careers or seeking work should likewise follow up any openings that appeal to them. These Water Oxen will also find the year producing some curious situations. They may be offered a position they did not expect to get or one in marked contrast to what they have done before. Whatever happens, the events of 2004 will have far-reaching results which will not only allow the Water Ox to further his career but also set it on a more satisfying path. For opportunities and key developments, March, April and October could all be significant.

The progress that the Water Ox makes in his work will lead to an increase in his income. In addition some Water Oxen may be able to take on extra work or put one of their interests or skills to good use. The Monkey year supports the enterprising well. However, while the year will bring more money in, the Water Ox does need to watch his outgoings. He has many obligations and where possible should try to reduce these as well as add to his assets. By managing his resources carefully, however, he will be able to improve his financial situation over the year.

The Monkey year will also see much activity in the Water Ox's personal life. If a parent, he will do much to help and encourage his children and will be pleased with the progress they make during the year. However, young children can be demanding and the Water Ox should take up any offers of help available to him. Also, if at any time he feels in need of extra assistance or an occasional break, he should ask. He may be a conscientious parent, but he does need to give consideration to his own well-being too.

Also, if during the year the Water Ox is worried about any matter or feels under pressure, he will find that talking with those he loves and trusts of great value. The one thing he should avoid is bottling up any pressures or anxieties. Family and friends *can* help and he can call on them if he should need to.

Although the year will bring its busy times, there will be a great deal to appreciate in the Water Ox's domestic life, including interests and activities he can share with family members, such as home and garden projects and breaks or holidays. The Monkey year will certainly give rise to many pleasant and agreeable occasions.

The Water Ox's social life is also favourably aspected, although with work activities and family commitments some Water Oxen may tend to restrict this just to meeting up with existing friends. However, whether he keeps his social life low key or goes out fairly regularly, the Water

Ox will enjoy himself. Those Water Oxen who may be lonely or have had some difficulty in their personal life will find that the year can usher in better times. For some, a new friendship or romance could transform the year and indeed their life.

Also, in spite of the many commitments on his time, the Water Ox should make sure he does not neglect his own interests over the year. He does deserve some time for himself!

Overall, this will be a favourable year for the Water Ox, bringing him the opportunity to make progress as well as develop his talents. And he will be well supported by the many who think so highly of him.

TIP FOR THE YEAR
You have many abilities and a fine future ahead of you. In 2004 aim to make progress towards some of your goals and aspirations. Positive and purposeful action *will* be rewarded.

The Wood Ox
This will be an exciting year for the Wood Ox. Keen to make the most of himself, he will enjoy the many opportunities the Monkey year will bring and will achieve a great deal as a result. Personal matters are particularly well aspected, with a lively social life and affairs of the heart often being significant.

In the Monkey year, the Wood Ox will really come into his own and his confidence, manner and qualities will certainly make an impression. He will find himself much in demand with existing friends as well as having the opportunity to widen his social circle. Many Wood Oxen will find themselves in new situations over the year, perhaps having moved for the purposes of education or work, and will find themselves building up new friendships and contacts as the year progresses. Some of those the Wood Ox meets will become special, with a few even meeting their future partner over the year. Any Wood Ox who has had a recent romance turn sour, or was obviously not meant to be, will find the Monkey year can heal the scars, perhaps with someone new entering their life. For personal and social matters April, May and the months from August to November are particularly favourable.

During the year, the Wood Ox will have good reason to be grateful for the support of family members. Although he may desire more independence now and feel that some relatives may not be completely in tune with his ideas or situation, they may well understand and empathize more than he may realize, and if he is open about his aspirations and listens to the advice and encouragement he is given, he will gain a great deal. To benefit, though, he does need to be forthcoming. The Wood Ox will also be helped by those he has impressed over the years, whether his tutors, people he has worked for or those who know him and sense his potential. He will gain both from the advice they offer to his face and the good words they put in for him behind his back. Both academically and professionally, the Monkey year offers good prospects to the Wood Ox.

The many Wood Oxen studying for qualifications will find that by working conscientiously throughout the year, they will not only make pleasing progress but also often be able to decide upon their future vocation. In some cases their decision may be different from their earlier ideas, but it is often a legacy of the Monkey year to set the Wood Ox off on an exciting new path.

For those Wood Oxen already in work, the year will also bring significant change, with the opportunity to make progress in their present company or, if dissatisfied with their present role, the chance to try something different. Almost all Wood Oxen in employment at the start of the year will end it in a different and more satisfying position. And even though they may be at the beginning of their working life, already many will have given an indication of their potential.

For those Wood Oxen seeking work, the Monkey year will again bring some interesting opportunities, and while these may not always be exactly what the Wood Ox was hoping for, they will prove a valuable platform on which to build and will provide experience which can indeed prove helpful in the future.

Care will be needed with finance, though, and the Wood Ox should avoid unnecessary risks and keep a close watch on his spending. Many Wood Oxen will, however, be able to supplement their income by taking on some extra work or giving assistance when needed. The Monkey year does provide good opportunities for the enterprising and hardworking.

In many respects, 2004 will be a positive and encouraging year for the Wood Ox. On a personal level he will enjoy himself a great deal, forging new friendships and in many cases finding romance. He will also be able to make good progress, and what he achieves now, either academically or in his career, will be important for his future prospects.

TIP FOR THE YEAR
Be flexible and make the most of the opportunities that arise. Experience gained now will often be to your long-term advantage.

The Fire Ox

As the Monkey year starts, the Fire Ox would do well to bear in mind the Chinese proverb 'The whole year's work depends on a good plan in the spring; the whole day's work depends on a good start in the morning.' The Monkey year does hold much promise for the Fire Ox, but to benefit from it he does need to plan his activities. By deciding early in 2004 what he would like to accomplish, he will find his ideas gathering momentum and leading to some positive developments. Also, throughout the year, the Fire Ox will be helped by those around him, and whenever he is mulling over ideas or would be grateful for some assistance (especially of a practical nature), he should be forthcoming and ask. He will find others not only willing to help but also able to offer constructive advice, and in addition the process of talking over his ideas can often help get them started.

For many Fire Oxen accommodation matters will feature prominently, with some choosing to move to somewhere more suitable for their present needs and others deciding to alter or add features to certain rooms. Although moving or making alterations will be disruptive, the Fire Ox will be satisfied with what is accomplished. Also, many Fire Oxen will decide to have a purge of items they have accumulated over the years. Whether this involves sorting out storage areas, thinning out old paperwork or discarding items no longer needed, the Fire Ox will again delight in what is achieved and in how much neater and better organized certain areas have become. This will also appeal to his methodical nature!

Another area which will bring the Fire Ox satisfaction is his own personal development. If there is a skill or subject he would like to learn more about, he should take steps to follow this up over the year, perhaps by reading up on it, enrolling on a course or contacting those able to give advice or instruction, maybe through a local society. He will find this both a pleasurable and rewarding use of his time. And there could be an additional benefit in that he may come into contact with other enthusiasts and, in time, make some good friends.

The Fire Ox's domestic life will see much activity over the year. In addition to the various home projects he decides to tackle, he will take a fond interest in the activities of his loved ones and will do much to help others, especially younger relations who may be leading busy and demanding lives. The assistance and sometimes counsel he is able to offer will be more appreciated than he may realize.

Although the Fire Ox may not be the most active of socializers, much preferring to spend time with those he knows well, he will find himself with quite a few invitations and opportunities to go out over the year. His social life offers some fine prospects, with the events he does attend leading to some enjoyable times and a widening of his social circle. Any Fire Ox who may feel lonely or desire more companionship will find that an interest he takes up or event he is invited to will often lead to a welcome upturn in his social life. Again, the Monkey year is an encouraging one for the Fire Ox.

One area that does need special attention, though, is bureaucratic matters. The Fire Ox does need to be vigilant when dealing with important paperwork and should check carefully the implications of any agreement he enters into. If in doubt, it would be worth him seeking advice, especially where finance and possible benefits are concerned.

In most respects, however, this will be a positive year for the Fire Ox and by following through his ideas and using his time well, he will be able to achieve a great deal and feel highly satisfied as a result.

TIP FOR THE YEAR
Aim to develop yourself and your interests in some way. These will not only be satisfying and pleasurable but can often bring other benefits too.

The Earth Ox

The Monkey year holds encouraging prospects for Earth Ox, particularly as it will allow him to make good use of his strengths and ideas as well as reap the rewards of some of his more recent activities. Also, the year will have an element of surprise to it, with certain events occurring and opportunities arising which the Earth Ox may not have envisaged but which will be to his long-term advantage. Overall, this is a year for positive and far-reaching change.

One area which will see much activity will be the Earth Ox's work, and although quite a few Earth Oxen will have changed the nature of their duties over the last 12 months, there could be yet further opportunities. Sometimes the Earth Ox will find the work he has been doing has expanded to such a level that he will be given the chance to channel his efforts into something more specific and a position he is more suited for. Alternatively, as more senior colleagues move on, he could find himself well placed to take over. Quite a few Earth Oxen will win well-deserved promotion this year.

Another feature of the Monkey year is that it will give the Earth Ox more chance to take his career into his own hands and concentrate on activities he prefers. Many of those who are keen to change what they do or who are looking for work will be successful in securing an opportunity which is ideal for them. Admittedly, their quest will take considerable effort, but by remaining resolute they will often find events working out in a fortuitous manner.

There will also be some Earth Oxen who, in their desire for change, will opt to work fewer hours, perhaps taking a job share, or even early retirement. Again, these Earth Oxen will find that events will unfold in a way that will give them greater opportunity to carry out activities of their own choosing.

The months of April, May, August and October could see some key developments relating to the Earth Ox's work and prospects, but overall the Monkey year will give most Earth Oxen the chance to move forward in the way that they want.

Another area the Earth Ox should give consideration to is his own development. He will find that setting himself something interesting and purposeful to do, whether learning or furthering a skill or tackling a practical project, will add another enjoyable element to the year. In the process, some Earth Oxen could find themselves discovering talents they never realized they had. The Monkey year *is* an encouraging one for the Earth Ox and the discovery and development of a skill or talent could be another important bonus.

This will also be a positive year for financial matters, although the Earth Ox would do well to keep a watchful eye over his outgoings, and if he has borrowings, to try to reduce them. By managing his finances carefully, he will be able to improve his position over the year, and he will find that allowing for forthcoming expenses can prevent certain pressures or shortfalls from arising later. The attention he can give to his finances will reward him well.

On a domestic level this will be a busy but pleasing year, with the Earth Ox's methodical nature proving a great asset. Those close to him will appreciate his ability to organize and oversee a great deal, as well as how his efforts help in the efficient running of the household. His considerate nature will also be valued, with those close to him being grateful for the help and advice he so generously gives. In addition to the more practical aspects of home life, the Earth Ox himself will value those interests and projects that can be shared as well as some of the more agreeable occasions that take place, many of which he will have been instrumental in organizing. For family life to go well it does need everyone to balance out their commitments and contribute, and in this respect the Earth Ox will certainly play his full part.

The Earth Ox's social life is, though, very much in his own hands. Over the year some Earth Oxen will prefer to keep this quiet, simply meeting up with friends occasionally, while those who desire more companionship could find that a chance meeting or joining a society brings just the contact they desire. And this does sum up the nature of the Monkey year for the Earth Ox. The aspects are on his side and it rests with him to decide what *he* wants to achieve. The clearer his plans, the better he will fare.

TIP FOR THE YEAR
Follow through your ideas and see where they lead. It is better to take action now rather than be left wondering 'What if?' Be bold, seize the initiative and make the most of the opportunities the year will bring.

FAMOUS OXEN

King Abdullah of Jordan, Robert Altman, Hans Christian Andersen, Johann Sebastian Bach, Warren Beatty, Kate Beckinsale, Napoleon Bonaparte, Rory Bremner, Albert Camus, Jim Carrey, Johnny Carson, Charlie Chaplin, Melanie Chisholm, George Clooney, Martin Clunes, Jean Cocteau, Natalie Cole, Bill Cosby, Tom Courtenay, Tony Curtis, Diana, Princess of Wales, Marlene Dietrich, Walt Disney, Patrick Duffy, Harry Enfield, Jane Fonda, Gerald Ford, Edward Fox, Michael J. Fox, Peter Gabriel, Richard Gere, Robin Gibb, Handel, King Harald V of Norway,

Adolf Hitler, Dustin Hoffman, Anthony Hopkins, Saddam Hussein, Billy Joel, King Juan Carlos of Spain, B. B. King, Mark Knopfler, Burt Lancaster, Jessica Lange, Kate Moss, Alison Moyet, Eddie Murphy, Paul Newman, Jack Nicholson, Leslie Nielsen, Gwyneth Paltrow, Oscar Peterson, Colin Powell, Paula Radcliffe, Robert Redford, Lionel Richie, Rubens, Greg Rusedski, Meg Ryan, Jean Sibelius, Sissy Spacek, Bruce Springsteen, Meryl Streep, Lady Thatcher, Alan Titchmarsh, Scott F. Turow, Vincent van Gogh, Gore Vidal, Minette Walters, Zoë Wanamaker, Sigourney Weaver, the Duke of Wellington, Barbara Windsor, W. B. Yeats.

26 JANUARY 1914 ～ 13 FEBRUARY 1915   *Wood Tiger*

13 FEBRUARY 1926 ～ 1 FEBRUARY 1927   *Fire Tiger*

31 JANUARY 1938 ～ 18 FEBRUARY 1939   *Earth Tiger*

17 FEBRUARY 1950 ～ 5 FEBRUARY 1951   *Metal Tiger*

5 FEBRUARY 1962 ～ 24 JANUARY 1963   *Water Tiger*

23 JANUARY 1974 ～ 10 FEBRUARY 1975   *Wood Tiger*

9 FEBRUARY 1986 ～ 28 JANUARY 1987   *Fire Tiger*

28 JANUARY 1998 ～ 15 FEBRUARY 1999   *Earth Tiger*

THE
TIGER

THE PERSONALITY OF THE TIGER

The aim of life is self-development, to realize one's nature perfectly.

Oscar Wilde, a Tiger

The Tiger is born under the sign of courage. He is a charismatic figure and usually holds very firm views. He is strong-willed and determined, and sets about most of his activities with tremendous energy and enthusiasm. He is very alert and quick-witted and his mind is forever active. He is a highly original thinker and is nearly always brimming with new ideas or full of enthusiasm for some new project or scheme.

The Tiger adores challenges and he loves to get involved in anything which he thinks has an exciting future or which catches his imagination. He is prepared to take risks and does not like to be bound either by convention or the dictates of others. He likes to be free to act as he chooses and at least once during his life he will throw caution to the wind and go off and do the things he wants to do.

The Tiger does, however, have a somewhat restless nature. Even though he is often prepared to throw himself wholeheartedly into a project, his initial enthusiasm can soon wane if he sees something more appealing. He can also be rather impulsive and there will be occasions in his life when he acts in a manner he later regrets. If the Tiger were to think things through or be prepared to persevere in his various activities, he would almost certainly enjoy a greater degree of success.

Fortunately the Tiger is lucky in most of his enterprises, but should things not work out as he had hoped, he is liable to suffer from severe bouts of depression and it will often take him a long time to recover. His life often consists of a series of ups and downs.

The Tiger is, however, very adaptable. He has an adventurous spirit and rarely stays in the same place for long. In the early stages of his life he is likely to try his hand at several different jobs and he will also change his residence fairly frequently.

The Tiger is very honest and open in his dealings with others. He hates any sort of hypocrisy or falsehood. He is also well known for being blunt and forthright and has no hesitation in speaking his mind. He can be rebellious at times, particularly against any form of petty authority, and while this can lead him into conflict with others, he is never one to shrink from an argument or avoid standing up for what he believes is right.

The Tiger is a natural leader and can invariably rise to the top of his chosen profession. He does not, however, care for anything too bureaucratic or detailed and he also does not like to obey orders. He can be stubborn and obstinate and throughout his life he likes to retain a certain amount of independence in his actions and be responsible to no one but himself. He likes to consider that all his achievements are due to his own efforts and unless he cannot avoid it, he will rarely ask for support from others.

Ironically, despite his self-confidence and leadership qualities, the Tiger can be indecisive and will often delay making a major decision until the very last moment. He can also be sensitive to criticism.

Although the Tiger is capable of earning large sums of money, he is rather a spendthrift and does not always put his money to its best use. He can also be most generous and will often shower lavish gifts on friends and relations.

The Tiger cares very much for his reputation and the image that he tries to project. He carries himself with an air of dignity and authority and enjoys being the centre of attention. He is very adept at attracting publicity, both for himself and for the causes he supports.

The Tiger often marries young and he will find himself best suited to those born under the signs of the Pig, Dog, Horse and Goat. He can also get on well with the Rat, Rabbit and Rooster, but will find the Ox and Snake a bit too quiet and serious for his liking, and he will be highly irritated by the Monkey's rather mischievous and inquisitive ways. He will also find it difficult to get on with another Tiger or a Dragon – both partners will want to dominate the relationship and could find it difficult to compromise on even the smallest of matters.

The Tigress is lively, witty and a marvellous hostess at parties. She takes great care over her appearance and is usually most attractive. She can be a very doting mother and while she believes in letting her children have their freedom, she makes an excellent teacher and will ensure that her children are well brought up and want for nothing. Like her male counterpart, she has numerous interests and likes to have sufficient independence and freedom to go off and do the things she wants to do. She has a most caring and generous nature.

The Tiger has many commendable qualities. He is honest, courageous and often a source of inspiration to others. Providing he can curb the wilder excesses of his restless nature, he is almost certain to lead a fulfilling and satisfying life.

THE FIVE DIFFERENT TYPES OF TIGER

In addition to the 12 signs of the Chinese zodiac there are five elements, and these have a strengthening or moderating influence on the sign. The effects of the five elements on the Tiger are described below, together with the years in which the elements were exercising their influence. Therefore all Tigers born in 1950 are Metal Tigers, those born in 1962 are Water Tigers, and so on.

Metal Tiger: 1950
The Metal Tiger has an assertive and outgoing personality. He is very ambitious and while his aims may change from time to time, he will work relentlessly until he has obtained what he wants. He can, however, be impatient for results and become highly strung if things do not work out as he would like. He is distinctive in his appearance and is admired and respected by many.

Water Tiger: 1962
This Tiger has a wide variety of interests and is always eager to experiment with new ideas or satisfy his adventurous

nature by going off to explore distant lands. He is versatile, shrewd and has a kindly nature. He tends to remain calm in a crisis, although he can be annoyingly indecisive at times. He communicates well with others and through his many capabilities and persuasive nature he usually achieves what he wants in life. He is also highly imaginative and is often a gifted orator or writer.

Wood Tiger: 1914, 1974

The Wood Tiger has a friendly and pleasant personality. He is less independent than some of the other types of Tiger and is more prepared to work with others to secure a desired objective. However, he does have a tendency to jump from one thing to another and can easily become distracted. He is usually very popular, has a large circle of friends and invariably leads a busy and enjoyable social life. He also has a good sense of humour.

Fire Tiger: 1926, 1986

The Fire Tiger sets about everything he does with great verve and enthusiasm. He loves action and is always ready to throw himself wholeheartedly into anything which catches his imagination. He has many leadership qualities and is capable of communicating his ideas and enthusiasm to others. He is very much an optimist and can be most generous. He has a likeable nature and can be a witty and persuasive speaker.

Earth Tiger: 1938, 1998
This Tiger is responsible and level-headed. He studies everything objectively and tries to be scrupulously fair in all his dealings. Unlike other Tigers, he is prepared to specialize in certain areas rather than get distracted by other matters, but he can become so involved with what he is doing that he does not always take into account the opinions of those around him. He has good business sense and is usually very successful in later life. He has a large circle of friends and pays great attention to both his appearance and his reputation.

PROSPECTS FOR THE TIGER
IN 2004

The Chinese New Year starts on 22 January 2004. Until then, the old year, the Year of the Goat, is still making its presence felt.

The Year of the Goat (1 February 2003 to 21 January 2004) will have been a reasonable one for the Tiger, although he could have found it lacking the activity and pace he likes so much. The Tiger is all for action and for getting things done, but during the Goat year he will have found progress slow and not always easy.

However, despite the frustrations, the Goat year will still have brought its benefits, with the closing months being a more constructive period for the Tiger. In particular, if he has the opportunity to widen his experience by taking on other duties or is offered the chance of training, he should follow this through. What he learns at this time can be useful for his later progress. For those Tigers seeking work or wanting to advance their career, September could bring some interesting opportunities. Travel is also favoured and if the Tiger has the chance to go away, perhaps to visit family or friends, he should take this up. He will find his trips working out well.

The Tiger's domestic and social life is also set to become busier as the year draws to a close and he will be heavily involved in organizing some get-togethers and domestic projects. Although he may be under pressure at this time, he will often welcome the increased pace and the buzz of activity. On a personal level, the last quarter could be one of the busiest but most satisfying parts of the Goat year.

Although the Tiger may have wished to have accomplished more in the Goat year, he can take comfort in the knowledge that much of what he has done and learned will be to his advantage over the next 12 months.

The Year of the Monkey starts on 22 January and while it holds some pleasing developments for the Tiger, it is also one which requires some care. However, provided the Tiger remains aware of the traps that the Monkey year can spring, he will make good progress and be able to use his talents well.

One feature of the Monkey year is that it encourages the enterprising, and as the Tiger is usually so keen and a source of so many ideas, he is well placed to benefit from the prevailing aspects. In his work he can make good progress and there will certainly be chances for him to take on greater responsibilities, be promoted, or move to a position which allows him to make better use of his talents. Work-wise, the Monkey year is a time for change and progress. Also, when he has ideas he should put these forward. Again his initiative can lead to some interesting results.

Tigers who are seeking work, either as the year starts or during it, will also find that their experience and keenness will lead to them securing an interesting position. While it may not always be exactly what they were hoping for, by making the most of the opportunities they are given, they will not only be able to further their skills but also discover new strengths which they can build upon. For some Tigers, 2004 can bring a change in direction which they can capitalize on over the next few years. For work opportunities the months of April, June, September and November are particularly favourable.

However, while the Monkey year will allow the Tiger to make progress, some words of caution do need to be sounded. In particular, the Tiger does need to remain disciplined. With his wide interests and desire to be involved in so much, there is a risk that he could spread his energies too widely or take on more than he can properly handle. Similarly, in his desire to get results, the Tiger should be wary of taking short cuts or risks. When carrying out his duties he needs to remain thorough and focused. In addition, he could face some niggling irritations as a result of delays, bureaucracy or even the petty-mindedness of certain individuals. Although annoying, these situations should be handled with care. A considered response will yield far more than words said in haste. With care, though, the Tiger's handling of difficult situations could ultimately enhance his reputation.

The progress that the Tiger makes in his work will lead to an increase in his income, but again a certain care is needed. Over the year the Tiger will want to do and acquire a great deal, but he does need to plan his spending as well as allow for any new financial obligations he may take on. While he may feel he deserves to enjoy the rewards of his efforts, too many spending sprees could quickly mount up. Money-wise, this can be a good year, but it does call for careful management.

This need for care and consideration also extends to the Tiger's personal life. Although both domestically and socially the year will give rise to many happy and memorable occasions, the Tiger does need to remain mindful of others. In particular he could find that those around him do not always share his enthusiasm for some of his ideas and plans. To prevent problems, he must take note of their views and be prepared to show some flexibility. Dialogue and compromise really can make a great difference in certain situations. Also, the Tiger should be careful that his work and interests do not intrude too much into his family life. To be too preoccupied with other activities could again lead to some tensions. Fortunately the Tiger is usually considerate in this respect, but it is something he does need to watch over the year.

However, despite these warnings, the Tiger can look forward to some great moments in his domestic and social life. There will be much in his family life for him to enjoy, including the interests and activities he can share with others. His social life too will bring him considerable pleasure, with invitations to parties and other events. On a personal level, the months of April and May and the last quarter of the year could be some of the best and most active times.

Throughout the Monkey year the Tiger should bear in mind that there are many who think highly of him, and when he does have any problems and concerns, he should raise them. With dialogue being so important this year, he does need to be forthcoming.

The Monkey year favours travel and the Tiger should try to go away for a holiday or break at some time. As he will find, his travels will not only take him to some interesting destinations but also give him the chance to unwind and enjoy himself.

Overall, this can be a rewarding year for the Tiger, giving him the chance to make progress, use his skills well and sometimes identify new strengths. He will enjoy many of the activities he gets involved in, but he does need to remain aware of the traps the Monkey year can spring and should be careful and thorough in all he does. If he bears this in mind, then he can certainly benefit from the opportunities this interesting and generally positive year will bring.

The Metal Tiger

As far as the different types of Tiger are concerned, the Monkey year holds interesting prospects for the Metal Tiger, allowing him to make good use of his skills as well as take pleasure in many of his undertakings. However, as with all Tigers, the Metal Tiger does need to remain aware of the year's trickier aspects and avoid complacency or unnecessary risks. It can be a constructive and satisfying year, but some caution is necessary.

In his work, the Metal Tiger can look forward to some positive developments. In view of his long years of experience as well as more recent achievements, he is likely to find himself being earmarked for new responsibilities and well placed for promotion. Indeed, some Metal Tigers will be able to secure a position they have sought for some time. Admittedly, some of the tasks the Metal Tiger will be given will be daunting, especially when taking over a new role, but by rising to the challenge he will quickly make his mark. He, too, will find his innovative approach a real asset and over the year his resourcefulness will serve him well.

Metal Tigers who are seeking work or considering a career change will also find this a year of interesting developments. By keeping alert for openings, many will be able to secure a position which represents an interesting change and allows them to use their experience in a new and more rewarding manner. For work opportunities April, June, September and November are especially favourable.

However, while the Metal Tiger can make good progress in his work, he does need to take note of the views and advice of colleagues. He may like to set about his activities in his own way, but to be too independent could be to his detriment. Also, situations could arise which try his patience, and he needs to handle these with tact. Metal Tigers, take note. This is a good year for progress, but care is still required.

The Monkey year is generally positive for financial matters and many Metal Tigers will enjoy a noticeable increase in income as well as sometimes benefit from an additional sum of money, often from a different source. While this upturn will be welcome, the Metal Tiger should still manage his finances with care. He could find it helpful to set funds aside for certain requirements (including travel) and, if he is able, to add to his long-term savings. By managing his money carefully, rather than proceeding in an ad hoc way, he will find he is often able to do more as well as improve his general position.

Many Metal Tigers have an adventurous streak and in the Monkey year travel can turn out to be both satisfying and enjoyable, so the Metal Tiger should aim to go away at some time over the year. He should also set a regular time aside for other recreational pursuits. Sometimes these can be an outlet for his creative talents as well as provide an important balance to all his other activities.

The Monkey year can also bring some fine domestic and social occasions. The Metal Tiger will enjoy helping and encouraging those close to him as well as keeping himself busy with various projects in his home and garden. He will watch the progress of younger relations with fond interest and if he is able to offer any help, especially to those with young children, it will often be greatly appreciated. However, while there is so much that will bring the Metal Tiger pleasure, there will be times when pressures could lead to him feeling tired and irritable. At such times the Metal Tiger would find it helpful to talk over any matters giving him concern and ask for assistance when required. As he will find, dialogue and support at busy times really can make a difference over the year.

On a social level, the Metal Tiger will welcome the chance to meet up with friends over the year and will enjoy many of the social events he attends. Many Metal Tigers will also find that their interests or some of their travels will allow them to meet others and an important friendship can be forged as a result.

Overall, the Monkey year holds much promise for the Metal Tiger. It will allow him to make progress as well as to develop his skills. But he does need to remain careful in all his activities and be mindful of others.

TIP FOR THE YEAR
Be enterprising and make the most of your ideas. However, do be sure to consult others and build up support.

The Water Tiger

This will be a promising year for the Water Tiger, particularly as it will give him the chance to make more of his talents and ideas.

As the year begins, Water Tigers who are keen to advance in their work should actively start to look for new openings. These can be within the organization in which they are based – and here their internal knowledge could be an advantage – or elsewhere, but by making the decision to progress, many will find new possibilities emerging.

This also applies to those Water Tigers seeking work. Although some may have become disillusioned as a result of recent events or feel that their old spark has diminished, this is a year for drawing a firm line under past disappointments and moving ahead. It will take effort and determination, but by persisting these Water Tigers will find themselves being given an opportunity which could set them off on an interesting and more rewarding career path. For work opportunities, late March, April, June and September are especially favourable.

However, while the year offers good opportunities for progress, it will not be without its pressures. At work there could be deadlines to meet, new initiatives and procedures to learn or complex tasks to carry out, and these could demand a lot from the Water Tiger. However, by concentrating on what needs to be done and giving his best, he will be able to show his true strength and sometimes discover new skills in the process. The Monkey year will be a good test of his abilities and will give him the chances and the incentive which could have been lacking in recent years.

The progress that the Water Tiger makes in his work will lead to an increase in income and generally this will be a positive year for financial matters. However, to benefit fully from this upturn, the Water Tiger will need to remain disciplined and budget well, setting funds aside to cover his obligations and the more substantial purchases he may want to make. By controlling his spending and if possible reducing some of his borrowings, he will find his situation much improved by the end of the year.

As far as the Water Tiger's relations with others are concerned, this will be a positive year, but again a certain care will be needed. At times the Water Tiger could become preoccupied with work and other activities, and failure to give time to family life could lead to some edginess and strain. Others in his household could also have busy schedules and feel under pressure, and the Water Tiger should aim to show some support and understanding and encourage everyone to help each other. He would also do well to encourage activities that everyone can enjoy, perhaps a project or shared interest, going out to some form of entertainment or for a special meal, having friends around or holding a party. Such activities will lead to some pleasurable occasions and be much appreciated.

Over the year, many Water Tigers will also take considerable pride in the success of younger relations. While the Water Tiger may not wish to be seen as interfering, any support and advice he feels able to give will be valued.

The Water Tiger will have many demands on his time during the year, but he should take care that his social life and interests do not suffer. Both provide a valuable balance to his life and can lead to some enjoyable occasions. Water Tigers who may have had some difficulty in their personal life or desire more companionship can take heart in the Monkey year. By making the effort to go out, they will soon find themselves meeting others and often striking up a significant friendship or romance, with the months of April and May and the last quarter of the year seeing much social activity.

Overall, the Monkey year holds much potential for the Water Tiger and by making the most of his strengths and the opportunities the year will bring, he will make good headway. Also, by spending time with those important to him and balancing out his activities, he will enjoy many satisfying and pleasurable occasions.

TIP FOR THE YEAR
Show the true Water Tiger spirit. Move forward. Strive for better things. Use your strengths, experience and ideas well and your efforts will be rewarded.

The Wood Tiger

This marks the Wood Tiger's thirtieth year and it promises to be a significant one, allowing him to make good use of his talents as well as enjoy a pleasing personal life. The aspects are mostly on his side, although the year could nevertheless spring some surprises which could cause him to look again at some of his plans and activities.

Work-wise, there will be some key developments. Although many Wood Tigers will have made progress and gained useful experience in recent years, there will be quite a few who feel they could be doing better and hanker after more responsible positions. As the Wood Tiger enters his thirties, he will feel impelled to take action, sensing that if he does not put himself forward now opportunities could be lost. As a result, many Wood Tigers will actively pursue promotion opportunities or openings which they feel offer greater potential. However, with the Monkey year containing its share of surprises, there could be some unexpected twists. Sometimes, by indicating his desire to move on, the Wood Tiger could find his present employers singling him out for a new and more rewarding role, as they try to avoid losing someone so experienced. Alternatively, he may see a position advertised which represents a welcome change but still allows him to profit from the experience he has built up. Whatever happens, by looking to advance, the Wood Tiger will be able to make headway, sometimes in an unexpected but fortuitous manner.

The year also holds good prospects for those Wood Tigers seeking work. By remaining alert and following up any vacancies that interest them, many will be successful in gaining a position which allows them to use their skills and also opens up interesting possibilities for the future. Opportunities could arise at almost any time, such is the favourable nature of the Monkey year, but April, June, September and November could see particularly interesting developments.

This is also a favourable year for self-development and the Wood Tiger should take advantage of any training he may be offered or any other means of developing his skills. Even if this involves reading or studying in his own time, it will be helpful both now and in the near future.

Similarly, the Wood Tiger should also not overlook his personal interests. By developing them further, he will learn a lot as well as take greater pleasure in them. Wood Tigers who have creative interests should consider promoting their work. In some cases it could attract an encouraging response.

The progress that the Wood Tiger makes over the year will lead to a welcome increase in his income, but with his many obligations, he does need to watch his outgoings. With care and good financial housekeeping this can be a much improved year, but to benefit fully the Wood Tiger does need to manage his finances well and budget for forthcoming expenses. He should also avoid unnecessary risks, remembering that the Monkey year can spring traps for the unwary.

As far as the Wood Tiger's domestic life is concerned, this will be an active year. There will be many calls upon his time, both from younger and more senior relations, and although he may sometimes despair of all that is required of him, the advice and assistance he is able to give others will be greatly valued. At particularly busy times, rather than pushing himself, he would find it helpful to prioritize what needs to be done and, if necessary, defer certain household projects until he has more time. Also, he should not hesitate to draw on offers of assistance, and if he feels others could help more with certain household tasks, he should make sure they do so. Home life in 2004 will require good time management and a fair sharing of responsibilities, but in return there will be a great deal that will mean a lot to the Wood Tiger, including some wonderful family occasions. The Monkey year will certainly contain its pleasures and memorable moments.

The Wood Tiger will also appreciate his social life and while this may not be as active as some years, he will enjoy meeting up with friends as well as some of the events he is invited to. Wood Tigers who may desire more company or romance or who are eager to put past disappointments behind them can do much to bring some sparkle back into their lives by going out more, with many meeting someone who will become special to them. April, May and the last quarter of the year are particularly favourable for meeting others.

Generally, the Monkey year holds fine prospects for the Wood Tiger and by making the most of his talents and looking to advance his career, he can achieve a great deal. Although on a domestic level this may be a busy year, the love, support and encouragement the Wood Tiger receives from those around him will mean a great deal to him and will spur him on.

TIP FOR THE YEAR
This is a time for action. Make the most of your talents and ideas and the opportunities the year will bring. Also, at busy times, prioritize and concentrate on the essentials.

The Fire Tiger

Enthusiastic, eager and keen, the Fire Tiger will want to make much of his eighteenth year, and it does hold considerable promise. In 2004 he will enjoy some great personal successes as well as form a clearer idea of what he wants to do over the next few years. However, he should still be mindful of some of the traps the Monkey year can spring, and if he pushes his luck too far or rests on his laurels too much, he could face some disappointments. This is a year to enjoy and to make progress, but to be careful too.

For many Fire Tigers much of the year will be dominated by study and approaching exams. Although there will be times when the Fire Tiger may be disheartened by the amount he needs to learn, by working consistently and keeping the end result in mind, he *will* do well. He will also find it helpful to remain disciplined, perhaps giving himself a timetable of what needs to be covered and for when. The more organized he is, the better he will fare.

Many Fire Tigers will also be giving thought to their future and will have important decisions to take. Some will be debating whether to carry on with their education. Given its importance, this is not a decision that they can take lightly or without advice, and they would do well to speak to their tutors and career advisers about the various options and courses available. But by taking time to consider what would be most suitable, many Fire Tigers will be content with the decisions they make.

For those Fire Tigers already in employment or those who decide to seek a job during the year, again the Monkey year will bring some interesting developments. Those seeking work will need to be persistent and while they will naturally be disappointed when certain applications do not go their way, with each job they try for they will be strengthening their application techniques and discovering more about what employers require. And once the Fire Tiger is given a position – possibly one he was not expecting to get – he will find it will give him a valuable foothold on the employment ladder as well as some useful experience, and such is the nature of the Monkey year that one position can quickly lead to another. The Monkey year can produce some swift changes, particularly in the second half.

The Fire Tiger will, though, need to be careful when dealing with money matters and avoid taking unnecessary risks. Although he may be eager to supplement his income, he should be wary of 'get rich quick' schemes or committing his money to undertakings he has not fully investigated or knows little about. This is very much a year for care and should he have any doubts over any financial matter, it really would be worth him seeking advice. Fire Tigers, take note and remain vigilant.

As far as the Fire Tiger's personal life is concerned, this will be a special year and he will enjoy himself with friends both old and new. With his breezy and genial nature, he will find he is very much in demand and he will enjoy going out partying as well as joining in with various social activities. Fire Tigers in youth groups, clubs or sports teams could find their contribution singles them out for an increased role. On a personal level, the Fire Tiger will be in demand and on great form.

The Monkey year will also give the Fire Tiger the chance to develop some of his ideas, and whether these relate to his interests or to some travel plans, by taking them further he will find that a great deal is possible. Again, though, he should talk to others (especially family members) about what he has in mind. He will find he is supported and encouraged in a great many ways. For those keen on travel, the year is especially favourable.

Generally, the Monkey year holds encouraging prospects for the Fire Tiger and by setting about his studies and work in his usual enthusiastic way, he will do well and also be helping his future. And on a personal level, this is a year he will enjoy.

TIP FOR THE YEAR
Remain disciplined and focus your attention on what needs to be done, particularly in regard to exam preparation or work responsibilities. The effort and commitment made now will pay considerable dividends in the future.

The Earth Tiger
This will be a busy and satisfying year for the Earth Tiger, with his home life seeing much activity.

For quite some time many Earth Tigers will have been having thoughts about their accommodation. For some this could involve moving to somewhere more appropriate for their present needs, while others will have projects they would like to carry out. For those who do move, much time will be spent in finding a new home and then in the process of moving and settling in. This will be a demanding time, but with the opportunities and amenities their new home and area offer, these Earth Tigers will feel that the move is the right thing. They will also find it helpful to draw on the help of others rather than take on too much single-handed. This not only includes getting advice on the legalities involved, but also asking for help with some of the more strenuous activities. As these Earth Tigers will find, moving is a demanding process, but help and support can make it all the easier.

Earth Tigers who remain where they are will also find their practical nature getting the better of them and they will decide to go ahead with household projects they have long had in mind. This could include refurbishing certain rooms or adding new features and comforts to their home. Again, some disruption could result, but to compensate, they will be satisfied with what is achieved.

In view of the expense his domestic activities will involve, the Earth Tiger does need to be aware of the costs he is taking on and should obtain several quotations for work and services as well as a written breakdown of all that is covered. Without adequate care and attention, he could find he is sometimes paying more than is necessary or that not all he wanted was included in the price. Important agreements and financial transactions *do* need to be checked thoroughly if problems are to be avoided.

Similarly, the Earth Tiger could be required to complete several forms relating to tax, pension or benefits over the year and these need to be completed carefully and on time. In 2004 matters involving finance and important paperwork cannot be left to chance. Earth Tigers, do take note.

Despite the considerable domestic expense of the year, the Earth Tiger should still try to set some funds aside for travel. A holiday or change of scene will not only do him good but could also be great fun. The Earth Tiger will enjoy the places he visits and the opportunity to meet others while away, some of whom could become friends. He should also take advantage of any invitation to visit family or friends living some distance away. As he will find, travel in 2004 will lead to some very agreeable times.

On a domestic level, although some of the year will be dominated by practical activities, the Earth Tiger will be grateful for the support he is given by family members and will follow the progress of those close to him with fond interest. Some of the family occasions that take place will mean a great deal to him, including the successes of some younger relations.

This will also be a pleasant year socially, with the Earth Tiger appreciating the chances to meet friends as well as the support and assistance they are able to give. Those Earth Tigers who move or may desire more companionship will find that by getting involved in various activities, they will soon get to meet and befriend others with similar interests and outlooks. On a social level, the Monkey year will hold some very enjoyable and gratifying times, with April, May and the last quarter being especially favourable.

Despite the activity of the year, the Earth Tiger should also make sure his own personal interests are not neglected. Outdoor pursuits such as gardening or walking, creative activities or taking up new skills can all be fulfilling and rewarding. And if the Earth Tiger can join fellow enthusiasts at a local group or society, he will find this can add to the pleasure his interests already bring.

Overall, the Monkey year will be a busy one for Earth Tiger, particularly in view of some of the domestic plans he will be keen to carry out. However, with support, he will be pleased with what he accomplishes and will be delighted at seeing so many of his ideas take shape. And his relations with others and his personal interests will mean much to him over the year.

TIP FOR THE YEAR

Involve others in your activities and draw on the assistance they may offer. With support, this can be a gratifying and significant time.

FAMOUS TIGERS

Debbie Allen, Kofi Annan, Sir David Attenborough, Queen Beatrix of the Netherlands, Victoria Beckham, Beethoven, Tony Bennett, Tom Berenger, Chuck Berry, Jon Bon Jovi, Sir Richard Branson, Emily Brontë, Garth Brooks, Mel Brooks, Isambard Kingdom Brunel, Agatha Christie, Charlotte Church, Phil Collins, Robbie Coltrane, Sheryl Crow, Tom Cruise, Penelope Cruz, Charles de Gaulle, Leonardo DiCaprio, Emily Dickinson, David Dimbleby, Dwight Eisenhower, Queen Elizabeth II, Enya, Roberta Flack, E. M. Forster, Frederick Forsyth, Jodie

Foster, Crystal Gayle, Elliott Gould, Buddy Greco, Alan Greenspan, Germaine Greer, Ed Harris, Hugh Hefner, Tim Henman, William Hurt, Natalie Imbruglia, Jewel, Ray Kroc, Stan Laurel, Jay Leno, Groucho Marx, Karl Marx, Marilyn Monroe, Demi Moore, Alanis Morissette, Jeremy Paxman, Marco Polo, Beatrix Potter, John Prescott, Renoir, Kenny Rogers, the Princess Royal, Dame Joan Sutherland, Dylan Thomas, Liv Ullman, Jon Voight, Julie Walters, H. G. Wells, Oscar Wilde, Robbie Williams, Tennessee Williams, Terry Wogan, Stevie Wonder, William Wordsworth.

29 JANUARY 1903 ∼ 15 FEBRUARY 1904   *Water Rabbit*

14 FEBRUARY 1915 ∼ 2 FEBRUARY 1916   *Wood Rabbit*

2 FEBRUARY 1927 ∼ 22 JANUARY 1928   *Fire Rabbit*

19 FEBRUARY 1939 ∼ 7 FEBRUARY 1940   *Earth Rabbit*

6 FEBRUARY 1951 ∼ 26 JANUARY 1952   *Metal Rabbit*

25 JANUARY 1963 ∼ 12 FEBRUARY 1964   *Water Rabbit*

11 FEBRUARY 1975 ∼ 30 JANUARY 1976   *Wood Rabbit*

29 JANUARY 1987 ∼ 16 FEBRUARY 1988   *Fire Rabbit*

16 FEBRUARY 1999 ∼ 4 FEBRUARY 2000   *Earth Rabbit*

THE
RABBIT

THE PERSONALITY OF THE RABBIT

Whatever you are by nature, keep to it; never desert your line of talent. Be what nature intended you for, and you will succeed.

Sydney Smith, a Rabbit

The Rabbit is born under the signs of virtue and prudence. He is intelligent, well-mannered and prefers a quiet and peaceful existence. He dislikes any sort of unpleasantness and will try to steer clear of arguments and disputes. He is very much a pacifist and tends to have a calming influence on those around him. He has wide interests and usually has a good appreciation of the arts and the finer things in life. He also knows how to enjoy himself and will often gravitate to the best restaurants and night spots in town.

The Rabbit is a witty and intelligent speaker and loves being involved in a good discussion. His views and advice are often sought by others and he can be relied upon to be discreet and diplomatic. He will rarely raise his voice in anger and will even turn a blind eye to matters which displease him just to preserve the peace. The Rabbit likes to remain on good terms with everyone, but he can be rather sensitive and takes any form of criticism very badly. He will also be the first to get out of the way if he sees any form of trouble brewing.

The Rabbit is a quiet and efficient worker and has an extremely good memory. He is very astute in business and financial matters, but his degree of success often depends on the conditions that prevail. He hates being in a situation which is fraught with tension or where he has to make sudden decisions. Wherever possible he will plan his various activities with the utmost care and a good deal of caution. He does not like to take risks and does not take kindly to changes. Basically, he seeks a secure, calm and stable environment, and when conditions are right he is more than happy to leave things as they are.

The Rabbit is conscientious and because of his methodical and ever-watchful nature he can often do well in his chosen profession. He makes a good diplomat, lawyer, shopkeeper, administrator or priest, and he excels in any job where he can use his superb skills as a communicator. He tends to be loyal to his employers and is respected for his integrity and honesty, but if he ever finds himself in a position of great power he can become rather intransigent and authoritarian.

The Rabbit attaches great importance to his home and will often spend a lot of time and money maintaining and furnishing it and fitting it with all the latest comforts – the Rabbit is very much a creature of comfort! He is also something of a collector and there are many Rabbits who derive much pleasure from collecting antiques, stamps, coins, *objets d'art* or anything else which catches their eye or particularly interests them.

The female Rabbit has a friendly, caring and considerate nature, and will do all in her power to give her home a happy and loving atmosphere. She is also very sociable and enjoys holding parties and entertaining. She has a great ability to make the maximum use of her time and although she involves herself in numerous activities, she always manages to find time to sit back and enjoy a good read or a chat. She has a great sense of humour, is very artistic and is often a talented gardener.

The Rabbit takes considerable care over his appearance and is usually smart and well turned out. He also attaches great importance to his relations with others and matters of the heart are particularly important to him. He will rarely be short of admirers and will often have several serious romances before he settles down. The Rabbit is not the most faithful of signs, but he will find that he is especially well suited to those born under the signs of the Goat, Snake, Pig and Ox. Due to his sociable and easy-going manner he can also get on well with the Tiger, Dragon, Horse, Monkey, Dog and another Rabbit, but he will feel ill at ease with the Rat and Rooster as both these signs tend to speak their mind and be critical in their comments, and the Rabbit just loathes any form of criticism or unpleasantness.

The Rabbit is usually lucky in life and often has the happy knack of being in the right place at the right time. He is talented and quick-witted, but he does sometimes put pleasure before work, and wherever possible will tend to opt for the easy life. He can at times be a little reserved and suspicious of the motives of others, but generally will lead a long and contented life and one which – as far as possible – will be free of strife and discord.

THE FIVE DIFFERENT TYPES OF RABBIT

In addition to the 12 signs of the Chinese zodiac there are five elements, and these have a strengthening or moderating influence on the sign. The effects of the five elements on the Rabbit are described below, together with the years in which the elements were exercising their influence. Therefore all Rabbits born in 1951 are Metal Rabbits, those born in 1903 and 1963 are Water Rabbits, and so on.

Metal Rabbit: 1951

This Rabbit is capable, ambitious and has very definite views on what he wants to achieve in life. He can occasionally appear reserved and aloof, but this is mainly because he likes to keep his thoughts to himself. He has a quick and alert mind and is particularly shrewd in business matters. He can also be very cunning in his actions. The Metal Rabbit has a good appreciation of the arts and likes to mix in the best circles. He usually has a small but very loyal group of friends.

Water Rabbit: 1903, 1963

The Water Rabbit is popular, intuitive and keenly aware of the feelings of those around him. He can, however, be rather sensitive and tends to take things too much to heart. He is very precise and thorough in everything he does and has an exceedingly good memory. He tends to be quiet and at times rather withdrawn, but he expresses his ideas well and is highly regarded by his family, friends and colleagues.

Wood Rabbit: 1915, 1975

The Wood Rabbit is likeable, easy-going and very adaptable. He prefers to work in groups rather than on his own and likes to have the support and encouragement of others. He can, however, be rather reticent in expressing his views and it would be in his own interests to become a little more open and let others know how he feels on certain matters. He usually has many friends, enjoys an active social life and is noted for his generosity.

Fire Rabbit: 1927, 1987

The Fire Rabbit has a friendly, outgoing personality. He likes socializing and being on good terms with everyone. He is discreet and diplomatic and has a very good understanding of human nature. He is also strong-willed and provided he has the necessary backing he can go far in life. He does, not, however, suffer adversity well and can become moody and depressed when things are not working out as he would like. He has a particularly good manner with children, is very intuitive and there are some Fire Rabbits who are even noted for their psychic ability.

Earth Rabbit: 1939, 1999

The Earth Rabbit is a quiet individual, but he is nevertheless very astute. He is realistic in his aims and is prepared to work long and hard in order to achieve his objectives. He has good business sense and is invariably lucky in financial matters. He also has a most persuasive manner and usually experiences little difficulty in getting others to fall in with his plans. He is held in high esteem by his friends and colleagues and his views are often sought and highly valued.

PROSPECTS FOR THE RABBIT IN 2004

The Chinese New Year starts on 22 January 2004. Until then, the old year, the Year of the Goat, is still making its presence felt.

The Year of the Goat (1 February 2003 to 21 January 2004) is a generally favourable one for the Rabbit. He is likely to achieve a great deal in his work, both furthering his experience and obtaining some often impressive results. Many Rabbits will have made good headway over the year, but for those seeking work or looking to make further advances, September and November could hold interesting prospects.

In the closing months of the Goat year the Rabbit should also spend time on his personal interests. Goat years do favour creative and cultural pursuits, and with his talents in these areas the Rabbit is well placed to benefit. If he has a creative project or ideas he can promote at this time, he should do so.

The Rabbit's personal life is also well aspected and he can look forward to many happy and meaningful occasions in the company of both family and friends. However, with so much happening, he should try to spread his commitments out. The last quarter of the year will require good time management. Yet despite its activity, the Rabbit will enjoy a great deal of what happens as well as the love and companionship of those who mean much to him. The last few months of the year will also be a splendid time for meeting others and, in some cases, a significant friendship will be born.

This will, though, be an expensive time and the Rabbit would do well to watch his spending and avoid unnecessary risks. This warning apart, much can go in his favour and by making the most of his ideas and strengths, he can make progress as well as enjoy himself.

The Year of the Monkey starts on 22 January and although a reasonable one for the Rabbit, it will not be without its trickier moments.

One of the more awkward areas concerns finance. Over the year the Rabbit will face many demands on his resources, including family, accommodation and transport costs as well as some large purchases. Fortunately the Rabbit is usually quite adept when dealing with money matters, but this is not a year for taking risks or entering into important agreements without studying all the implications. Should the Rabbit have any reservations or questions about a transaction he is considering, he *must* resolve these before proceeding.

This need for care also extends to any important forms that the Rabbit receives, especially if related to finance, tax or possible benefits. Again, these need to be dealt with thoroughly, otherwise there is a chance that the Rabbit could find himself at a disadvantage. Fortunately his conscientious nature can help prevent mistakes from arising, but the Monkey year does require him to be on his guard and it can be unforgiving over lapses or errors of judgement.

The Rabbit will enjoy better prospects in his work. In 2004 he will be able to build on his present position and extend his experience. With the Monkey year favouring enterprise, he should put forward any work-related ideas or schemes he has. His initiative will be appreciated and can often lead to interesting results.

Rabbits who want to advance their career or who are seeking work will find that they will fare best by following up positions which draw on their skills and experience rather than trying for anything too different. Sometimes a great deal of persistence will be required, but the effort will be worthwhile, with the months of March, May, October and November bringing the best opportunities.

However, while there will be chances to make progress at work, the Rabbit should not forget the year's more awkward elements. Although he may like to immerse himself in his own activities, this is not a year to close himself off from other developments, and he should take note of unfolding situations, proposals under consideration and the views of his colleagues. The better informed he is, the better prepared he will be to adapt to any changes that take place.

The Rabbit should also take full advantage of any training opportunities that may be offered and consider ways in which he can add to his skills, perhaps by enrolling on a course or taking on some additional study. Keeping his skills up to date and learning new ones will not only be helpful for his current position but also open up possibilities for the future.

In addition, the Rabbit should set a regular time aside for his own personal interests, again possibly extending them in some way. By setting himself an interesting project to do or skill to learn, he will find his interests can be especially rewarding and can often develop in an encouraging manner.

The Rabbit will also take much satisfaction from his domestic life and will, as always, play a major part. He will do much to assist both younger and more senior relations and others will often look to him for advice as well as practical support. In addition, the help and understanding he is able to show to someone who may have an awkward problem will be of more value than he may realize. If, though, any problem should arise which the Rabbit may not feel sufficiently able to deal with, he would find it helpful to contact someone more qualified to advise. The Rabbit may have a willing disposition, but he should remember that expert help *is* available should he need it, and it can, in some cases, help ease any burden or obligation he may feel under. No year is completely free from its problems or pressures, but the Rabbit will still find his home life bringing many rewarding occasions. As well as encouraging the progress of those around him, he will take pleasure in shared projects and interests. A holiday or break too could lead to some particularly enjoyable times, especially in the third quarter of the year.

The Rabbit's social life will also bring him much pleasure, particularly the chances he gets to meet up with friends and attend parties and other social events. There will be excellent opportunities for him to extend his social circle and, for the unattached, significant romance could beckon. The months of March and April and August to October are particularly favourable for making new friends. For the Rabbit, affairs of the heart are one of the most favourably aspected areas of the Monkey year.

Overall, this will be a generally satisfying year for the Rabbit and while he will need to be careful when dealing with financial and bureaucratic matters, his domestic and social life and personal interests will all be rewarding.

The Metal Rabbit

As far as the different types of Rabbit are concerned, this will be a reasonable year for the Metal Rabbit. He can look forward to making useful progress as well as enjoying some moments of great personal success, but the year could also bring a few problems. The Metal Rabbit will need to tread carefully and cautiously.

At work many Metal Rabbits will decide to remain in their present position, especially as they will be able to use their knowledge and experience to good effect. By carrying out their duties in their usual conscientious way, they can look forward to achieving some pleasing and often personally satisfying results. Also, some could find their experience leads to them taking on other responsibilities or becoming involved in new projects. As a worker, the Metal Rabbit has a fine reputation and the Monkey year will certainly allow him to use his talents well.

The Metal Rabbit who is seeking work or anxious to change his position will also find that the Monkey year can provide him with some interesting opportunities. Although he will have to strive hard for these, once he does secure a new position he will quickly impress others and make much of his new duties.

Another positive feature of the year is the chance it will give the Metal Rabbit to extend his skills, and regardless of whether he is well established in his position or new to it, he should take full advantage of any training opportunities offered. They will not only assist him with his present duties but could also open up possibilities for the future.

While the Metal Rabbit will take a good deal of satisfaction in his work, he does still need to be aware of the trickier elements of the Monkey year. Problems could suddenly flare up or certain colleagues could prove awkward. At such times the Metal Rabbit will need to deal with the situation as best and as tactfully as he can. He will often find it helpful to encourage dialogue rather than let problems simmer in the background. Rather than ignoring any unpleasantness – which Rabbits tend to do – he will find that by addressing the situation he can do much to defuse it. Also, taking the initiative can win him the respect of others.

Another area which requires care is finance. The Metal Rabbit's generally cautious nature will be an advantage here, but if he enters into any large transaction, he does need to check the small print carefully. This is not a year for risks, and important paperwork, especially if related to finance, does require close attention. The Metal Rabbit would also find it helpful to make early provision for any large expenses. Careful budgeting will not only help him to spread the costs but also enable him to manage his general financial situation that much better.

More favourably aspected is the Metal Rabbit's domestic life. He will take a fond interest in the activities of family members and they in turn will value the advice and assistance he so generously gives. He will also enjoy some of the more practical activities he undertakes, such as adding new comforts to his home and tackling projects in his garden. Any breaks or holidays will also be pleasurable and the Metal Rabbit will benefit from the rest and change of routine that they bring.

The Metal Rabbit's social life, too, will bring him a good deal of pleasure. Whether attending parties and other social occasions, spending time with friends or going out for a meal or to some form of entertainment, the Metal Rabbit will enjoy himself and add to his social circle in the process. Those who may desire more companionship or have had some personal difficulties of late will find that the Monkey year can certainly bring some happiness back into their life. The months from March to early May and August and October are especially favourable for social activities.

Although the Monkey year will not be without its awkward moments, provided the Metal Rabbit remains his careful self he can do much to avoid or minimize some of the more challenging aspects and can take much satisfaction in his many activities.

TIP FOR THE YEAR
Make the most of your strengths and aim to develop them. They are not only an asset but also an investment for the future.

The Water Rabbit

This will be an important year for the Water Rabbit with what he achieves often being to his long-term benefit.

Work-wise, though, this can be quite a challenging year, with the prospect of an increased workload or having to adapt to new techniques and procedures. There will be times when the Water Rabbit will despair of all he has to do and of some of the petty and niggling problems he has to face, but by remaining his disciplined and conscientious self he will not only deal with a great many things but also add to his experience and help his future prospects in the process.

Throughout the year, however, the Water Rabbit does need to work closely with others rather than be too independent in his actions. By liaising with others, he will find he becomes more involved in what is going on as well as better able to build up support.

In view of the changes many Water Rabbits will have seen in the preceding Goat year, many will choose to remain in their present position this year. However, for those seeking to move on or looking for work, the Monkey year will produce some interesting opportunities. Admittedly, it could take the Water Rabbit several attempts to secure a position, but once in a new post, he will find it will not only help him to extend his skills but could also open up other possibilities for the future. As with all Rabbits, the Water Rabbit will find that progress in the Monkey year will require considerable effort, but what he is able to achieve now *will* be of long-term benefit.

Also, if he has any ideas relating to his work or something extra he could do, he should take them further. With the Monkey year so favouring enterprise, one of the Water Rabbit's ideas could bring an interesting response.

The best months for work activities are from March to May and October and November, but generally this is a year for working in consultation with others and for using and developing existing skills rather than looking to make major career leaps.

As far as finance is concerned, this is a year for caution. In 2004 the Water Rabbit could face several periods of considerable outlay, especially involving family members, accommodation and transport costs. In addition, as with almost all Rabbits in 2004, the Water Rabbit's practical nature will often get the better of him and he will embark on some home improvements. Throughout the year, he should make allowances for this, and would find it helpful to set regular funds aside. Also, when involved in any large expenditure, he should check that he is getting the best terms available. Extra care when managing his finances really will be worthwhile. Also, should the Water Rabbit have any uncertainties over any transaction he is about to enter into, he should check the details and small print and, if necessary, seek further advice. Money-wise, this *is* a year to remain vigilant.

The Water Rabbit's home life will, though, bring him a great deal of pleasure. Whether this is by undertaking household projects, developing mutual interests, entertaining friends, taking holidays or celebrating the progress and success of family members, the Monkey year will certainly give rise to some good occasions. Also, the Water Rabbit should remember that others are keen to help him, and if he would welcome more assistance with certain activities or chores or would find it helpful to talk about any pressures he may be under, he should be forthcoming. He does, after all, give so much to others and in 2004 he must be receptive to the help they can give in return.

The Water Rabbit's social life, too, will give rise to many agreeable times over the year. He will enjoy various parties and other occasions – with the second half of the year being particularly active – as well as the chance to chat with friends. Again, if he is troubled by any matter and has a friend or contact with the knowledge to help or advise, he should be forthcoming. As he will find, he does have friends who can provide valuable help should he need it. With the aspects so good for personal relations, he will also find his social circle increasing quite widely as the year progresses. For some Water Rabbits the Monkey year can bring the gift of significant romance. March, April and the months from August to October are well aspected for meeting others.

Overall, this will be a constructive year for the Water Rabbit, allowing him to further his skills and experience. Domestic and social matters will go well. It is with finance that the greatest care is required.

TIP FOR THE YEAR
Be forthcoming and gain from the help and support that others can give.

The Wood Rabbit

This will be an interesting year for the Wood Rabbit and although it will not be free from its pressures and problems, there will be much for him to enjoy.

The Wood Rabbit's personal life is especially well aspected and over the year he will value the love and encouragement of those who mean much to him. For those Wood Rabbits with a partner, the Monkey year will bring some truly special times, and despite the pressures of work and other activities, by supporting each other and sharing concerns and thoughts, they will find their rapport will often be strengthened. Also, if the Wood Rabbit is able to involve his partner and others in his household in some of his activities and projects, he will value the assistance they can give. For domestic life to go well, there does have to be input and communication, and the role the Wood Rabbit plays in this can indeed make this a rewarding year. Wood Rabbits who are parents will also take pleasure in the progress their children make as well as treasure some of the wonderful moments young children can bring.

Home life for the Wood Rabbit can certainly go well in 2004, but with everything else he has to do there will be times when he feels tired or under pressure. At such times, if he can draw on offers of help, he should do so, and if certain activities can be deferred until he has more time, he should consider it. The Wood Rabbit may be conscientious, but he does need to give himself some consideration rather than drive himself relentlessly. Also, if he is sedentary for much of the day, he could find some suitable and appropriate exercise could help to keep him in good form.

The Wood Rabbit's social life is well aspected and again he will enjoy the camaraderie and support offered by his friends. In addition, he will enjoy a wide variety of social events over the year. For any Wood Rabbit who may desire new friendships or romance, or may have had recent difficulties in his personal life, the Monkey year can mark the start of an exciting new chapter, with a chance introduction bringing a new and very special person into his life. As far as personal relationships are concerned, this is a very positive year for the Wood Rabbit.

Work-wise, this will also be an interesting year. Although it will bring demands and pressures, by rising to the challenges set him the Wood Rabbit will acquit himself well and do his reputation and prospects much good. He will also gain from any training he can undertake and by keeping his skills up to date, he will find this to his advantage when he chooses to move on. In addition, he should aim to build up his circle of contacts. By getting himself known and impressing those he meets, he will not only mark himself out as someone eager to progress but will also benefit from the advice he receives.

However, while the Wood Rabbit will accomplish a great deal over the year, he will need to work hard for his results. Wood Rabbits who are seeking work or keen to move from their current position could find it takes several attempts to secure a position they are happy with. Once they do so, however, they will quickly impress others in the way they set about their new duties and in their ability to learn. The Wood Rabbit knows he has the talents and skills to achieve much in his working life and what he accomplishes in 2004 will certainly be to his future advantage.

As with all Rabbits, though, this could be a tricky year for financial matters. Over the year the Wood Rabbit will face many expenses, especially relating to his accommodation, as well as having to meet various commitments and obligations. In view of these, he should manage his finances carefully and watch his outgoings. This is not a year for risks or needless extravagance. And when he is planning any major expenditure, perhaps something for his home or a holiday away, he should try to save towards it in advance and so help spread the cost. By dealing with financial matters efficiently and carefully, he can often prevent problems from arising. Wood Rabbits, take note.

Overall, this will be an agreeable year for the Wood Rabbit, with the love and support of others meaning a great deal to him. Although the nature of his work will often place many demands on him, by rising to the challenges and furthering his experience, he will be doing much to prepare for his future progress.

TIP FOR THE YEAR
Do not neglect yourself over the year and make sure you give yourself time to relax and unwind as well as take sufficient exercise. To be at your best you do need to give consideration to your own well-being.

The Fire Rabbit
This will be an interesting and generally positive year for the Fire Rabbit. Most of his activities will go well and his personal life will bring him a great deal of pleasure, but

such is the nature of the Monkey year that he cannot afford to be complacent or take undue risks.

For many Fire Rabbits the year will bring exams, with the results often having an important bearing on the future. In view of their significance the Fire Rabbit should aim to work consistently over the year rather than leave revision to the last moment. Even if he has had good results in any mock or practice exams he may have taken, he must not rest on his laurels. With his future at stake, he owes it to himself to give of his best.

With his enquiring mind the Fire Rabbit will often find the subject matter he has to study interesting, and some Fire Rabbits could become especially inspired by some course work they have to do. However, should the Fire Rabbit have any problems, he should not hesitate to seek additional guidance. Sometimes just one more explanation can make difficult areas much easier to understand and can improve the Fire Rabbit's overall performance considerably. Also, during his studying, he could find it helpful to keep in mind the opportunities that good grades will bring. With his talents and personality, the Fire Rabbit does have a great future ahead of him and what he does now will help prepare the way to that future.

Indeed, during the year many Fire Rabbits will need to consider what they will do next – whether to continue their education (and if so, which subjects to choose), have a gap year or enter the world of work. Given the importance of his choice, the Fire Rabbit should take his time in coming to a decision and also seek the advice of his family and tutors. By considering and talking over his options, he will feel that the decision he does ultimately take is the right one for him and once it has been taken he will feel better able to turn his attention to what lies ahead. The one thing the Fire Rabbit does have to be careful of is allowing himself to drift. Without a sense of direction he could find he is not only losing out on opportunities but also lacking his usual zest. Fortunately most Fire Rabbits will become clear in their intentions over the year, but the Monkey year can provide some sharp reminders to those who do not make the most of their potential.

For those in work or seeking, there will, however, be some excellent opportunities for the Fire Rabbit to gain experience. Although some of the tasks he is given may be routine, by setting about them in an earnest way and being willing to learn, he will soon find himself being rewarded with additional responsibilities. Although this may only be the beginning of his working life, he can still make quite an impact and at the same time give himself the confidence to progress further when better opportunities become available. For work matters late March to May, October and November hold encouraging prospects.

The Fire Rabbit does, though, need to be careful in money matters. Over the year he will want to do a great deal on often limited means. As a result, he will need to think carefully about some of his purchases and avoid succumbing to too many impulsive buys. With prudence, he can make his resources go far, but he does need to be disciplined and avoid unnecessary risks.

The Fire Rabbit's personal life is, though, splendidly aspected. He will thoroughly enjoy many parties and other lively and spirited social occasions. The year will also bring its romances, and although some will quickly fade, one could come to mean much. On a social level, the Monkey year can bring the Fire Rabbit some great times.

The Fire Rabbit will also derive much satisfaction from his interests, especially those that involve others. For those Fire Rabbits who enjoy sport or are members of a club or group, the year will give rise to some memorable occasions. Any Fire Rabbit who has a particular interest he wishes to make more of will benefit by contacting fellow enthusiasts or an appropriate society, or simply finding out more. However, the onus to take action does rest with him.

The year certainly holds potential for the Fire Rabbit and by making the most of his talents and the opportunities available to him, he will find himself well rewarded and will sow some significant seeds for the future.

TIP FOR THE YEAR
Always give your best. This is not a year to let standards slip or allow earlier efforts to come to nothing. What is achieved now can be important for the long term.

The Earth Rabbit

This will be a promising year for the Earth Rabbit, although how he fares is very much in his own hands. To get the best from the year, he should give some thought to what he would like to do during it. With some aims in mind, this can be a very satisfying time.

The Earth Rabbit's plans can concern almost any area of his life – accommodation, travel, personal interests and his own development as well as some projects he may have thought about for some time. Whatever he decides upon, by discussing his thoughts with those around him, he will find that many of his ideas are able to move ahead in an encouraging manner. The Monkey year is definitely a call for action.

One area which will particularly please the Earth Rabbit is his own personal development. If there is a subject or skill he would like to learn or take further, he should follow this up over the year, perhaps through reading up on it, enrolling on a course, joining an appropriate group or learning through the media. By taking positive action, he will not only gain from the practical benefits his new knowledge will bring but may also discover a new talent. His new interest may even lead to a new circle of friends. The aspects are particularly encouraging and all Earth Rabbits should take advantage of the opportunities for personal development over the year.

Another area the Earth Rabbit should give some thought to is travel. If there is a particular place he would like to visit, he should discuss this with family members and see what is possible. Sometimes just by mentioning his thoughts, he could find his plans starting to move in quite surprising ways. In addition he could be tempted by a holiday or break on the spur of the moment and his time away will often be made all the more special by the spontaneity.

In so much of what he does, the Earth Rabbit will be well supported by those around him. However, to benefit from their help and love, he does need to be forthcoming and speak of any worries or concerns. He in turn will be pleased to help others, perhaps by looking after grandchildren or giving advice or extra assistance, and his kindness and generosity will be appreciated. The Earth Rabbit will also enjoy the activities he can share with those around him and whether these are projects in the home or garden, mutual interests or just time spent enjoying each other's company, the Monkey year will give rise to many pleasing occasions.

The Earth Rabbit's social life can also bring much pleasure and can receive quite a fillip over the year, perhaps from new interests he takes up or, should he move, from opportunities to meet others in his new neighbourhood. There will certainly be many chances to make new friends and acquaintances, and Earth Rabbits who may start the Monkey year at a low ebb will find it can bring some happiness and meaning back into their lives.

The trickiest aspect of the year relates to finance and important paperwork, and in this great care is required. Should the Earth Rabbit have any doubts over any transaction or financial forms he may have to complete, he must check and perhaps seek professional advice. This is not a year to take risks or be less than thorough when his financial interests are at stake. Also, given the poor aspects concerning bureaucratic matters, the Earth Rabbit should keep his paperwork in order and keep receipts and guarantees safe. This could prevent problems later.

In many other respects, though, the Monkey year holds much promise for the Earth Rabbit and by deciding on what he would like to do and then setting his plans in motion, he will find this a satisfying time. He will also derive considerable pleasure from both his domestic and social life.

Set yourself some interesting projects and activities to do, especially in the area of self-development. With time well spent, this can be a rewarding year.

FAMOUS RABBITS

Bertie Ahern, Margaret Atwood, Drew Barrymore, David Beckham, Harry Belafonte, Ingrid Bergman, St Bernadette, Gordon Brown, Melanie Brown, Emma Bunton, James Caan, Nicolas Cage, Lewis Carroll, Fidel Castro, John Cleese, Confucius, Marie Curie, Johnny Depp, Albert Einstein, George Eliot, W. C. Fields, James Fox, Sir David Frost, James Galway, Cary Grant, Edvard Grieg, Oliver Hardy, Seamus Heaney, John Howard, Bob Hope, Whitney Houston, Helen Hunt, John Hurt, Anjelica Huston, Chrissie Hynde, Enrique Inglesias, Clive James, Henry James, David Jason, Angelina Jolie, Michael Jordan, Michael Keaton, John Keats, Judith Krantz, Danny La Rue, Cheryl Ladd, Patrick Lichfield, Gina Lollobrigida, Sir Trevor McDonald, George Michael, Arthur Miller, Colin Montgomerie, Roger Moore, Mike Myers, Brigitte Nielsen, Jamie Oliver, George Orwell, John Peel, Edith Piaf, Sidney Poitier, Romano Prodi, Ken Russell, Mort Sahl, Elisabeth Schwarzkopf, Neil Sedaka, Jane Seymour, Neil Simon, Frank Sinatra, Fatboy Slim, Sting, J. R. R. Tolkien, Arturo Toscanini, Tina Turner, Luther Vandross, Queen Victoria, Muddy Waters, Orson Welles, Walt Whitman, Robin Williams, Kate Winslet, Tiger Woods.

16 FEBRUARY 1904 ⌢ 3 FEBRUARY 1905   *Wood Dragon*

3 FEBRUARY 1916 ⌢ 22 JANUARY 1917   *Fire Dragon*

23 JANUARY 1928 ⌢ 9 FEBRUARY 1929   *Earth Dragon*

8 FEBRUARY 1940 ⌢ 26 JANUARY 1941   *Metal Dragon*

27 JANUARY 1952 ⌢ 13 FEBRUARY 1953   *Water Dragon*

13 FEBRUARY 1964 ⌢ 1 FEBRUARY 1965   *Wood Dragon*

31 JANUARY 1976 ⌢ 17 FEBRUARY 1977   *Fire Dragon*

17 FEBRUARY 1988 ⌢ 5 FEBRUARY 1989   *Earth Dragon*

5 FEBRUARY 2000 ⌢ 23 JANUARY 2001   *Metal Dragon*

THE
DRAGON

THE PERSONALITY OF THE DRAGON

> Ever since I was a child I have had this instinctive urge for
> expansion and growth. To me, the function and duty of a
> quality human being is the sincere and honest develop-
> ment of one's potential.
>
> *Bruce Lee, a Dragon*

The Dragon is born under the sign of luck. He is a proud
and lively character and has a tremendous amount of self-
confidence. He is also highly intelligent and very quick to
take advantage of any opportunities. He is ambitious and
determined and will do well in practically anything he
attempts. He is also something of a perfectionist and will
always try to maintain the high standards he sets himself.

The Dragon does not suffer fools gladly and will be
quick to criticize anyone or anything that displeases him.
He can be blunt and forthright in his views and is certainly
not renowned for being either tactful or diplomatic. He
does, however, often take people at their word and can
occasionally be rather gullible. If he ever feels that his trust
has been abused or his dignity wounded, he can sometimes
become very bitter and it will take him a long time to
forgive and forget.

The Dragon is usually very outgoing and is particularly
adept at attracting attention and publicity. He enjoys being
in the limelight and is often at his best when he is
confronted by a difficult problem or tense situation. In
some respects he is a showman and he rarely lacks an
audience. His views are highly valued and he invariably

has something interesting – and sometimes controversial – to say.

He has considerable energy and is often prepared to work long and unsocial hours in order to achieve what he wants. He can, however, be rather impulsive and does not always consider the consequences of his actions. He also has a tendency to live for the moment and there is nothing that riles him more than to be kept waiting. The Dragon hates delay and can get extremely impatient and irritable over even the smallest of hold-ups.

The Dragon has an enormous faith in his abilities, but he does run the risk of becoming over-confident and unless he is careful he can sometimes make grave errors of judgement. While this may prove disastrous at the time, he does have the tenacity and ability to bounce back and pick up the pieces again.

The Dragon has such an assertive personality, so much willpower and such a desire to succeed that he will often reach the top of his chosen profession. He has considerable leadership qualities and will do well in positions where he can put his own ideas and policies into practice. He is usually successful in politics, show business, as the manager of his own department or business, and in any job which brings him into contact with the media.

The Dragon relies a tremendous amount on his own judgement and can be scornful of other people's advice. He likes to feel self-sufficient and there are many Dragons who cherish their independence to such a degree that they prefer to remain single throughout their lives. However, the Dragon will often have numerous admirers and many will be attracted by his flamboyant personality and striking looks. If he does marry, he will usually marry young, and will find himself particularly well suited to those born under the signs of the Snake, Rat, Monkey and Rooster. He will also find that the Rabbit, Pig, Horse and Goat make ideal companions and will readily join in with many of his escapades. Two Dragons will also get on well together, as they understand each other, but the Dragon may not find things so easy with the Ox and Dog, as both will be critical of his impulsive and somewhat extrovert manner. He will also find it difficult to form an alliance with the Tiger, for the Tiger, like the Dragon, tends to speak his mind, is very strong-willed and likes to take the lead.

The female Dragon knows what she wants in life and sets about everything she does in a determined and positive manner. No job is too small for her and she is often prepared to work extremely hard until she has secured her objective. She is immensely practical and somewhat liberated. She hates being bound by routine and petty restrictions and likes to have sufficient freedom to be able to go off and do what she wants to do. She will keep her house tidy, but is not one for spending hours on housework – there are far too many other things that she prefers to do. Like her male counterpart, she has a tendency to speak her mind.

The Dragon usually has many interests and enjoys sport and other outdoor activities. He also likes to travel and often prefers to visit places that are off the beaten track rather than head for popular tourist attractions. He has a very adventurous streak in him and providing his financial circumstances permit – and the Dragon is usually sensible with his money – he will travel considerable distances during his lifetime.

The Dragon is a very flamboyant character and while he can be demanding of others and in his early years rather precocious, he will have many friends and will nearly always be the centre of attention. He has charisma and so much confidence that he can often become a source of inspiration to others. In China he is the leader of the carnival and he is also blessed with an inordinate share of luck.

THE FIVE DIFFERENT TYPES OF DRAGON

In addition to the 12 signs of the Chinese zodiac there are five elements, and these have a strengthening or moderating influence on the sign. The effects of the five elements on the Dragon are described below, together with the years in which the elements were exercising their influence. Therefore all Dragons born in 1940 and 2000 are Metal Dragons, those born in 1952 are Water Dragons, and so on.

Metal Dragon: 1940, 2000

This Dragon is very strong-willed and has a particularly forceful personality. He is energetic, ambitious and tries to be scrupulous in his dealings with others. He can also be blunt and to the point and usually has no hesitation in speaking his mind. If people disagree with him or are not prepared to co-operate, he is more than happy to go his own way. The Metal Dragon usually has very high moral values and is held in great esteem by his friends and colleagues.

Water Dragon: 1952

This Dragon is friendly, easy-going and intelligent. He is quick-witted and rarely lets an opportunity slip by. However, he is not as impatient as some of the other types of Dragon and is prepared to wait for results rather than expect everything to happen at once. He has an understanding nature and is prepared to share his ideas and co-operate with others. His main failing is a tendency to jump from one thing to another rather than concentrate on the job in hand. He has a good sense of humour and is an effective speaker.

Wood Dragon: 1904, 1964

The Wood Dragon is practical, imaginative and inquisitive. He loves delving into all manner of subjects and can quite often come up with some highly original ideas. He is a thinker and a doer and he has the drive and commitment to put many of his ideas into practice. He is more diplomatic than some of the other types of Dragon and has a good sense of humour. He is very astute in business matters and can also be most generous.

Fire Dragon: 1916, 1976

This Dragon is ambitious, articulate and has a tremendous desire to succeed. He is a hard and conscientious worker and is often admired for his integrity and forthright nature. He is very strong-willed and has considerable leadership qualities. He can, however, rely a bit too much on his own judgement and not take into account the views and feelings of others. He can also be rather aloof and it would certainly be in his own interests to let others join in more with his various activities. The Fire Dragon usually enjoys music, literature and the arts.

Earth Dragon: 1928, 1988

The Earth Dragon tends to be quieter and more reflective than some of the other types of Dragon. He has a wide variety of interests and is keenly aware of what is going on around him. He also has clear objectives and usually has no problems in obtaining support and backing for any of his ventures. He is very astute in financial matters and is often able to accumulate considerable wealth. He is a good organizer, although he can at times be rather bureaucratic and fussy. He mixes well with others and has a large circle of friends.

PROSPECTS FOR THE DRAGON IN 2004

The Chinese New Year starts on 22 January 2004. Until then, the old year, the Year of the Goat, is still making its presence felt.

The Year of the Goat (1 February 2003 to 21 January 2004) will have been a reasonable one for the Dragon and in what remains of it most of his activities will go well.

In his work the Dragon can look forward to making useful headway, although if asked to take on additional responsibilities or seeking to advance, he does need to show some flexibility in outlook and make the most of situations as they are rather than as he would like them to be. September and November can be two important months work-wise.

The Dragon does, though, need to handle money matters with especial care. In the last quarter of the Goat year he will have an increasing number of expenses and, when possible, should try to make early provision for them. He should also avoid taking risks or committing his money to ventures he has not properly investigated. Money-wise, the Goat year is one for care.

More positively aspected is travel, and as the Goat year draws to a close the Dragon will have the opportunity to go on several pleasant journeys, visiting places of interest as well as relations and friends he does not often get the chance to see.

The last quarter of the year will also bring much domestic and social activity. In his home life the Dragon will spend much time assisting others as well as getting involved in the many activities that take place. Socially, he will find himself in demand and will enjoy the opportunities to meet friends, make some new ones and attend various parties and other social occasions.

Overall, the last few months of the year will be active and rewarding ones.

The Year of the Monkey starts on 22 January and will be a positive one for the Dragon. Encouraged by the opportunities that will come his way, he will be able to make useful progress as well as enjoy a full and active personal life.

As the Monkey year starts, though, the Dragon should spend some time reflecting on his present situation and the way in which he would like to move forward. Both in his work and his own personal development this is a time when he should look to take on new challenges and he will find that deciding on some objectives for the next 12 months will help give him more direction. In his deliberations the Dragon would find it helpful to discuss his thoughts with others. This will not only lead to him receiving useful advice but also give him some interesting suggestions to consider.

As far as work is concerned, many Dragons will find their standing and knowledge will lead to promotion or a transfer to more interesting and remunerative duties in their present organization. However, for those who feel their prospects could be improved by moving elsewhere or who are seeking work, the Monkey year can produce some excellent opportunities. When an interesting opening does appear, the Dragon should be quick to act. Events will move swiftly in 2004 and so must he. Even if not all his applications go his way, the Dragon should persist. The Monkey year does move in curious ways and some rejections, despite the hurt they may cause, can turn out to be blessings in disguise as something better appears in their wake. For work opportunities, April, May and the period from late August to October are particularly favourable.

However, while the Dragon can make good progress, a warning does need to be sounded. When everything seems to be going well, there can be a danger of the Dragon becoming over-complacent, taking an unnecessary risk or being less than thorough with a certain matter. Should he let this happen, he could find that others will be quick to notice any lapse. In 2004 he does need to remain on his mettle and maintain his standards.

The Dragon will gain a great deal by furthering his skills over the year and should take advantage of any training opportunities. Keeping his skills up to date will not only increase his efficiency and output but also help his prospects. And if the Dragon has a particular position or vocation in mind for the future, even if it is very different from what he is doing now, any study or work he can do to keep his aspiration alive will be of value.

Over the year the Dragon will derive much pleasure from his personal interests, often being tempted to take up a new activity in his spare time. This can relate to general fitness – perhaps a suitable course or exercise programme – or an absorbing project he has set himself. By giving himself something worthwhile to do, the Dragon will find his recreational pursuits will be another rewarding aspect of the year.

The Dragon does, though, need to be careful in his financial undertakings. Over the year many Dragons will decide to spend quite heavily on their accommodation, particularly in replacing equipment and furnishings and adding new comforts to their home. Although the Dragon will be pleased with the improvements, large purchases do need to be budgeted for. And in view of the often heavy outlay, the Dragon does need to be controlled in his spending and avoid taking unnecessary risks.

The Dragon's personal life does, though, hold much promise and will bring him many rewarding times. He will see much activity in his home life and while those in his household will often be involved with their various commitments, the Dragon will value their support, interest and encouragement. In turn, by giving time to those who are important and showing he cares, the Dragon will find his domestic life going well. While some pressures or problems will inevitably arise over the year, by being willing to address any difficulties – and compromise in certain cases – the Dragon will find they can be quickly dealt with and will certainly not interfere with the more agreeable aspects of the year.

The Dragon's social life will also bring him much pleasure. In addition to building up new contacts in his work, he will find himself making some new friends as the year progresses, either as a result of his work, his interests or his contacts. On a social level, he will be in good form and will enjoy the many social opportunities the year will bring.

The year is also wonderfully aspected for romance, with many unattached Dragons meeting someone who will quickly become special. However in the early days of any romance, the Dragon should take the time to get to know and understand the other person. Sometimes his exuberant personality can get the better of him and without some consideration, there is the danger that an otherwise promising romance could sour. The Dragon should watch this. However, this warning apart, he will find his relations with others will mean much to him over the year. The months of April, May, September and December will be especially active for social matters.

Overall, the Monkey year holds good prospects for the Dragon and by making the most of his many strengths and the opportunities that arise, he will find this a pleasing and satisfying year.

The Metal Dragon

As far as the different types of Dragon are concerned, this will be a busy year for the Metal Dragon.

One area which will see much activity will be his home life. Some Metal Dragons will decide to move to accommodation more suitable to their present needs over the year and will find this taking up a good deal of their time. They would do well to draw on the assistance of others during the move as well as obtain advice on the legalities and paperwork involved. Also, with the variable aspects concerning finance this year, the Metal Dragon needs to take especial notice of the costs he is incurring as well as any new financial obligations he is taking on. Although he is usually vigilant in financial matters, this is not a year for risks or neglecting to keep a close check on his position. The moving process may be demanding and at times the Metal Dragon may despair of what he has embarked upon, but once settled in his new home, he will consider it the start of an exciting new chapter in his life.

Metal Dragons who remain where they are will also often busy themselves with home projects. These could be quite ambitious, including adding new features, redecorating or installing equipment and new comforts. Again, what the Metal Dragon has in mind could take some time to carry out and be disruptive. However, by taking his time and drawing on the help and advice of others, he will be pleased with what he achieves.

As well as seeking help with domestic projects, the Metal Dragon should be forthcoming about his ideas throughout the year. Although he may sometimes like to keep his own counsel, given the ambitious nature of some of his ideas, he should make an effort to discuss them fully with those around him. This will not only lead to useful suggestions and greater support, but can also help prevent misunderstandings from arising later. And should any of the Metal Dragon's proposals meet with dissension, he should be prepared to look at them again and see whether another approach would be more acceptable.

In addition to the practical sides of domestic life, the Metal Dragon will take a keen interest in the progress of loved ones, often helping younger relations, particularly those bringing up children or those under pressure. His caring attitude will be of more value than he may realize. And amid all the activity there will also be good cause for a family celebration, possibly involving a younger relation who means much to the Metal Dragon.

Although this will be an expensive year, the Metal Dragon should ensure he goes away for a holiday over the year. The change of scene will do him good and give him the opportunity to rest and unwind.

The Metal Dragon's social life is also favourably aspected and he will not only enjoy meeting his friends but also some of the social events he goes to. In some cases his personal interests will bring him into contact with others and he will value the social element his recreational pursuits will bring. The months of April, May and the last quarter of the year will be both active and interesting times socially and those seeking more companionship can do much to bring about an upturn in their social life by going out and involving themselves in different activities, with many building what can be a significant new friendship.

For those Metal Dragons in work, the Monkey year can be a time of change as well as progress. Some will retire and take up interests they have long considered, while for others, new projects and responsibilities will beckon. For work matters, April and the period from August to October will be significant, but throughout the year, the Metal Dragon will be given excellent opportunities to use his experience to good effect. Again, the chances are there for him.

In fact in 2004 the Metal Dragon is very much in charge of his destiny and whether he moves, retires, takes up new interests or launches projects, by following his ideas through he can achieve a great deal. However, at all times, he should consult others and heed the advice they are so willing to give.

TIP FOR THE YEAR

Allow plenty of time to realize your projects and plans. Being too hasty could lead to risks and mistakes.

The Water Dragon

This will be an interesting year for the Water Dragon, particularly as it will give him more opportunity to use his strengths and develop some of his ideas. The Monkey year offers him both scope *and* potential.

Work aspects are especially encouraging. Given his experience and reputation, the Water Dragon will find others will look to him to take on further responsibilities and play a greater role. For the Water Dragon who is keen to progress, promotion will beckon, and with it will come the opportunity for him to draw more fully on his skills and training and demonstrate his true potential. Work-wise, this can be a much more fulfilling year for him. In addition, he should be forthcoming with any ideas he may have, as some of his proposals could be particularly well received.

For those Water Dragons seeking work, again the year will bring some positive developments. Although obtaining a position will require persistence, an opening discovered almost by chance will not only prove ideal but also offer far greater potential than the Water Dragon may initially realize. For work opportunities, the months of April and May and from August to October are favourable.

The progress that the Water Dragon makes in his work will lead to an increase in his income, but although this will be welcome, he must be careful not to let it lull him into a period of extravagance or carelessness. Money matters do need watching. In this the Water Dragon could find it helpful to set certain amounts aside for specific requirements as well as add to his savings. This is not a year for risks and should the Water Dragon have any uncertainty over a financial matter he should check and, if need be, obtain further advice. The more attention he can give to his finances, the more he will find he can do and the better his overall position will be.

The Monkey year will, however, be a positive time for the Water Dragon's personal interests and despite other pressures he should aim to set a regular time aside for these. Creative and practical pursuits can bring him much pleasure over the year, as can those that take him out of doors or allow him to get some additional exercise. If there is a subject or skill the Water Dragon would like to find out more about, he should follow it up. As he will find, his interests and personal development can help to make the year all the more fulfilling.

In his domestic life the Water Dragon will also enjoy the interests and practical projects that he carries out with others. Spending time with those important to him and on activities that can be enjoyed will not only help general domestic life but also maintain the rapport and under-standing the Water Dragon so values.

The one danger that he should guard against is becoming preoccupied or irritable when pressures mount, otherwise minor disagreements could escalate and spoil an otherwise agreeable year. At busy times, when he or others may be tired, he should encourage a spirit of under-standing and co-operation. Here the Water Dragon's considerate manner will prove a great asset. Taking a holiday or break with loved ones over the year will also do much good.

This can be a promising year for social matters, although just how the Water Dragon's social life shapes does rest in his own hands. Some Water Dragons will prefer to keep it low key, deciding just to go out occasionally, while others could find an interest they have or a society they belong to will lead to their going out often and in some cases becoming more heavily involved in what they do. Any Water Dragon who may have had some recent personal sadness or be feeling lonely will find that the Monkey year can bring the chance to build up some new friendships and, in some cases, romance too. However, for the Monkey year to work its magic, these Water Dragons must be prepared to move their lives forward and go out more and give themselves the opportunity to meet others. Their efforts *will* be rewarded.

In most respects the Water Dragon will find the Monkey year an encouraging one. In his work he will be able to make good use of his strengths, while his interests and personal life offer some fine times. Provided he is careful in financial matters and sets about his activities in his usual diligent way, this can prove a satisfying and successful year.

TIP FOR THE YEAR
Make the most of your talents and ideas. This is a year to be enterprising and bold.

The Wood Dragon

The Monkey year holds good prospects for the Wood Dragon and will allow him to make important progress as well as lead an agreeable personal life.

The aspects are especially encouraging in the Wood Dragon's work and over the year he will be able to build on his recent achievements. Many Wood Dragons will find that they have made such an impression in their present duties that they are singled out for further responsibilities. Alternatively, others could decide that having become proficient in one aspect of their work it is now time to move to something different and more challenging. However, for almost all Wood Dragons, this is a year for positive and often substantial change. Also, the Wood Dragon knows that if he is to realize his longer-term ambitions, he must put himself forward. In the Monkey year his initiative *will* be rewarded.

This also applies to those Wood Dragons seeking work or feeling disillusioned in their present role. Again, this is the year to seize the initiative. With his experience and determined nature, the Wood Dragon will find his efforts will often lead to an important position which will set his career off on an exciting new path. The Monkey year can have long-term significance. For work matters, the months of April, May, September and October are especially promising.

The Wood Dragon will also gain by furthering his skills over the year, whether through training offered by his employer, an evening class or personal study. In this way the Wood Dragon will not only feel that he is moving himself forward but will also enhance and sometimes widen his future prospects.

However, while the Wood Dragon's prospects are favourable, at no time should he become complacent or, if asked to help with additional duties, appear unaccommodating. This is a time when he must show himself in the best possible light if he is to benefit from the chances the year will bring.

The headway that the Wood Dragon makes at work will bring an increase in his income, but money matters do need to be handled with care. In addition to his existing obligations, he could find the activities of family members (including education), travel, transport and items he wants for his home all add to his outgoings. In view of this, he does need to manage his finances well and at times would find it prudent to cut down on expenses that are not really necessary. Also, he should avoid any risky undertakings. Financially, this is a year for care.

The Wood Dragon will, though, gain much from his personal interests over the year and although he will have a lot to occupy his time, he should not neglect them. Not only will they give his lifestyle greater balance, but they could also give him additional exercise, get him out of doors and lead to some fine social occasions with fellow enthusiasts. Some could even provide an additional source of income, perhaps through freelance writing, teaching or in some other way. For those Wood Dragons with an enterprising disposition, the Monkey year can have some surprises in store.

The Wood Dragon will also see much activity in his domestic life and will do much to help others, particularly those who may be under pressure. This includes those more senior to him as well as younger relations who may be studying or facing important decisions. By listening, encouraging and assisting, the Wood Dragon will play an appreciated role. Despite the often busy lifestyle that he and others in his household may lead, he will find that by devoting time to family activities and helping each other, everyone can enjoy some very agreeable occasions. A family holiday or break taken over the year can turn out to be one of the best for a long time.

The Wood Dragon's social life will also go well and he will enjoy meeting up with his close friends and some of the events he attends. His social life can be a good way for him to unwind. Also, for the unattached or those who may feel lonely, the Monkey year can bring an important new romance or friendship. Again, the Monkey year serves the Wood Dragon's interests well.

In almost all respects this is a favourable year for the Wood Dragon and provided he is careful in money matters and remains flexible in his attitude, he is set to impress others and make good progress as well as enjoy himself.

TIP FOR THE YEAR
Organize your time and make sure your lifestyle has balance. Too much attention to one area could cause problems in another. Also, do give time to those who are important to you.

The Fire Dragon

This will be a busy and rewarding year for the Fire Dragon and one in which he can look forward to making substantial progress.

Work prospects are especially encouraging. The preceding Goat year will not only have allowed many Fire Dragons to add to their skills and prove themselves in their duties but also helped them establish some useful contacts and enhance their reputation. The rewards for all their efforts will soon become apparent. As colleagues move on and new opportunities arise, the Fire Dragon will find himself ideally placed to take advantage of the situation. Late March to May could see some particularly interesting developments, with further opportunities arising in the third quarter of the year.

The encouraging aspects also apply to Fire Dragons who are seeking work, feeling in a rut or considering that their present position has limited prospects. By actively following up vacancies that interest them, many will be able to secure a position which will not only allow them to use and develop their skills but also offer scope for the future. This is a year which offers excellent possibilities and the Fire Dragon's persistence and faith in himself will lead to some important advances.

The Fire Dragon will also be helped by the supportive attitude of colleagues. By being willing to discuss his thoughts and ideas he will not only gain from advice he is given but may also benefit from others putting in a good word for him. With 2004 being a year for progress, the Fire Dragon's initiative and ability to get on well with others can prove a great asset.

However, while work prospects are good, one area which does require care is finance. This is not a year for risks or for proceeding in an ad hoc manner. The Fire Dragon should keep track of his spending and, as far as possible, budget for forthcoming expenses. The better he can manage his financial situation, the more he will be able to do, including taking what can be a pleasing and in some cases unusual holiday. In addition, the Fire Dragon could decide to spend a great deal on his home during the year, particularly on replacing some equipment and furnishings. Although he may be eager to proceed with this, he could save himself considerable outlay by waiting for sales or more favourable buying opportunities. Again, patience and careful consideration would be to his advantage.

The Fire Dragon will, however, derive much pleasure from his home life in 2004. Not only will he be grateful for the support he is given, but he will also delight in the many fine domestic occasions that take place and in the progress of his loved ones. Some activities arranged on the spur of the moment will be especially appreciated. Domestically, this can be a happy year but, as with all years, some difficult matters will arise. At such times the Fire Dragon should show understanding and encourage dialogue. And, while he may possess definite views and like to hold sway, when differences of opinion occur he could find it helpful to show some flexibility. Too stubborn an attitude could jeopardize an otherwise harmonious time. Fire Dragons, take note.

Also, Fire Dragons with young children who find they are getting tired or feel that certain household tasks are mounting up should ask for help rather than try to do too much single-handed. Others will be willing to assist, but sometimes need prompting!

The Fire Dragon will enjoy his social life over the year and can look forward to going to a variety of parties, events and other social gatherings. With his sociable nature, he will often find himself in demand both with existing friends and new acquaintances. For the unattached and those who may start the year feeling lonely, there may be the prospect of an exciting romance or important new friendship. April, May, September and December are favourably aspected for meeting others and general social activities.

Overall, this will be an important year for the Fire Dragon, offering him the chance to make more of his talents as well as enjoy an often rewarding domestic and social life. It is a year to make the most of opportunities.

You have experience, talents and ideas. Show others your true worth and potential. Look to advance and your efforts will be rewarded well.

The Earth Dragon

This year holds good prospects for the Earth Dragon, although to make the most of himself and the fine opportunities that are available to him, he needs to stay organized as well as be willing to take advantage of the chances that arise. For the keen and enterprising, this can be a splendid year.

Many Earth Dragons will be involved in important exams over the year and to do themselves justice they should work steadily in the months leading up to the exams rather than leave too much to the last moment. The better organized the Earth Dragon is with his revision, the more likely he is to get the results he desires. He could also find it helpful, especially when facing a particularly heavy period of revision or schoolwork, to think of the benefits his studying will bring. The exams he passes can prove important to his future progress.

If at any time the Earth Dragon feels under too much pressure or has subject areas he does not understand, he should not hesitate to tell others. Those around will be keen to help and a further explanation from his tutors can often help the Earth Dragon overcome some of his difficulties.

While the attention of many Earth Dragons will be focused on academic matters, there will also be some who decide not to take their education further and enter the world of work instead. These Earth Dragons will also find that the Monkey year can teach them a great deal. Although the positions they are offered may sometimes be routine, by demonstrating a willingness to learn and develop, they will often single themselves out for advancement. As the Earth Dragon will discover, by making the effort and doing all that is required, he can greatly improve his prospects. And this lesson will serve him well throughout his working life.

Many of those Earth Dragons remaining in education will also take on a job for a few hours a week. Again, the tasks they are given may not be the most inspiring, but the additional money will be welcome and the work could also lead to meeting others of a similar age and making new friends. There will certainly be chances for the enterprising Earth Dragon to earn and learn.

As with all Dragons, though, the Earth Dragon does need to be careful in money matters this year. He will want to do a great deal on limited means and at times he will have to decide on his priorities and forgo certain indulgences. However, he is resourceful and with careful management he will be pleased and sometimes surprised what he is able to do, given his position. He does, though, need to avoid unnecessary risks or making sizeable purchases without first seeking advice.

The Monkey year will, however, certainly contain its pleasures. The Earth Dragon will enjoy the camaraderie of his friends and can look forward to some lively social occasions. Those who may not have anything particular with which to fill their spare time should make enquiries about what is available. A local youth or special interest group or an after-school activity could not only lead to some fine occasions and new friendships but also be a good use of their time. However, it rests with the Earth Dragon to find out what is available and to become involved.

The Earth Dragon should also aim to develop his personal interests over the year and if he can do this under the guidance of others, he will gain a great deal. For sports enthusiasts, a group they belong to or coaching they take will allow them to become more proficient in what they do, while for the keen musician or those who prefer more creative pursuits, extra time spent developing their skills will not only add to their pleasure but also allow them to make considerable advances.

As far as the Earth Dragon's home life is concerned, however, he will again need to tread carefully. Although he will be grateful for the support and guidance he is given as well as enjoy some of the family activities that take place, he will at times need to be accommodating in his attitude. Sometimes his views or plans may not have the backing or approval he was hoping for. At such times, the Earth Dragon should see whether some understanding could be reached or accept that the time is not actually right for his plans. To remain unyielding or stubborn could lead to some difficult moments and undermine his rapport with others. To prevent problems, the Earth Dragon does need to show some flexibility and should not let what could be relatively small issues mar what can be a positive and generally agreeable year. Earth Dragons, take note.

In many respects, though, the Monkey year does have great potential for the Earth Dragon and by making the most of himself and the opportunities that are available, he will be enhancing his future prospects.

TIP FOR THE YEAR
Set about your studies, revision and work in an organized and thorough manner. What is achieved this year can have long-term significance.

FAMOUS DRAGONS

Clive Anderson, Maya Angelou, Jeffrey Archer, Joan Armatrading, Joan Baez, Roseanne Barr, Count Basie, Maeve Binchy, Sandra Bullock, Julie Christie, James Coburn, Courteney Cox, Randy Crawford, Bing Crosby, Russell Crowe, Roald Dahl, Salvador Dali, Charles Darwin, Lindsay Davenport, Neil Diamond, Bo Diddley, Matt Dillon, Christian Dior, Placido Domingo, Fats Domino, Kirk Douglas, Faye Dunaway, Bruce Forsyth, Sigmund Freud, Graham Greene, Che Guevara, David Hasselhoff, Sir Edward Heath, James Herriot, Paul Hogan, Joan of Arc, Tom Jones, Immanuel Kant, Martin Luther King, Eartha Kitt, Bruce Lee, John Lennon, Abraham Lincoln, Elle MacPherson, Queen Margrethe II of Denmark, Yehudi Menhuin, François Mitterrand, Bob Monkhouse, Andrew Motion, Hosni Mubarak, Florence Nightingale, Nick Nolte, Al Pacino, Gregory Peck, Pelé, Edgar Allan Poe, Vladimir Putin, Christopher Reeve, Keanu Reeves, Sir Cliff Richard, Harold Robbins, George Bernard Shaw, Martin Sheen, Alicia Silverstone, Ringo Starr, Princess Stephanie of Monaco, Dave Stewart, Karlheinz Stockhausen, Shirley

Temple, Maria von Trapp, Andy Warhol, Johnny Weissmüller, Raquel Welch, Mae West, Earl of Wessex, Frank Zappa.

4 FEBRUARY 1905 ∼ 24 JANUARY 1906		Wood Snake
23 JANUARY 1917 ∼ 10 FEBRUARY 1918		Fire Snake
10 FEBRUARY 1929 ∼ 29 JANUARY 1930		Earth Snake
27 JANUARY 1941 ∼ 14 FEBRUARY 1942		Metal Snake
14 FEBRUARY 1953 ∼ 2 FEBRUARY 1954		Water Snake
2 FEBRUARY 1965 ∼ 20 JANUARY 1966		Wood Snake
18 FEBRUARY 1977 ∼ 6 FEBRUARY 1978		Fire Snake
6 FEBRUARY 1989 ∼ 26 JANUARY 1990		Earth Snake
24 JANUARY 2001 ∼ 11 FEBRUARY 2002		Metal Snake

THE
SNAKE

THE PERSONALITY OF THE SNAKE

As soon as you trust yourself you will know how to live.
Johann Wolfgang von Goethe, a Snake

The Snake is born under the sign of wisdom. He is highly intelligent and his mind is forever active. He is always planning and always looking for ways in which he can use his considerable skills. He is a deep thinker and likes to meditate and reflect.

Many times during his life he will shed one of his famous Snake skins and take up new interests or start a completely different job. The Snake enjoys a challenge and he rarely makes mistakes. He is a skilful organizer, has considerable business acumen and is usually lucky in money matters. Most Snakes are financially secure in their later years, provided they do not gamble – the Snake has the distinction of being the worst gambler in the whole of the Chinese zodiac!

The Snake generally has a calm and placid nature and prefers the quieter things in life. He does not like to be in a frenzied atmosphere and hates being hurried into making a quick decision. He also does not like interference in his affairs and tends to rely on his own judgement rather than listen to advice.

The Snake can at times appear solitary. He is quiet, reserved and sometimes has difficulty in communicating with others. He has little time for idle gossip and will certainly not suffer fools gladly. He does, however, have a good sense of humour and this is particularly appreciated in times of crisis.

The Snake is certainly not afraid of hard work and is thorough in all that he does. He is very determined and can occasionally be ruthless in order to achieve his aims. His confidence, willpower and quick thinking usually ensure his success, but should he fail it will often take a long time for him to recover. He cannot bear failure and is a very bad loser.

The Snake can also be evasive and does not willingly let people into his confidence. This secrecy and distrust can sometimes work against him and it is a trait which all Snakes should try to overcome.

Another characteristic of the Snake is his tendency to rest after any sudden or prolonged bout of activity. He burns up so much nervous energy that he can, if he is not careful, be susceptible to high blood pressure and nervous disorders.

It has sometimes been said that the Snake is a late starter in life and this is mainly because it often takes him a while to find a job in which he is genuinely happy. However, the Snake will usually do well in any position which involves research and writing and where he is given sufficient freedom to develop his own ideas and plans. He makes a good teacher, politician, personnel manager and social adviser.

The Snake chooses his friends carefully and while he keeps a tight control over his finances, he can be particularly generous to those he likes. He will think nothing of buying expensive gifts or treating his friends or loved ones to the best theatre seats in town. In return he demands loyalty. The Snake is very possessive and he can become extremely jealous and hurt if he finds his trust has been abused.

The Snake is also renowned for his good looks and is never short of admirers. The female Snake in particular is most alluring. She has style, grace and excellent (and usually expensive) taste in clothes. A keen socializer, she is likely to have a wide range of friends and a happy knack of impressing those who matter. She has numerous interests and her opinions are often highly valued. She is generally a calm-natured person and while she involves herself in many activities, she likes to retain a certain amount of privacy in her undertakings.

Affairs of the heart are very important to the Snake and he will often have many romances before he finally settles down. He will find that he is particularly well suited to those born under the signs of the Ox, Dragon, Rabbit and Rooster. Provided he is allowed sufficient freedom to pursue his own interests he can also build up a very satis-factory relationship with the Rat, Horse, Goat, Monkey and Dog, but he should try to steer clear of another Snake as they could very easily become jealous of each other. The Snake will also have difficulty in getting on with the honest and down-to-earth Pig, and will find the Tiger far too much of a disruptive influence on his quiet and peace-loving ways.

The Snake certainly appreciates the finer things in life. He enjoys good food and often take a keen interest in the arts. He also enjoys reading and is invariably drawn to subjects such as philosophy, political thought, religion or the occult. He is fascinated by the unknown and his enquiring mind is always looking for answers. Some of the world's most original thinkers have been Snakes, and although he may not readily admit it, the Snake is often psychic and relies a lot on intuition.

The Snake is certainly not the most energetic member of the Chinese zodiac. He prefers to proceed at his own pace and to do what he wants. He is very much his own master and throughout his life he will try his hand at many things. He is something of a dabbler, but at some time – usually when he least expects it – his hard work and efforts will be recognized and he will invariably meet with the success and the financial security which he so desires.

THE FIVE DIFFERENT TYPES OF SNAKE

In addition to the 12 signs of the Chinese zodiac there are five elements, and these have a strengthening or moderating influence on the sign. The effects of the five elements on the Snake are described below, together with the years in which the elements were exercising their influence. Therefore all Snakes born in 1941 and 2001 are Metal Snakes, those born in 1953 are Water Snakes, and so on.

Metal Snake: 1941, 2001
This Snake is quiet, confident and fiercely independent. He often prefers to work on his own and will only let a privileged few into his confidence. He is quick to spot

opportunities and will set about achieving his objectives with an awesome determination. He is astute in financial matters and will often invest his money well. He also has a liking for the finer things in life and a good appreciation of the arts, literature, music and good food. He usually has a small group of extremely good friends and can be generous to his loved ones.

Water Snake: 1953

This Snake has a wide variety of interests. He enjoys studying all manner of subjects and is capable of undertaking quite detailed research and becoming a specialist in his chosen area. He is highly intelligent, has a good memory and is particularly astute when dealing with business and financial matters. He tends to be quietly spoken and a little reserved, but he does have sufficient strength of character to make his views known and attain his ambitions. He is very loyal to his family and friends.

Wood Snake: 1905, 1965

The Wood Snake has a friendly temperament and a good understanding of human nature. He is able to communicate well and often has many friends and admirers. He is witty, intelligent and ambitious. He has numerous interests and prefers to live in a quiet, stable environment where he can work without too much interference. He enjoys the arts and usually derives much pleasure from collecting paintings and antiques. His advice is often highly valued, particularly on social and domestic matters.

Fire Snake: 1917, 1977

The Fire Snake tends to be more forceful, outgoing and energetic than some of the other types of Snake. He is ambitious, confident and never slow in voicing his opinions – and he can be very abrasive to those he does not like. He does, however, have many leadership qualities and can win the respect and support of many with his firm and resolute manner. He usually has a good sense of humour, a wide circle of friends and a very active social life. He is also a keen traveller.

Earth Snake: 1929, 1989

The Earth Snake is charming, amusing and has a very amiable manner. He is conscientious and reliable in his work and approaches everything he does in a level-headed and sensible way. He can, however, tend to err on the cautious side and never likes to be hassled into making a decision. He is adept in dealing with financial matters and is a shrewd investor. He has many friends and is very supportive towards the members of his family.

PROSPECTS FOR THE SNAKE IN 2004

The Chinese New Year starts on 22 January 2004. Until then, the old year, the Year of the Goat, is still making its presence felt.

The Year of the Goat (1 February 2003 to 21 January 2004) will have been one of mixed fortunes for the Snake.

Many aspects of his life will have gone well, but the year could also have been tinged with some sadness or disappointment. However, the closing stages can turn out to be a more satisfying time.

In his work the Snake will get the best results from concentrating on the areas he knows well and making the most of his experience. If his work allows him to develop his ideas, his often distinctive approach can bring him much credit. The Goat year certainly favours creativity and in what remains of it the Snake should make the most of his talents. September and November are two particularly encouraging months for work matters.

Although usually careful in money matters, the Snake should be prudent in the closing months of the Goat year and think carefully about any sizeable purchases. Too many impulsive or expensive buys could quickly eat into his resources and he would do well to be patient and wait for more favourable buying opportunities.

The Snake's personal life will see a lot of activity at this time and while he might prefer a less demanding pace, there will still be much for him to enjoy, including family gatherings and opportunities to go out and meet friends. For the unattached, a new friendship or romance can add a definite sparkle to the end of the Goat year.

The Year of the Monkey starts on 22 January and will be a reasonably good one for the Snake. Progress is certainly possible and on a personal level the year can bring happiness, but it is not a time for risks or for being too independent.

As far as his work is concerned, the Snake will be able to build on his experience and make useful headway. As with the previous year, his greatest successes will come from areas which draw on his expertise rather than from anything new. The Snake's contacts and the knowledge and reputation he has built up will often lead to more responsibilities or promotion. The Monkey year will offer good chances to progress, with March, June, September and October being encouraging for work opportunities.

Snakes who are seeking work or feeling limited in their current position will also find that by drawing on their knowledge and experience they will be able to secure a position they are well suited for and which they will find more fulfilling.

While his progress may be good, the Snake does, however, need to watch his independent tendencies. To benefit from the support and co-operation of others, he needs to show himself a good team member rather than keep himself to himself. Otherwise, should any difficulties arise, he could find himself isolated. Snakes, do take note of this.

In addition, the Snake should keep his knowledge and skills up to date, even though he may feel he is already proficient in what he does. By taking advantage of training opportunities and being prepared to develop himself, he will gain a great deal and will find his future progress that much easier. Personal development *is* a key area in 2004.

This will be a generally good year for money matters, with the Snake not only enjoying a noticeable increase in income but also receiving additional funds from another source. Some Snakes may find they are able to supplement their income by freelance work or putting a skill or talent to profitable use. The enterprising could find their initiative well rewarded. The upturn in finances will also allow the Snake to spend money on his home, his interests and loved ones, whom he can sometimes spoil quite considerably. Also, if he is able, he should try to add to his savings. By managing his finances well, he will not only appreciate the rewards of his efforts but also improve his overall assets.

The Snake's relations with others are also well aspected. Many of those Snakes already enjoying romance, perhaps started in the previous Goat year, will decide to get engaged, married or settle down together. And for the unattached, serious romance can beckon. The Monkey year is excellently aspected for affairs of the heart, with March, April, July and August bringing good chances to meet others. For any Snake who has had a recent disappointment in his love life, this is the time to move forward, go out and make new friends. Many of these Snakes will meet someone who will quickly become important to them.

All Snakes, regardless of their situation, can gain much from their social life in 2004 and it will provide an important balance to all their other activities. Snakes have a tendency to keep themselves to themselves, but this really is a year when they should make every effort to lose some of their reserve and go out more. Their life will be so much richer as a result. And with his quiet humour and kindly ways, the Snake does have so much to offer.

This also applies to the Snake's home life. His love and care will do much to encourage family members over the year. And whether he is assisting those who may be involved in study, have important decisions to make or are grappling with problems related to work, the Snake's considerate nature and advice will be appreciated. Some of his suggestions for family activities can also lead to some pleasurable occasions. Home life means much to the Snake and his contribution will certainly make a difference in the Monkey year.

One warning that does need to be sounded, though, relates to any practical projects the Snake may start, especially any home improvements. In some instances such projects will be more disruptive than he originally envisaged and could lead to some fraught moments. When planning such projects, the Snake should allow plenty of time and avoid starting too much at once. Practical activities can lead to some tricky domestic moments! Snakes, take note.

Overall, this can be a positive year for the Snake, although he does need to watch his more independent tendencies. In his work, he can look forward to making good progress by making the most of his strengths and working well with others, while domestically, socially and romantically, this can be a pleasing and rewarding year.

The Metal Snake

As far as the different types of Snake are concerned, the Monkey year will be an interesting one for the Metal Snake. However, to make the most of the generally encouraging trends, he should map out what he would like to do over the year. If he uses his time constructively, in pursuits he enjoys and feels are purposeful, he will feel satisfied with how the year develops.

One area which is particularly well aspected is personal interests, and the Metal Snake will be keen to develop these further, perhaps by reading and study, trying new techniques, experimenting with his skills or taking up something new. In some cases enrolling on a course, perhaps with others, will be rewarding and fun. The Metal Snake's interests can certainly bring him great satisfaction in the Monkey year.

In addition, the Metal Snake will be keen to undertake a number of projects in his home and here his eye for colour and style will be to the fore. Quite a few Metal Snakes will decide to redecorate or alter the layout of certain rooms as well as add new comforts, and again the Metal Snake will enjoy setting his ideas in motion. However, he does need to allow plenty of time for practical projects as well as be prepared for some disruption. Also, in planning such projects, he should listen carefully to the views of others. Not only will the pooling of ideas lead to better results, but early discussion could also prevent disagreements from arising later. And should the Metal Snake be involved in any strenuous activity, particularly involving lifting or digging in the garden, he does need to take care as well as draw on the assistance of others. A strain or pulled muscle could cause him considerable discomfort and take time to mend. Metal Snakes, take care.

While the Metal Snake will see a lot of practical activity in his home life, most of it at his instigation, he will also delight in other aspects, including following the progress of family members and helping and advising them. In particular, if a grandparent, he could enjoy the time he spends with grandchildren. Family life for the Metal Snake can certainly be rewarding, but, as with all years, difficult situations could sometimes arise. In some instances the Metal Snake could find himself in disagreement with others or be concerned about the attitude of certain family members. At such times he should let his views be known. As he will find, an open approach is more likely to defuse a problem than letting it linger on and cause continuing concern.

The Metal Snake will value his social life over the year and will again find his interests, either old or new, giving rise to some enjoyable occasions with fellow enthusiasts. Any Metal Snake seeking company, perhaps after moving to a new area, could find joining a local group a good way to make new friends. This also applies to those who may be a little more reserved or who, either because of their work or lifestyle, have let their social life lapse. In 2004 they really should make an effort to go out and enjoy themselves more. This would add another positive element to the year as well as put an important ingredient back into their lives, one that some Metal Snakes may have neglected in recent times.

Over the year the Metal Snake will enjoy some good fortune in money matters, often in the form of a gift, unexpected payment or bonus for work completed earlier. This upturn will tempt many Metal Snakes into proceeding with plans for their accommodation as well as buying some home comforts. However, if the Metal Snake has funds he does not immediately need, he would be wise to set some aside for the longer term rather than letting them 'burn a hole in his pocket'. Some Metal Snakes could also enjoy a stroke of luck in a competition they enter.

Generally, the Monkey year holds good prospects for the Metal Snake and by furthering his interests and spending time on activities he enjoys, he will find it a satisfying and constructive year. His domestic and social life will bring him much pleasure.

TIP FOR THE YEAR

Aim to develop yourself in some way, possibly through a new interest or skill. This will not only satisfy your enquiring mind but have other benefits too.

The Water Snake

This will be an important year for the Water Snake and one in which he can make significant strides. However, the key message for him during the Monkey year is that he must remain focused on his objectives. To go off on a tangent or get distracted – and the Monkey year can put quite a few distractions his way – will not only mean he will achieve much less but also that he could miss out on some excellent opportunities. This is very much a year for self-discipline.

In his work the Water Snake should concentrate on the activities he does best and in which he is most experienced. By using his skills and strengths well, he will not only achieve some impressive results but also feel much more inspired. He will be helped by the enterprising nature of the Monkey year and if his work is in any way creative or allows him to further his ideas, he can again look forward to some encouraging results.

Throughout the year the Water Snake will also be helped by working closely with colleagues and other useful contacts he may have. In order to get support as well as further his aims he *does* need to show himself a good team member (or leader) and be mindful of others. This is not a year for being too independent.

In view of the changes many Water Snakes will have seen in their work in the preceding Goat year, most will be content to remain in their existing position and continue to develop their skills. However, for those keen to move on, the Monkey year will hold some excellent opportunities. In many cases, the Water Snake's existing duties will make him a strong candidate for some of the promotion opportunities that become available.

Water Snakes who are seeking work or wanting to change employer should also focus on positions which draw on their experience rather than look for anything too different. As the Water Snake will find, his strengths and skills will stand him in good stead, with March, June, September and October bringing good opportunities.

The Water Snake also possesses an enquiring mind and over the year he should spend some time in study, perhaps furthering his knowledge in areas related to his work or following up something of a more recreational nature. Whatever he does, he will find that setting a regular time aside for reading and personal development will be rewarding and beneficial.

The Water Snake should also pay attention to his well-being over the year, especially if he does not get much exercise. He could find walking more or perhaps swimming, cycling or some other form of exercise helpful. If necessary, he should seek medical guidance on the best way to proceed. With regular exercise as well as improvements to his diet and general lifestyle, he will often feel much better in himself.

The year will also see an upturn in the Water Snake's financial situation. As well as an increase in income, many Water Snakes could receive an additional sum from another source. Usually the Water Snake is careful when dealing with money, but in the Monkey year he should be wary of succumbing to too many temptations and impulsive buys. Without care, he could find he is spending more than he intended, sometimes on items which he may not need or which he might have found cheaper elsewhere. Also, if he is able, he would do well to add to his longer-term savings.

The year also holds much promise for personal matters. As always, the Water Snake will take a fond interest in the progress of those around him and the academic or career success of a younger family member will particularly delight him. Also, he will find that others place much confidence in his views and advice, and his ability to empathize with others, sometimes despite a considerable gap in years, will count for a good deal. Although the Monkey year will bring its busy times and pressures, the Water Snake's organized manner and calm temperament will again be valued. An occasional family treat could also ease some of the tensions during busy times and restore a certain balance.

The Water Snake will appreciate the social events he attends over the year, and whether meeting friends or going to an interest group that he belongs to (or decides to join), his social activities can bring him pleasure as well as do him good. Water Snakes who tend not to go out much should try to rectify this, as they will find they will benefit greatly from having more contact with others. If you are feeling lonely, Water Snake, *do* bear these words in mind.

In so many respects, the Monkey year holds considerable promise for the Water Snake and by using his skills well and spending time with others as well as on activities he enjoys, he will be pleased with how it proceeds.

TIP FOR THE YEAR
Pay attention to others. Much will be gained by listening to those around you and involving them in your plans and activities.

The Wood Snake

The Wood Snake likes to be his own master, setting about his activities in his own way and style. And because of his considered approach and amiable personality, he often enjoys a great deal of success. However, he could find the Monkey year a demanding one, with a lot being asked of him. The rewards, though, for what he does and the experience he gains will often be considerable.

At work this will be a busy year, with many Wood Snakes dealing with an increased workload, having to learn new procedures or sorting out problems that have arisen. Some of the situations that occur will certainly challenge the Wood Snake, but in the process he will come up with new ideas and try different approaches as well as add considerably to his experience. By making the most of the situations that arise, he will learn much and impress many, both with his industry and his ingenuity.

In view of some of the challenges he will face over the year, it is important the Wood Snake maintains the support of those around him. He should consult his colleagues regularly and listen carefully to their views, as well as continue to add to his circle of contacts. The effort he puts into maintaining good working relationships really can pay big dividends over the year.

Despite the increased pressures, many Wood Snakes will decide to remain in their present position this year, knowing that the experience they are gaining will stand them in good stead for when they do decide to move. However, for those who feel the time is right for a change or who are seeking work, the Monkey year can bring some interesting developments. While not all their applications may go their way and they may at times feel discouraged, by remaining persistent and focusing on areas which would make good use of their experience, many Wood Snakes will succeed in gaining a position which offers excellent scope for development. For work opportunities, March, June, September and October are especially favourable.

This will be a positive year for financial matters, with the Wood Snake enjoying an increase in income and an improvement in his overall situation. While he may decide to reward himself and his loved ones with some well-deserved treats, he could find it helpful to use this financial upturn to reduce some of his borrowings and set some funds aside for his future. If he manages his finances well, he will often feel much more comfortable with his position as a result.

In his domestic life the Wood Snake will see much activity, with the year bringing some happy times but a few awkward ones as well. On the positive side, there will be some successes to celebrate, including not only the Wood Snake's own achievements but also those of family members. The progress of younger family members, in particular, will delight the Wood Snake, even though there may be occasions when he will despair over their activities and attitude. The Wood Snake does, after all, appreciate a peaceable existence! However, by taking an interest and showing he cares, he can enjoy a good rapport with younger relations as well as help and support them.

The Wood Snake will also enjoy some of the more pleasurable family activities, such as going for a day out somewhere or having friends round. However, with the pressures of work as well as sometimes helping more senior family members, there will be times when he will feel tired and on edge. Rather than struggle along unaided, he should let others know how he feels and ask for additional help. It is also important that he does not neglect himself over the year and gives himself the chance to relax and unwind. His conscientious nature may keep reminding him of tasks that need be done, but he *must* devote time to his own well-being this year.

In this respect, the Wood Snake's social life will be important and he will appreciate meeting up with friends and going to parties and other events. For Wood Snakes who may desire more companionship or have had recent disappointments in their personal life, the Monkey year holds excellent prospects. By taking up new interests, joining a local group or just going out more, they will soon get to meet others and can form what can be a very significant friendship or romance. March, April and June to August are particularly favourable for socializing.

Although the Monkey year will demand a great deal of the Wood Snake, it will give him an excellent chance to further himself and gain experience as well as enjoy many of his undertakings.

TIP FOR THE YEAR

Have faith in your talents and rise to the challenges the year will bring. In mastering them you can learn much, gain experience and enhance your prospects. The benefits of what is accomplished now will be great indeed.

The Fire Snake

The Fire Snake can do well over the year, but to benefit from the prevailing trends he will need to be adaptable in his approach. This is a time for making the most of situations as they arise rather than sticking rigidly to existing plans.

The Fire Snake will find that some particularly interesting and sometimes unexpected opportunities will be in the offing at work. In some cases the sudden departure or promotion of colleagues could provide new openings for him or new positions could be created. By taking advantage of these opportunities, even though they may not be what he was originally aiming for, the Fire Snake will not only be able to further his experience and become better known among more senior figures but also help his future career prospects.

There will also be other ways for the Fire Snake to show his worth. Sometimes new schemes and ideas will be introduced, and by being willing to learn what is necessary, the Fire Snake will find his attitude noted *and* appreciated. Similarly, at busy times, showing commitment and being prepared to work longer than usual will result in the Fire Snake's standing with colleagues being much enhanced, and this, in turn, will be useful when he next looks to advance.

The Fire Snake will also be helped by his ability to get

on with his colleagues and throughout the year the effort he puts into maintaining good working relationships and building new ones really will repay him handsomely.

The Monkey year holds good prospects for those Fire Snakes who are currently seeking work or who decide to change employers over the year. However, these Fire Snakes should concentrate their efforts on positions which allow them to draw on their experience rather than try for anything too different. In this way, many will secure a position which will become an important stepping-stone in their career.

The progress that the Fire Snake makes at work will also lead to an improvement in his financial situation. However to benefit, he should still manage his finances with care, making allowance for his commitments and forthcoming expenses, and planning any major purchases carefully. By keeping on top of his financial situation, he will not only find himself able to do more but also, in some instances, to build up his assets and savings.

Another area which the Fire Snake should pay close attention to is his own personal development. Although he may lead a full and active life, he really would find it in his interest to set some time aside to further himself in some way. This could be by learning a work-related or academic skill or by doing something that is more recreational, but whatever he decides upon, the Fire Snake will benefit from the feeling that he is moving himself forward. Similarly, he should pay attention to his own well-being over the year and make sure he gets regular exercise and eats a balanced and healthy diet. In such an active year, he does need to look after himself in order to keep on good form.

Also, despite his commitment to his work and eagerness to do well, he must make sure that his home and social life do not suffer as a result. Fortunately most Fire Snakes are aware of this and do give time to those who are important to them, but during busy periods the Fire Snake would do well to remember this and to preserve some time for family, recreational and social pursuits.

In the Fire Snake's home life there will indeed be some splendid occasions, particularly as he follows and encourages the activities of those dear to him. However, as with all Snakes in 2004, if the Fire Snake embarks on any practical projects or decides to move, he should allow plenty of time and be prepared for a great deal of disruption. Practical activities can bring problems.

Despite all the pressures on his time, the Fire Snake should not neglect his social life over the year. Not only will it give rise to some agreeable occasions and allow him to benefit from the company of friends, but it will bring an important balance to his life. Even those Fire Snakes who tend to keep themselves to themselves will find that making the effort to go out and meet others can make this year all the more special.

Overall, the Monkey year holds some fine prospects for the Fire Snake, but to benefit he does need to make the most of the opportunities that arise. But with his skills, commitment and a willingness to adapt, this can prove a rewarding and successful year.

TIP FOR THE YEAR

Make sure you spend time with those important to you, sharing your successes, interests, hopes and joys. Also, ensure your lifestyle has balance.

The Earth Snake

This will be a promising year for the Earth Snake, although for those born in 1989, attitude is going to be a crucial factor. With a positive and adaptable approach the young Earth Snake can make pleasing strides and do himself considerable good. However, if he lets opportunities slip by or does not rise to the challenges set him, then there could be some uncomfortable moments in store. How he fares is very much in his own hands.

The year will, though, be an important one as far as the young Earth Snake's education is concerned. There will be new topics to be covered, tests and exams to be revised for and course work to do. There will certainly be times when the Earth Snake will be faced with work he does not find easy and he may despair of what is being asked of him. However, this is when his attitude becomes so crucial. By trying hard and making the best of his abilities, the Earth Snake will not only cope well but also learn the value of persistence and effort, something which will serve him well throughout his life. In addition, he will find that by having to apply himself he learns far more than he would if his work were too easy. He should, however, not allow himself to get discouraged by subjects that may be giving difficulty, as he does, after all, have some particularly strong areas which he will continue to do well in and enjoy.

He will also be well supported and if he finds a subject difficult, a word with his tutors can often help.

The Earth Snake should also take advantage of some of the other opportunities and facilities available to him over the year. Whether joining an after-school club or a social, sports or special interest group or developing a skill, he will find that getting involved in activities that interest him can bring him a great deal of fun and pleasure.

The Earth Snake can also look forward to many fine times with his friends, and with his sense of humour and ability to get on with others, he will find himself a popular member of any group. As far as socializing is concerned, this is a very positive year.

The Earth Snake's home life will also go well and although he may sometimes desire a little more independence, he will be grateful for the encouragement he is given. If he has any worries, he should be open and willing to ask for help, as those around him will be understanding and can do much to allay his concerns. The Earth Snake will also be able to help more with some household tasks that need to be done this year, and this will be appreciated. In addition, he will enjoy some of the family activities that take place. However, there could be also occasions when the Earth Snake may find some of his ideas do not meet with the approval he was hoping for. While disappointed, he should realize that decisions are often made with his interests at heart. If any disagreements do arise, he should try to settle them early rather than let them sour family relations. Without care, a small issue could escalate. However, in most respects, both as far as his home and social life are concerned, this will be a year the Earth Snake will enjoy.

He will, though, need to be careful with his spending. He will be tempted by a great many things, but given his position it would be wise for him to reflect on some of the purchases he may be considering as well as avoid spending too much on the spur of the moment. Indeed, by planning and saving towards specific items, he will find they will mean much more to him than if he were to spend his money too hastily.

For those Earth Snakes born in 1929 again the Monkey year holds fine prospects. However, these Earth Snakes should make a point of involving others in their activities and being forthcoming with their ideas. This way they will not only find that more is possible but they will also gain from the support and input that others are able to give. These Earth Snakes will also find their own personal interests bringing them much pleasure, especially if they draw on their more creative talents.

The Snake does not tend to travel far in Monkey years, but if the Earth Snake does get the chance to go away, he should go well prepared. This includes making sure he has everything he is likely to need as well as sorting out his itinerary beforehand. Thorough preparation can help avert possible problems as well as make his time away that much more enjoyable.

Although 2004 will demand much of the Earth Snake, by developing his skills and knowledge and making the most of the chances that are available, he will find this a positive and constructive time. And his efforts will reward him well both now *and* in the future.

TIP FOR THE YEAR
Be earnest and be willing to learn and discover. With a positive attitude you will benefit, particularly in your own personal development.

FAMOUS SNAKES

Muhammad Ali, Ann-Margret, Yasser Arafat, Lord Baden-Powell, Ronnie Barker, Kim Basinger, Björk, Tony Blair, Michael Bloomberg, Heinrich Böll, Michael Bolton, Brahms, Pierce Brosnan, Casanova, Chubby Checker, Dick Cheney, Jackie Collins, Tom Conti, Jim Davidson, Bob Dylan, Elgar, Sir Alex Ferguson, Sir Alexander Fleming, Henry Fonda, Mahatma Gandhi, Greta Garbo, Art Garfunkel, J. Paul Getty, Dizzy Gillespie, W. E. Gladstone, Goethe, Princess Grace of Monaco, Stephen Hawking, Audrey Hepburn, Jack Higgins, Howard Hughes, Tom Hulce, Liz Hurley, James Joyce, Stacy Keach, Ronan Keating, Howard Keel, J. F. Kennedy, Carole King, Cyndi Lauper, Courtney Love, Dame Vera Lynn, Mao Tse-tung, Henri Matisse, Cecil B. de Mille, Robert Mitchum, Nasser, Bob Newhart, Alfred Nobel, Mike Oldfield, Aristotle Onassis, Jacqueline Onassis, Pablo Picasso, Mary Pickford, Brad Pitt, André Prévin, Daniel Radcliffe, Franklin D. Roosevelt, Mickey Rourke, J. K. Rowling, Jean-Paul Sartre, Franz Schubert, Brooke Shields, Paul Simon, Delia Smith, Paul Theroux, Madame Tussaud, Shania Twain, Dionne Warwick, Charlie Watts, Ruby Wax, Oprah Winfrey, Victoria Wood, Virginia Woolf.

25 JANUARY 1906 ⌢ 12 FEBRUARY 1907   *Fire Horse*

11 FEBRUARY 1918 ⌢ 31 JANUARY 1919   *Earth Horse*

30 JANUARY 1930 ⌢ 16 FEBRUARY 1931   *Metal Horse*

15 FEBRUARY 1942 ⌢ 4 FEBRUARY 1943   *Water Horse*

3 FEBRUARY 1954 ⌢ 23 JANUARY 1955   *Wood Horse*

21 JANUARY 1966 ⌢ 8 FEBRUARY 1967   *Fire Horse*

7 FEBRUARY 1978 ⌢ 27 JANUARY 1979   *Earth Horse*

27 JANUARY 1990 ⌢ 14 FEBRUARY 1991   *Metal Horse*

12 FEBRUARY 2002 ⌢ 31 JANUARY 2003   *Water Horse*

THE
HORSE

THE PERSONALITY OF THE HORSE

Everyone has talent. What is rare is the courage to follow the talent to the dark place where it leads.

Erica Jong, a Horse

The Horse is born under the signs of elegance and ardour. He has a most engaging and charming manner and is usually very popular. He loves meeting people and likes attending parties and other large social gatherings.

The Horse is a lively character and enjoys being the centre of attention. He has considerable leadership qualities and is much admired for his honest and straightforward manner. He is an eloquent and persuasive speaker and has a great love of discussion and debate. He also has a particularly agile mind and can assimilate facts remarkably quickly.

He does, however, have a fiery temper and although his outbursts are usually short-lived, he can often say things which he will later regret. He is also not particularly good at keeping secrets.

The Horse has many interests and involves himself in a wide variety of activities. He can, however, get involved in so much that he can often waste his energies on projects which he never has time to complete. He also has a tendency to change his interests rather frequently and will often get caught up with the latest craze or 'in thing' until something better or more exciting turns up.

The Horse also likes to have a certain amount of freedom and independence. He hates being bound by petty rules and regulations and as far as possible he likes to feel that he is answerable to no one but himself. But despite this spirit of freedom, he still likes to have the support and encouragement of others in his various enterprises.

Due to his many talents and likeable nature, the Horse will often go far in life. He enjoys challenges and is a methodical and tireless worker. However, should things work against him and he fail with any of his enterprises, it will take a long time for him to recover and pick up the pieces again. Success to the Horse means everything. To fail is a disaster and a humiliation.

The Horse likes to have variety in his life and he will try his hand at many different things before he settles down to one particular job. Even then, he will probably remain alert to see whether there are any better opportunities for him to take up. The Horse has a restless nature and can easily get bored. He does, however, excel in any position which allows him sufficient freedom to act on his own initiative or which brings him into contact with a lot of people.

Although the Horse is not particularly bothered about accumulating great wealth, he handles his finances with care and will rarely experience any serious financial problems.

The Horse also enjoys travel and he loves visiting new and faraway places. At some stage during his life he will be tempted to live abroad for a short period of time and due to his adaptable nature he will find that he will fit in well wherever he goes.

The Horse pays a great deal of attention to his appearance and usually likes to wear smart, colourful and rather distinctive clothes. He is very attractive to others and will often have many romances before he settles down. He is loyal and protective to his partner, but despite his family commitments he still likes to retain a certain measure of independence and have the freedom to carry on with his own interests and hobbies. He will find that he is especially well suited to those born under the signs of the Tiger, Goat, Rooster and Dog. The Horse can also get on well with the Rabbit, Dragon, Snake, Pig and another Horse, but he will find the Ox too serious and intolerant for his liking. The Horse will also have difficulty in getting on with the Monkey and the Rat – the Monkey is very inquisitive and the Rat seeks security, and both will resent the Horse's rather independent ways.

The female Horse is usually most attractive and has a friendly, outgoing personality. She is highly intelligent, has many interests and is alert to everything that is going on around her. She particularly enjoys outdoor pursuits and often likes to take part in sport and keep-fit activities. She also enjoys travel, literature and the arts, and is a very good conversationalist.

Although the Horse can be stubborn and rather self-centred, he does have a considerate nature and is often willing to help others. He has a good sense of humour and will usually make a favourable impression wherever he goes. Provided he can curb his slightly restless nature and keep a tight control over his temper, he will go through life making friends, taking part in a multitude of different activities and generally achieving many of his objectives. His life will rarely be dull.

THE FIVE DIFFERENT TYPES OF HORSE

In addition to the 12 signs of the Chinese zodiac there are five elements, and these have a strengthening or moderating influence on the sign. The effects of the five elements on the Horse are described below, together with the years in which the elements were exercising their influence. Therefore all Horses born in 1930 and 1990 are Metal Horses, those born in 1942 and 2002 are Water Horses, and so on.

Metal Horse: 1930, 1990
This Horse is bold, confident and forthright. He is ambitious and a great innovator. He loves challenges and takes great delight in sorting out complicated problems. He likes to have a certain amount of independence and resents any outside interference in his affairs. The Metal Horse has charm and a certain charisma, but he can also be very stubborn and rather impulsive. He usually has many friends and enjoys an active social life.

Water Horse: 1942, 2002
The Water Horse has a friendly nature, a good sense of humour and is able to talk intelligently on a wide range of topics. He is astute in business matters and is quick to take advantage of any opportunities that arise. He does,

however, have a tendency to get easily distracted and can change his interests – and indeed his mind – rather frequently, and this can often work to his detriment. He is nevertheless very talented and can often go far in life. He pays a great deal of attention to his appearance and is usually smart and well turned out. He loves to travel and also enjoys sport and other outdoor activities.

Wood Horse: 1954

The Wood Horse has a most agreeable and amiable nature. He communicates well with others and is able to talk intelligently on many different subjects. He is a hard and conscientious worker and is held in high esteem by his friends and colleagues. His opinions are often sought and, given his imaginative nature, he can quite often come up with some very original and practical ideas. He is usually widely read and likes to lead a busy social life. He can also be most generous and often holds high moral views.

Fire Horse: 1906, 1966

The element of Fire combined with the temperament of the Horse creates one of the most powerful forces in the Chinese zodiac. The Fire Horse is destined to lead an exciting and eventful life and to make his mark in his chosen profession. He has a forceful personality and his intelligence and resolute manner bring him the support and admiration of many. He loves action and excitement and his life will rarely be quiet. He can, however, be rather blunt and forthright in his views and does not take kindly to interference in his own affairs or to obeying orders. He is a flamboyant character, has a good sense of humour and will lead a very active social life.

Earth Horse: 1918, 1978

This Horse is considerate and caring. He is more cautious than some of the other types of Horse, but he is wise, perceptive and extremely capable. Although he can be rather indecisive at times, he has considerable business acumen and is very astute in financial matters. He has a quiet, friendly nature and is well thought of by his family and friends.

PROSPECTS FOR THE HORSE
IN 2004

The Chinese New Year starts on 22 January 2004. Until then, the old year, the Year of the Goat, is still making its presence felt.

The Year of the Goat (1 February 2003 to 21 January 2004) is a generally rewarding one for the Horse and in the remaining months he can do himself much good.

At work this is very much a time for the Horse to make the most of his strengths and concentrate on the areas in which he has most experience. This way he will not only impress others but also enhance his prospects, particularly for the more favourable Monkey year that follows. For those Horses who are keen to progress or are seeking work, the last quarter of the year will certainly hold some interesting opportunities, but again, the real benefits will come in 2004.

The Goat year will, however, have been an expensive one and as it draws to a close the Horse would do well to keep a watchful eye on his spending. He could also find it helpful to spread out some of his more seasonal purchases.

The closing months will also be an active time for personal matters. In the Horse's home life there will be much for him to do, including arranging various activities, visiting others and keeping on top of his already busy schedule as well as fitting in with the arrangements of loved ones. The last quarter will certainly be busy, but despite the pressures and occasional fraught moment, the Horse will enjoy himself. He is, after all, never one to sit idly by when there is something of interest to do.

The Horse will also enjoy himself on a social level, particularly at some of the events and parties he is invited to. And for those newly in love or desiring romance, the closing months of the year can be an exciting and special time. The Goat year does favour affairs of the heart, as many Horses will, to their delight, discover.

The Year of the Monkey starts on 22 January and is one which will suit the Horse personality. The Horse likes things to happen quickly, and in the Monkey year they will. This will be a year in which the Horse can go ahead with his plans and ideas.

In his work the Horse can make great strides. Not only will he benefit from his hard work and the skills he has acquired in the preceding Goat year, but some exciting opportunities will also become available. In some cases, the Horse's high standing in his current organization will make him an ideal candidate for promotion or lead him to become involved in more rewarding duties. Opportunities will certainly beckon and will enable the Horse to take several rungs up the career ladder.

While some Horses will make important progress with their present employer, there will be those who will feel the time is right for a new challenge. For those who may feel they have done all they can in their existing post, who consider themselves in a rut or who are seeking work, again the Monkey year will provide some exciting possibilities. By considering the type of work they would now like to do and going after suitable openings, many Horses will be successful in securing a position which offers them the chance to extend their skills and find a greater fulfilment in what they do. For interesting work developments February, May, June and October are well aspected.

The Horse's progress at work will also lead to a welcome increase in his income. However, while money may flow into his accounts, it could flow out again all too easily. The Horse will be eager to carry out many plans which entail considerable expense and he could also find certain indulgences hard to resist. In many instances he will be pleased with his acquisitions, especially those which add to the comfort and décor of his home. He will also enjoy any holidays and breaks he takes, as well as spending money on recreational pursuits, but in some cases a little more moderation would not come amiss. Also, the Horse could find it to his advantage to set funds aside for specific requirements. By controlling his money, he will not only be able to improve his overall position but also appreciate his purchases that much more.

Also, a word of warning does need to be sounded about any risks or speculative ventures the Horse may be considering. Although this may be a generally favourable year, the Horse should still be wary of getting involved in any matter he has not investigated or does not understand properly. Without care, he could fall victim to one of the Monkey's scams and end up the loser. Horses, take note, and in important financial matters *do* tread carefully.

With this being a year for so much activity, some Horses will decide to move and, though the moving process will take up much time, once installed in their new home they will often feel invigorated by the change. Not only will their new accommodation suit their requirements better, but it can represent a new beginning and new possibilities as well as giving them more amenities to enjoy.

The Horse's relations with others are favourably aspected and over the year he will find himself much in demand. In his home life he will take pleasure in many of the shared activities and also in encouraging the progress of others. His willingness to contribute so much to family life really will be appreciated. Overall, this will be a busy but good year domestically, and by spending time with those important to him, the Horse will find this a rewarding aspect of his life.

With his outgoing nature the Horse also values his social life, and the Monkey year offers much activity and fun. Not only will the Horse enjoy the company of his close band of friends but by taking part in activities he enjoys and going to events that appeal to him, he will also enjoy many pleasurable occasions. For any Horse who may start the year in low spirits, the Monkey year can usher in some brighter times, with the chance of new friendships and, for some, significant romance. As far as his personal relations are concerned, the Horse will be in excellent form. April, June, September and December could be particularly busy.

With the Horse being involved in so much over the year, he does, though, need to keep an eye on his own well-being. If he does not get much exercise he should try to make up for this with some extra walking or by cycling, swimming or some other suitable activity. Similarly, if he is reliant on convenience foods, switching to a more balanced diet could make a difference. By getting medical advice on the best way to proceed he will find he can improve both his level of fitness and his lifestyle. Giving consideration to his well-being really would be to his advantage over the year.

Overall, the active nature of the Monkey year will suit the Horse. In his work there will be opportunities to progress and he will particularly appreciate the chances to develop his skills in a more satisfying way. His personal life too will be busy but rewarding, with family, friends and, for some, romance and a more active social life meaning a great deal.

The Metal Horse

As far as the different types of Horse are concerned, the Monkey year holds great potential for the Metal Horse. With his keen and lively nature he will revel in the many opportunities that the year will bring and will learn a great deal.

Those Metal Horses born in 1990 can look forward to making important strides in their education over the year. Although there will be many subjects to cover, with his enquiring nature and a willingness to learn, the Metal Horse will find himself enjoying many aspects of his schoolwork. He could also develop a particular fondness for certain subjects and his success in these will often filter through to other areas too.

The Metal Horse will also find the camaraderie of his close friends will add an enjoyable element to school life. He will also find himself becoming involved in a wide range of activities, both run by his school and out of school. By getting involved, the Metal Horse will have fun and enjoy many great occasions.

In addition he should further the skills he has been learning. These could be connected with sport, music or another creative activity, but whatever he does, by practising his skill and building on his knowledge the Metal Horse will take pleasure in the progress he makes. His increased knowledge will also help him to do more and can open up new possibilities for him. He will be well supported in his activities, although to benefit he does need to overcome his independent tendencies and be forthcoming. When he has ideas he wishes to pursue, he should put them forward. Similarly, if he is experiencing difficulties in his schoolwork, a word with those who can help can make a big difference.

The year will also bring some interesting travel opportunities for the Metal Horse and whether born in 1930 or

1990, he will enjoy the chance to go away and visit new areas. The opportunities that arise will often appeal to his adventurous nature. The more senior Metal Horse will also welcome the chance to visit relations or friends he may not have seen for some time. Whenever he receives invitations, he should take them up. This *is* a year for making the most of opportunities.

This will also be a generally positive year for money matters. The younger Metal Horse could find he is able to help his financial position by taking on a small but suitable job or by assisting others. By being willing and enterprising, he can do much to supplement his resources. He does, though, still need to be careful with his money and be wary of taking risks or believing all that others may tell him. If he has doubts over *any* money matter, he should check. This also applies to those Metal Horses born in 1930. While they can look forward to receiving a bonus or perhaps the maturing of a policy, the Monkey year does still require them to be on their guard. Where financially-related forms and new obligations are concerned, care *is* needed.

The Metal Horse will, however, value his home life, particularly the help and encouragement others are able to give. Although the younger Metal Horse may sometimes prefer a little more independence, by being willing to play a greater part in household activities he will find others are often able to help him too. As with so many aspects of his life in 2004, by being involved and making an effort, he will find his life all the more rewarding.

The more senior Metal Horse will also value the support given by family members and will often be able to recipro-cate kindnesses by helping out those with particularly young families or offering advice based on his years of experience. The Metal Horse really does hold a valuable place in the lives of many and over the year his family life will mean a great deal to him.

The Monkey year does hold considerable promise for the Metal Horse and by furthering his skills and interests and taking advantage of the many opportunities that will be available, he will find this a satisfying and pleasing year.

TIP FOR THE YEAR
Be adventurous and be willing to give new activities, subjects and interests a try. It is by trying that you discover. And by discovering, you will be furthering yourself.

The Water Horse

This will be a positive year for the Water Horse, giving him the chance to be involved in a wide range of activities as well as to develop himself and his interests.

Being such a forward thinker, the Water Horse will already have some idea of what he would like to do over the next 12 months, but as the year starts he would find it helpful to discuss his thoughts with those around him. Being forthcoming will not only help to clarify his own ideas but can also set some of them in motion. The Water Horse could also be alerted about a particular opportunity or advised on the best way to proceed, and certainly by being open he will find himself being helped and encouraged by many.

One area which the Water Horse will find especially satisfying will be the way in which he is able to develop his interests, both existing ones and any new ones he takes up. The Water Horse has a creative streak and he could find pleasure in activities that allow him to express himself in some way, perhaps through photography, art, writing, music, drama or something similarly creative. Whether his interests are practical, recreational or just allow him to enjoy the outdoors more, he will find they often do him a lot of good. Any Water Horse who, perhaps because of his work and/or general lifestyle has let his interests lapse, really should give more time to himself and to activities he enjoys over the Monkey year.

Another area the Water Horse will have plans for will be his home. Some Water Horses will decide to move while others will be keen to change the décor of certain rooms and replace furnishings and equipment. While the Water Horse may be keen to set his plans in motion, he could find it better to take the time to consider the various possibilities as well as wait for favourable buying opportunities. By proceeding steadily, he will find his plans working out far better than if he were to act too hastily.

In many cases the Water Horse's practical activities will also extend to his garden. He could decide to add new features and experiment with new stock. Again, he will have ideas aplenty and will certainly keep himself well occupied over the year.

In all the Water Horse sets out to do he will be grateful for the support of family members, with many of his undertakings benefiting from the pooling of ideas and from the practical assistance of others. He will also take a keen interest in the progress of family members and will do much to assist others, particularly those who may be under pressure or have young families. The practical and caring way in which he is able to help will be greatly appreciated.

In addition to the pleasures his family life will bring, the Water Horse will enjoy himself on a social level. By going out and becoming involved in activities that appeal to him, he can look forward to many pleasing occasions and to adding to his circle of friends. Any Water Horses who may be seeking more companionship or have had some recent personal difficulty will find the Monkey year can certainly bring some brightness and joy back into their lives, with the prospects of an important new friendship. For socializing and meeting others, the months from April to June and September hold good prospects.

The adventurous nature of the Monkey year will suit the Water Horse and he will make the most of the travel opportunities that arise over the year. In addition to taking a holiday in what could be, for him, an unusual destination, he will enjoy many of the short breaks or outings that he goes on.

This will also be a good year for financial matters, with many Water Horses receiving an additional sum of money during the course of the year. This will often tempt the Water Horse to go ahead with plans he has been considering, including travel, but where possible he should also consider setting something aside for the longer term. In years to come he will be grateful for savings made now.

The Monkey year will be an interesting one work-wise, with the Water Horse being able to make effective use of his skills. Not only will colleagues often look to him for guidance but also some of the activities he undertakes will benefit particularly from his insight and experience. The Monkey year can be a productive time as far as work is concerned, even for those Water Horses who may have recently retired, as they too will find they are often able to use their skills and knowledge in different ways or take on freelance work. There will certainly be opportunities for all Water Horses to use their talents well in 2004.

Overall, this year is well aspected for the Water Horse and by following through his ideas and making the most of opportunities, he will find this an enjoyable and satisfying time. In addition, he will gain greatly from the love, support and encouragement of others.

TIP FOR THE YEAR
Consider this a year for action and making the most of your ideas. A great deal can be gained by spending time developing personal interests. These can be of benefit in more ways than one.

The Wood Horse
The Monkey year holds much potential for the Wood Horse, with most aspects of his life going well.

With his keen and enquiring nature, one area which will particularly appeal to him will be his own personal development. By undertaking any training at work, following up interests and subjects by himself, reading, joining study groups or enrolling on courses, he will take much satisfaction in what he learns as well as in being able to put his new knowledge to practical use. The very knowledge that he is furthering himself will give him a sense of moving forward and, in the process, bring a constructive feel to the year.

In addition to his own development there will be other plans the Wood Horse will hope to realize. Many adventurous Wood Horses will be tempted to travel and by making enquiries and talking to others about where they would like to go, they could find some of their ideas more possible than they first thought. Quite a few Wood Horses could be tempted by bargain breaks or could decide to go away on the spur of the moment. Certainly, travel-wise, the Monkey year will hold some fine possibilities.

But the activity will not stop there. Over the year many Wood Horses will turn their attention to their home and garden and decide to make some alterations. However, for these to be successful, the Wood Horse should allow himself plenty of time as well as avoid starting too much at once. Occasionally the Wood Horse's over-zealous nature can get the better of him and he should heed the sometimes more cautionary advice of others in his household!

However, the Wood Horse's home life will bring him much contentment over the year. In addition to enjoying time spent with loved ones, he will find that shared interests and projects will lead to some fine occasions. The Wood Horse will also take a fond interest in the progress of family members, especially younger ones who may, over the year, be particularly grateful for the assistance and advice he feels able to give. Domestically, this can certainly be a fine year, although, with work sometimes demanding much of his time, the Wood Horse does need to be careful that his home life does not suffer through him being too preoccupied. Fortunately, most Wood Horses are aware of this and balance their commitments well, but at busy times, it is something to be aware of.

The Wood Horse will also enjoy going out over the year and whether he attends social occasions, meets up with friends or enjoys more cultural pursuits, again the Monkey year will give rise to many pleasurable occasions. Many Wood Horses could find their social circle widening as a result of their interests and could forge some important new friendships. The months of April, May, September and December could be particularly active socially.

In his work the Wood Horse will make good headway and will appreciate the opportunities to make more of his strengths. Although many Wood Horses will be content in their present role, should promotion opportunities appear or they decide to progress, they should seize the often very good opportunities the year will bring. February, May, June and October will contain interesting prospects. In addition the Wood Horse should make the most of any work-related ideas that he has. The Monkey year is all for enterprise and, with his knowledge and experience, some of the Wood Horse's suggestions could be well received.

For those Wood Horses seeking work, again this is a year to be bold, and although competition for some positions may be fierce, by persevering and emphasizing their strengths and the contribution they feel they can make, these Wood Horses will often be given what could turn out to be a significant opportunity.

The positive aspects also extend to finance, with many Wood Horses enjoying an improvement in their position over the year. In view of this, the Wood Horse will often feel able to proceed with some of his ideas, purchases and travel plans. However, if he is able, he should consider reducing some of his borrowings, as well as setting something aside for the longer term. To benefit from the year's positive trends, he does need to manage his financial situation with care.

Overall, this will be a fine year for the Wood Horse. With the support of others, his fine abilities and wide interests, he certainly has much in his favour, and by making the most of himself and the chances the year will bring, he will find this a positive and constructive time.

TIP FOR THE YEAR
Do give thought to your personal development. This is a time when you should be making the most of yourself and your potential. You do, after all, have so much to offer.

The Fire Horse

The Fire Horse likes activity and there will be activity aplenty in 2004, with this being a fulfilling and successful year for him. He will be encouraged by the support he receives for many of his activities and will find it easier to accomplish many of his goals.

In his home life the Fire Horse will enjoy the activities he carries out with family members, especially those of a practical nature. Many Fire Horses will pay particular attention to their accommodation over the year, either adding improvements or moving. While their plans will often take up much time and energy, they will be pleased with what they are able to accomplish.

The Fire Horse will also enjoy other aspects of his family life, including sharing interests, entertaining and any trips and treats that may be arranged. By playing a full part in family life, he will find many aspects of it both pleasurable and rewarding. He will do much to help others over the year, particularly in giving advice to a relation who may be involved in education or have important long-term decisions to make. His advice and interest will be appreciated, often more than he may realize.

However, while so much will go well domestically, there will be times of pressure as well as some differences of opinion. At such times the Fire Horse would find it helpful to discuss matters and see how they can be resolved, rather than to let them linger in the background. Should he himself feel under pressure or have problems, again he should tell others rather than letting his vexations and tensions stew.

On a social level, the Fire Horse will find himself in demand, with invitations to a wide range of events either connected with his work, his interests or arranged by friends. The months from April to June and September and December will be especially active. Any Fire Horses who may have had some difficulty in their personal life will find the Monkey year ushering in a happier phase, with the opportunity to meet others and build up a new social circle. For the unattached Fire Horse, there could be significant romance. Again, the Monkey year will be supportive of the Fire Horse.

The encouraging trends also extend to the Fire Horse's work prospects. Almost as soon as the Monkey year starts the Fire Horse will see some interesting developments.

Sometimes new projects will lead to openings for which his knowledge and experience will make him an ideal candidate, while the progression of colleagues could also open up promotion possibilities. This is a year to advance, with February, May, June and October being particularly well aspected.

This also applies to those Fire Horses seeking work or feeling they have achieved all they can in their present position. In 2004 they should actively follow up opportunities that interest them. By preparing well for interviews as well as emphasizing their experience, many will secure what will be an important opportunity with the potential for further development.

The progress the Fire Horse makes in his work will also help his financial position, with many Fire Horses enjoying an appreciable increase in income over the year. However, to benefit, the Fire Horse should manage his money carefully and keep a watchful eye on his spending. By controlling his outgoings, planning his larger purchases, setting money aside for specific purposes and adding to his savings, he will find his financial position can be much improved. However, while favourable, this is not a year for risks or pushing his luck too far. The Fire Horse should remember that the Monkey year can provide some salutary reminders if he takes one risk too many.

Overall, the Monkey year holds much promise for the Fire Horse and by making the most of his talents and the opportunities that arise, he will find this a rewarding and successful time. The aspects are on his side and he should seize the opportunities that the year will bring. In addition, he will be encouraged by the love and support of those who mean so much to him.

Look to advance and to make more of your strengths and experience. These are real assets which can prove of great value during the year.

The Earth Horse

The Monkey year holds considerable potential for the Earth Horse and he can look forward to pleasing developments in many areas of his life.

Especially well aspected are his work prospects. With his keen and ambitious nature the Earth Horse knows he has it within him to achieve much and by drawing on his experience and keeping alert for positions which will give him more responsibilities and scope, he will often be successful in gaining an important new role over the year and, in the process, advancing several rungs up the career ladder. Also, he could find events moving in fortuitous ways. Sometimes he will find himself ideally placed to put in for a position which becomes available or he could discover a suitable opportunity quite by chance. By acting quickly and making the most of the situations that arise, he can certainly make good headway. February, May, June and October could see some particularly interesting work opportunities.

The favourable aspects also extend to those Earth Horses who are seeking work or feel disillusioned with their present position. By going after vacancies that appeal to them, many will be able to set their career off on an exciting new path. Work-wise, the Monkey year *is* an encouraging one.

The Earth Horse will also benefit from any training and personal development courses he can go on. Keeping his skills up to date and staying abreast of developments in his line of work will not only be helpful in his present duties but could also open up other possibilities for the future. Personal development is also well aspected and if there is an interest or recreational pursuit which the Earth Horse could take further, perhaps through private study, joining a group of enthusiasts or enrolling on a course, he should do so. Some interests could have the added benefit of giving him extra exercise or taking him out of doors, both of which he will appreciate.

This is also a favourably aspected year for personal matters and in his home life the Earth Horse will do much to support others. Those who are parents will watch their children's development with much interest and encourage them in their various activities. Admittedly, the demands of young children may sometimes be tiring, but for many these will still be wonderful times. If the Earth Horse finds too many demands are being placed on him, he should not hesitate to ask others for help with household chores or to take up offers of assistance from friends or close relations. Although the Earth Horse may be willing, he should accept that there is a limit to the amount he can do!

While his domestic life will often be busy, there will also be much to enjoy. For those Earth Horses with a partner, there will be interests they can share and some of the projects they tackle together to enhance their home will mean a great deal. In addition, by supporting and giving time to each other, the Earth Horse and his partner will find great strength in the relationship. For personal relations, this can be a very positive year.

In view of the demands on his time, the Earth Horse may be more selective in his socializing this year. However, he should be careful his social life does not get squeezed out altogether, as it does provide an important balance to his life. Not only will he benefit from regularly meeting up with friends but some of the social events he attends will be particularly enjoyable. And with the Monkey year holding so much promise, those Earth Horses who are lonely or who have had some recent difficulty in their personal life can look forward to some exciting prospects. For many, the year could mark the start of a significant new romance and even marriage. On a personal level, the Monkey year is both an active and well-aspected one.

As far as financial matters are concerned, the progress the Earth Horse makes at work will lead to a noticeable increase in his income. However, with his existing obligations, as well as some of the plans and purchases he has in mind for his home, he does need to keep an eye on his outgoings. With careful budgeting and the avoidance of risks, however, he will find he will not only be able to do a great deal but also put his financial situation on a better footing.

Overall, the Monkey year holds a great deal of potential for the Earth Horse, allowing him to make good progress, further his skills and interests and lead a rewarding personal life. However, it does rest with him to take advantage of the favourable aspects and reap the often considerable rewards his efforts and enterprise will bring.

TIP FOR THE YEAR

This is a year to seize the initiative and to go after your aims and aspirations. As the saying goes, 'There is no time like the present,' and the present is a good time to advance.

FAMOUS HORSES

Neil Armstrong, Rowan Atkinson, Samuel Beckett, Ingmar Bergman, Leonard Bernstein, Karen Black, Cherie Blair, Helena Bonham Carter, James Cameron, Ray Charles, Chopin, Sir Sean Connery, Billy Connolly, Catherine Cookson, Ronnie Corbett, Elvis Costello, Kevin Costner, Cindy Crawford, Michael Crichton, James Dean, Iain Duncan Smith, Clint Eastwood, Thomas Alva Edison, Britt Ekland, Harrison Ford, Aretha Franklin, Bob Geldof, Samuel Goldwyn, Billy Graham, Gene Hackman, Rolf Harris, Rita Hayworth, Jimi Hendrix, John Edgar Hoover, Janet Jackson, Calvin Klein, Lenin, Annie Lennox, Desmond Lynam, Sir Paul McCartney, Nelson Mandela, Princess Margaret, Ben Murphy, Sir Isaac Newton, Louis Pasteur, Harold Pinter, Puccini, Lou Reed, Rembrandt, Ruth Rendell, Jean Renoir, Condoleezza Rice, Theodore Roosevelt, Helena Rubenstein, Peter Sissons, Lord Snowdon, Alexander Solzhenitsyn, Barbra Streisand, Kiefer Sutherland, Patrick Swayze, John Travolta, Kathleen Turner, Mike Tyson, Vivaldi, Robert Wagner, Denzil Washington, Billy Wilder, Andy Williams, the Duke of Windsor, Boris Yeltsin, Will Young.

13 FEBRUARY 1907 ~ 1 FEBRUARY 1908	*Fire Goat*
1 FEBRUARY 1919 ~ 19 FEBRUARY 1920	*Earth Goat*
17 FEBRUARY 1931 ~ 5 FEBRUARY 1932	*Metal Goat*
5 FEBRUARY 1943 ~ 24 JANUARY 1944	*Water Goat*
24 JANUARY 1955 ~ 11 FEBRUARY 1956	*Wood Goat*
9 FEBRUARY 1967 ~ 29 JANUARY 1968	*Fire Goat*
28 JANUARY 1979 ~ 15 FEBRUARY 1980	*Earth Goat*
15 FEBRUARY 1991 ~ 3 FEBRUARY 1992	*Metal Goat*
1 FEBRUARY 2003 ~ 21 JANUARY 2004	*Water Goat*

THE
GOAT

THE PERSONALITY OF THE GOAT

If you don't have a dream, how are you going to make a dream come true?

Oscar Hammerstein II, a Goat

The Goat is born under the sign of art. He is imaginative, creative and has a good appreciation of the finer things in life. He has an easy-going nature and prefers to live in a relaxed and pressure-free environment. He hates any sort of discord or unpleasantness and does not like to be bound by a strict routine or rigid timetable. The Goat is not one to be hurried against his will, but despite his seemingly relaxed approach to life, he is something of a perfectionist and when he starts work on a project he is certain to give of his best.

The Goat usually prefers to work in a team rather than on his own. He likes to have the support and encouragement of others and if left to deal with matters on his own he can get very worried and tend to view things rather pessimistically. Wherever possible he will leave major decision-making to others while he concentrates on his own pursuits. If, however, he feels particularly strongly about a certain matter or has to defend his position in any way, he will act with great fortitude and precision.

The Goat has a very persuasive nature and often uses his considerable charm to get his own way. He can, however, be rather hesitant about letting his true feelings be known and if he were prepared to be more forthright he would do much better as a result.

The Goat tends to have a quiet, somewhat reserved nature but when he is in company he likes he can often become the centre of attention. He can be highly amusing, a marvellous host at parties and a superb entertainer. Whenever the spotlight falls on him, his adrenalin starts to flow and he can be assured of giving a sparkling performance, particularly if he is allowed to use his creative skills in any way.

Of all the signs in the Chinese zodiac, the Goat is probably the most gifted artistically. Whether it is in the theatre, literature, music or art, he is certain to make a lasting impression. He is a born creator and is rarely happier than when occupied in some artistic pursuit. But even in this the Goat does well to work with others rather than on his own. He needs inspiration and a guiding influence, but when he has found his true *métier*, he can often receive widespread acclaim and recognition.

In addition to his liking for the arts, the Goat is usually quite religious and often has a deep interest in nature, animals and the countryside. He is also fairly athletic and there are many Goats who have excelled in some form of sporting activity or who have a great interest in sport.

Although the Goat is not particularly materialistic or concerned about finance, he will find that he will usually be lucky in financial matters and will rarely be short of the necessary funds to tide himself over. He is, however, rather indulgent and tends to spend his money as soon as he receives it rather than make provision for the future.

The Goat usually leaves home when he is young but he will always maintain strong links with his parents and the other members of his family. He is also rather nostalgic and is well known for keeping mementos of his childhood and souvenirs of places that he has visited. His home will not be particularly tidy but he knows where everything is and it will also be scrupulously clean.

Affairs of the heart are particularly important to the Goat and he will often have many romances before he finally settles down. Although he is fairly adaptable, he prefers to live in a secure and stable environment and he will find that he is best suited to those born under the signs of the Tiger, Horse, Monkey, Pig and Rabbit. He can also establish a good relationship with the Dragon, Snake, Rooster and another Goat, but he may find the Ox and Dog a little too serious for his liking. Neither will he care particularly for the Rat's rather thrifty ways.

The female Goat devotes all her time and energy to the needs of her family. She has excellent taste in home furnishings and often uses her considerable artistic skills to make clothes for herself and her children. She takes great care over her appearance and can be most attractive to others. Although she is not the most organized of people, her engaging manner and delightful sense of humour create a favourable impression wherever she goes. She is also a good cook and usually derives much pleasure from gardening and outdoor pursuits.

The Goat can win friends easily and people generally feel relaxed in his company. He has a kind and under-standing nature and although he can occasionally be stub-born, he can, with the right support and encouragement, live a happy and very satisfying life. And the more he can use his creative skills, the happier he will be.

THE FIVE DIFFERENT TYPES OF GOAT

In addition to the 12 signs of the Chinese zodiac there are five elements, and these have a strengthening or moderating influence on the sign. The effects of the five elements on the Goat are described below, together with the years in which the elements were exercising their influence. Therefore all Goats born in 1931 and 1991 are Metal Goats, those born in 1943 and 2003 are Water Goats, and so on.

Metal Goat: 1931, 1991

This Goat is thorough and conscientious in all that he does and is capable of doing very well in his chosen profession. Despite his confident manner, he can be a great worrier and he would find it helpful to discuss his concerns with others rather than keep them to himself. He is loyal to his family and employers and will have a small group of particularly close friends. He has good taste and is usually highly skilled in some aspect of the arts. He is often a collector of antiques and his home will be very tastefully furnished.

Water Goat: 1943, 2003

The Water Goat is very popular and makes friends with remarkable ease. He is good at spotting opportunities but does not always have the necessary confidence to follow them through. He likes to have security both in his home life and at work and does not take kindly to change. He is articulate, has a good sense of humour and is usually very good with children.

Wood Goat: 1955

This Goat is generous, kind-hearted and always eager to please. He usually has a large circle of friends and involves himself in a wide variety of activities. He has a very trusting nature but he can sometimes give in to the demands of others a little too easily and it would be in his own interests if he were to stand his ground more often. He is usually lucky in financial matters and, like the Water Goat, is very good with children.

Fire Goat: 1907, 1967

This Goat usually knows what he wants in life and he often uses his considerable charm and persuasive personality to achieve his aims. He can sometimes let his imagination run away with him and has a tendency to ignore matters which are not to his liking. He is rather extravagant in his spending and would do well to exercise a little more care when dealing with financial matters. He has a lively personality, many friends, and loves attending parties and social occasions.

Earth Goat: 1919, 1979

This Goat has a considerate and caring nature. He is particularly loyal to his family and friends and invariably creates a favourable impression wherever he goes. He is reliable and conscientious in his work but sometimes finds it difficult to save and never likes to deprive himself of any little luxury he might fancy. He has numerous interests and is often very well read. He usually derives much pleasure from following the activities of the various members of his family.

PROSPECTS FOR THE GOAT IN 2004

The Chinese New Year starts on 22 January 2004. Until then, the old year, the Year of the Goat, is still making its presence felt.

The Year of the Goat (1 February 2003 to 21 January 2004) holds great promise for its own sign and in the closing months, the Goat can accomplish much. To benefit, though, he does need to seize the initiative and make the most of his talents and ideas.

At work positive changes are indicated, with many Goats taking on greater responsibilities and moving their career forward at this time. Any Goat who may be seeking work or feeling disillusioned with his present role should make a determined effort to pursue any openings that appeal to him. The Goat year is one for positive action and many Goats will make good headway in the last quarter.

The Goat can also enjoy several strokes of good fortune at this time, perhaps in the form of an unexpected gift or bonus, buying something he has long wanted at a favourable price, or even a competition win.

On a personal level the Goat will find himself in demand. In his home life the closing months of the year will see much activity, with some fine family get-togethers, many of which the Goat will enjoy arranging. He does, after all, make an attentive host. Socially, too, he will be busy, with his diary often becoming full with friends to meet, activities to do and events to attend. For the unattached Goat or those newly in love, the last quarter of the year can be a special time, with the affairs of the heart being well aspected.

The Goat year is a favourable time for its own sign and by making the most of the opportunities that arise and using his strengths and ideas to good effect, the Goat can prosper and enjoy himself.

The Year of the Monkey starts on 22 January and will be a variable one for the Goat. He could find events happening quickly and disturbing the stability he likes so much. However, while the Goat may not find this the most comfortable of years, by showing a willingness to adapt he can still emerge from it with some impressive gains to his credit.

In view of the changes many Goats will have seen in their work in the preceding year, they will often be keen to remain in their present role, feeling comfortable with their present duties. However, while the Goat may desire a settled time, the Monkey year is one for change. Some Goats could find new schemes are introduced which alter what they do or, as colleagues move on, they could be offered greater responsibilities. Few Goats will find themselves with the same duties or in the same position by the year's end. However, while some of the changes may not have been what the Goat envisaged, or wanted, there will be a positive aspect to what takes place. The changes will not only help the Goat to widen his experience but also enable him to discover strengths he may not have been aware of, and these in turn could open up important possibilities for the future.

For Goats who are looking for work or keen to change their position, the year will again bring some interesting developments. Although some posts for which these Goats feel ideally suited may remain out of reach, many will be successful in securing a position which will enable them to develop their skills in other ways. Although such a change could initially seem daunting, it could set their career off on an interesting new path. Again, the message for the Goat is to remain adaptable and do his best in the situations in which he finds himself, even if, at first sight, they are not always ideal. For work developments, the months from April to June and September to November are especially favourable.

Financially, the Goat will see an improvement in 2004. Not only will he enjoy a rise in income but he could also receive money from another source. This could be through a gift, the fruition of a policy or even by being able to supplement his income in some way, but money-wise this will be a generally positive year. However, the Goat should not allow any upturn to lull him into a false sense of security. To prevent problems he does need to manage his money well, setting amounts aside for specific requirements and controlling his expenditure. Also, he should be wary of taking risks or entering into agreements without checking all that is involved. The Monkey year can cause problems for the unwary. Goats, do take note.

As far as the Goat's relations with others are concerned, this will be a generally favourable year. The Goat's home life will be particularly busy, with some notable family developments. These could include a wedding or birth in the family as well as other good reasons for a family celebration, possibly marking the Goat's own progress as well as the achievements of those close to him. The Goat will also value the encouragement he is given and will gain a great deal by talking to those close to him about his ideas, activities and any concerns.

He will also enjoy some of the practical domestic activities that take place, including projects to enhance his home or garden. However, in view of the busy nature of the year, if he does find himself with a great deal to do or household chores beginning to mount up, he should not hesitate to ask for additional help. Generally, though, this will be an agreeable year domestically, with the Goat valuing the love and affection shown him and enjoying many of the family occasions that take place, including any holidays or breaks.

Being sociable and outgoing, the Goat also sets much store by his social life and this too is favourably aspected. In addition to meeting up with friends, the Goat will often be tempted out to various social events. He could also find his interests leading him to meet fellow enthusiasts and forge some new friendships. On a social level, he will find himself in demand and generally enjoying himself. Any Goats who may be lonely, perhaps after moving to a new area or suffering some recent personal difficulty, will find that by going out and getting involved in activities, they can enjoy a major upturn in their social life and in some cases forge an important new friendship. The onus to make this happen rests with the Goat, but by taking action, he can certainly find the Monkey year bringing some happiness and meaning back into his life. For socializing, April, June, August and December could see much activity.

Although this will be a busy year for the Goat and, work-wise, bring its changes, by adapting to the situations that arise, asking for help if under pressure (particularly with household activities) and balancing out his activities, he will be pleased with how he fares. And his efforts will be rewarded both this year and in the Rooster year that follows.

The Metal Goat

As far as the different types of Goat are concerned, this will be an interesting year for the Metal Goat and with a willingness to make the most of the chances available to him, he can make good progress as well as enjoy himself.

The Metal Goat has a particularly enquiring nature and this will serve him well as the year progresses. In his schoolwork there will be new topics to cover and course work to deal with, and by tackling these in an earnest way, the Metal Goat will learn much and be satisfied with his progress. Certain topics may particularly inspire him and give him an indication of which subjects he should choose for more detailed study later.

However, while the Metal Goat will have strong subject areas, he should not close his mind to those he does not like. By making an effort to understand these more, he will not only stand more chance of getting better results but will also find the effort he makes having a positive effect on other areas of his schoolwork. If he does experience any difficulties, rather than struggle on in bewilderment, he should be forthcoming and ask his tutors for guidance. Not only will this gain him more assistance but it will also help relieve some of the anxieties he may have.

Being born under the sign of art, the Metal Goat will particularly enjoy subjects which draw on his creative abilities and he should aim to develop these further. Sometimes joining an interest group or spending time experimenting with his ideas will be rewarding, and those Metal Goats who enjoy art, writing, drama or something similarly expressive will find that developing their talents will bring them much pleasure. Similarly, for those who enjoy music, are learning an instrument or would like to learn one, time spent in learning and practising will be well rewarded. The Metal Goat certainly possesses some fine gifts and he should make the most of them.

With his genial nature and sense of fun, the Metal Goat will also find he is much in demand on a social level. Over the year he can look forward to some great times with his friends, particularly in sharing interests, playing games and engaging in sporting activities. One particular friendship will come to mean a great deal, both in the support the Metal Goat and his friend give to each other and in their rapport and shared interests.

There may, though, be a few Metal Goats who do not feel part of the social scene, perhaps because they have recently changed schools, are living in a new area or simply feel they are not in tune with those around them.

However, these young Metal Goats should not despair. In this, as in so many other aspects of their lives in 2004, they should have faith in themselves. By being true to themselves they can certainly meet and befriend others who have similar outlooks and over the year they will forge some valuable friendships. The Metal Goat has a great deal in his favour and much to offer.

For those Metal Goats born in 1931, again the Monkey year will be an active one – at times, more active than the more senior Metal Goat may appreciate! Accommodation matters will feature prominently, with some Metal Goats deciding to move somewhere more suitable for their present needs. In view of the upheaval any move will entail, these Metal Goats should take up offers of help from loved ones as well as ask for advice over any matter giving them concern. With assistance, they will be satisfied with the results of all their activity.

They will also appreciate some of the other opportunities that the Monkey year will bring. These will include invitations to visit family and friends living some distance away and other chances to travel. The Metal Goat will also take much pleasure from his interests, especially those of a more creative nature. Metal Goats certainly know how to put their time to good use and over the year they will find much to occupy them, often in a satisfying way.

Both for the young and more senior Metal Goat the Monkey year is a time of opportunity and by taking advantage of those available to them, they will be pleased with what they are able to accomplish.

TIP FOR THE YEAR
Take advantage of the help and support others are able to offer. Those around you can allay concerns and provide guidance, assistance and reassurance. To benefit, though, do be forthcoming.

The Water Goat

This will be a reasonable year for the Water Goat and while some of his ideas and plans may take longer and involve more effort than he anticipated, it will still contain a great many pleasures.

Many Water Goats will have seen considerable changes of late. Some will have retired, some moved and some will have experienced changes in their personal circumstances. The Monkey year will allow these Water Goats to adapt to what has taken place, although the changes are not quite over yet. The Monkey year is, after all, one of activity, and it is capable of bringing both surprising and interesting developments.

Those Water Goats who have moved recently, or who do so during the year, will spend time settling into their new accommodation and getting it as they would like. Their eye for style and detail will be appreciated and they will take much pleasure in seeing their ideas unfold. However, the Water Goat should accept that some of his plans could take longer to realize than he envisaged and if he has to authorize any work to be carried out, he should check the details and terms beforehand. Where accommodation matters and practical undertakings are concerned, the Water Goat will need to be thorough, vigilant *and* patient.

Many Water Goats who have gardens will also spend time experimenting with new stock and enjoying what they create. Again, once the Water Goat's creative instincts are aroused, he will be keen to put his ideas into practice. However when gardening, particularly if digging or moving heavy weights, he does need to be careful. A strain or pulled muscle could cause considerable discomfort. When setting about anything strenuous, he should either seek help or be sure he adopts the right postures. Water Goats, do take care.

The Water Goat will also appreciate the support he receives for his ideas, although he should always be receptive to suggestions made by others. Sometimes their methods may be easier than his own or they could point out factors which he may not have considered. By pooling thoughts and talents, the Water Goat will often find his plans easier to set in motion.

In addition to practical activities, the Water Goat will enjoy the interests and pursuits he can share with his loved ones. Some Water Goats may even decide to enrol on a course with a partner or friend as well as arrange visits and trips out, short breaks or other agreeable occasions. By putting such ideas forward, the Water Goat can make his domestic life and his relations with those around him all the more rewarding.

While so much of his domestic life will go well there will, though, be certain matters which do concern the Water Goat, and rather than keeping his thoughts to himself, he should let his views be known. Although this may be uncomfortable – and the Water Goat is never one who likes being in awkward atmospheres – he will find it better to be forthcoming and air his views than let concerns linger in the background. Fortunately such awkward moments will be relatively few and will not take the edge off what can be a generally constructive and agreeable year.

Socially, the Water Goat will not only enjoy meeting up with friends and attending social occasions but could also find his interests helping to add to his social circle. Any Water Goats who would welcome more companionship will find that joining an interest group could add a positive new element into their life and this is something they should seriously consider.

The Water Goat will fare well in money matters over the year, often benefiting from a bonus, gift, the fruition of a policy or even, for some, a competition win. However, while this upturn will tempt many Water Goats to go ahead with plans they have been considering, they should still watch their outgoings as well as check the details of any new commitments. The Water Goat also needs to be vigilant with any forms he has to complete, especially those related to finance, tax or benefits. A slip or delayed response could lead to some burdensome correspondence and be to his detriment. Water Goats, take note and be thorough.

This need for vigilance is one of the key messages for the Water Goat in 2004. While he can accomplish a great deal, he does need to be mindful of others and pay attention to details and practicalities. With care and support he can do well and enjoy himself, but he should always remember that the Monkey year can cause problems for the unwary.

TIP FOR THE YEAR

Consult others about your plans and ideas. Joint effort and activities will be well rewarded and will not only help to maintain a good rapport but also lead to constructive and rewarding results.

The Wood Goat

This will be a busy year for the Wood Goat and will bring both change and some fine opportunities.

In his work in particular the Wood Goat will see some interesting developments. Some Wood Goats, feeling they have accomplished all they can in their present role or that they are not making the most of their talents, will decide to look for another position. Their quest could have some surprises in store. Although not all the applications they make will go their way and there will be times when they may feel disheartened, one opening they see or learn of by chance, and which is different from what they have done before, will turn out to be ideal. This position may demand a lot from the Wood Goat but it will give him the chance to make more of himself and his skills and, in the process, give his career and prospects a new lease of life. The months from April to June and September and November are particularly favourable for career moves but, as the Wood Goat will quickly discover, events can move at a fast pace in the Monkey year and once he is offered a new position, he will be surprised at how quickly his situation is transformed.

Some Wood Goats, of course, will prefer to remain in their existing position rather than make a change. This is particularly the case for those who are relatively new to their position or feel satisfied in the way they are able to use their skills. However, the Monkey year is not one for standing still and often these Wood Goats will find their experience will lead to them being offered greater responsibilities or will find they are ideal candidates for promotion. Although change may not be something these Wood Goats had anticipated, what is offered can be a considerable fillip to their career and can do them much good in the longer term.

For those Wood Goats seeking work the Monkey year can give rise to some good opportunities, but to benefit the Wood Goat does need to be adaptable in his approach. Again, by making the most of situations that arise, what he achieves can have far-reaching effects.

The progress that the Wood Goat makes in his work will lead to a noticeable increase in income over the year. However, he would be wise to manage his money well, setting amounts aside for specific requirements and carefully considering his various purchases. The better he can manage his outgoings, the more satisfied he will be. Also, if he is able, he should consider setting a certain amount of money aside for his future. In years to come he could be grateful for savings made now. The Wood Goat also needs to be thorough with any new agreement he enters into or any important paperwork he receives. The Monkey year is not a time for risks or carelessness.

Although the Wood Goat will have much to occupy himself over the year, he should make sure he sets a regular time aside for his own interests and recreational pursuits. He could find those that take him out of doors or provide him with some additional exercise particularly beneficial. Also, some of his interests could lead to some pleasant social occasions with other enthusiasts.

As far as the Wood Goat's home life is concerned, this will be a busy and often rewarding year. He will do much to encourage and support those around him, particularly those much older than himself, and his care and consideration really will be appreciated. However, while the Wood Goat will give so much time to others, in return he will value the help he receives with some of his own ideas and plans. This not only includes domestic projects but also some of the other activities he wants to carry out, including visiting certain places. By making his thoughts known as well as helping organize so much, the Wood Goat will be content with how many of his ideas unfold. On a domestic level, the Monkey year can certainly bring some pleasing times.

The one word of warning that should be sounded, however, is that when the Wood Goat himself or others in his household are particularly busy or preoccupied, the Wood Goat should be prepared to show some flexibility, perhaps deferring certain plans to more appropriate times or helping more with household tasks. By showing understanding and support, he can ease pressures and sometimes avoid difficult situations.

Socially, with a possible change of work and invitations to go out, the Wood Goat will get the chance to build up new contacts. With his approachable manner and often interesting repartee, he is likely to make a favourable impression almost everywhere he goes, as well as enjoy himself. The Monkey year holds excellent prospects for those Wood Goats seeking new friends and companionship, with April, June, August and December being busy on a social level.

Overall, the Monkey year does hold interesting prospects for the Wood Goat, but to benefit he will need to make the most of the opportunities that come his way. By being willing and enterprising, however, he can do himself a lot of good.

TIP FOR THE YEAR
Make the most of your skills and aim to develop them further. You have real talents and should make much of the opportunities that arise.

The Fire Goat

This will be a significant year for the Fire Goat and while he may have misgivings about some of what takes place, he will emerge with some useful gains to his credit. The Fire Goat likes order and stability, and the Monkey year will not always respect this. This is a time for action, sometimes change, and for moving forward.

In the Fire Goat's work a considerable amount is likely to happen. Although he may start the year content and settled, change is on the way. As colleagues move on or new projects are started, others will look to the Fire Goat to take on more responsibilities or adapt his role. While this will often bring promotion and increased remuneration, the Fire Goat could find what he is now expected to do will be considerably more demanding than his previous duties. As with any change, it could take the Fire Goat some time to settle into his new role, but by rising to the challenge before him, he will not only add to his experience but also help his future prospects.

This will also be a positive year for those Fire Goats who are seeking work or who feel the time is right to do something new. By considering what they want to do and the different ways in which they can draw on their experience, they will be able to come up with some interesting possibilities, and by following up suitable vacancies, many will be successful in gaining what will be an important position with long-term significance. The months from April to June and September and November could all see interesting developments, but generally, given the fast pace of the Monkey year, change can happen quickly and often take the Fire Goat by surprise.

In addition to the progress the Fire Goat will make in his work, he should also consider his own personal development. This includes any training offered by his work as well as furthering his own personal interests. He could set himself some interesting challenges, for instance learning more about an interest, tackling a new project or enrolling on a course. Whatever he does, he will find doing something purposeful and that he enjoys will help to give his life more balance as well as be satisfying.

Another area the Fire Goat should not neglect is his own well-being. If he is sedentary for much of the day or relies on convenience foods, he could find taking more exercise and switching to a more balanced diet will bring an improvement in how he feels as well as in his energy levels. Before proceeding, he should seek medical guidance, but the attention he can give to himself, particularly in terms of exercise, will generally be beneficial.

The Fire Goat's domestic life will see much activity over the year and sometimes his beloved peace and quiet will not always be easy to obtain. In the Monkey year many in his household will be busy with their own activities and there could be times when preoccupation, tiredness or tension could lead to some fraught moments. Also, the Fire Goat could find himself having differences of opinion with others, particularly younger members in his household, over certain issues. However, every year does bring its more awkward moments and by being willing to address these, talk over any disagreements and show understanding, the Fire Goat can do much to ease any tension. He does have a good way with others and his care and concern will be recognized and appreciated. The Fire Goat can also help make his domestic life that much more rewarding by ensuring that there its time for spending together and sharing interests. He should also make sure he goes away for a holiday with his loved ones over the year. The change of scene and break will do everyone a lot of good.

The Fire Goat will also derive much benefit from his social life, not only appreciating the camaraderie of his friends but also the chance to go out and unwind. Fire Goats who are feeling lonely will find that they can do much to improve their social lives by going out and getting involved in activities they enjoy, perhaps with a special interest group or through charity or social work. Over the year there will be excellent prospects for building up new friendships and, for some, significant romance could result.

As far as finances are concerned, this will be a much improved year, with many Fire Goats benefiting from increased income or an additional sum of money. However, rather than be tempted to spend all too readily, the Fire Goat should plan his major purchases as well as consider setting something aside for the longer term. To benefit from the financial upturn, he does need to manage his money well rather than proceed in an ad hoc fashion. And, as with all Goats in 2004, he should be wary of taking risks or committing his money to ventures he has not properly investigated.

The Monkey year will be an active one for the Fire Goat and a lot will happen. By rising to the challenge, the Fire Goat will learn a great deal and improve himself and his position as well as enjoy much that takes place.

TIP FOR THE YEAR
Be willing to adapt and develop. The changes that occur can give rise to some new possibilities as well as often have long-term significance.

The Earth Goat

The Earth Goat is always keen to make the most of himself and as the Monkey year begins he will be hoping to build on his recent achievements. However, the Monkey year will not always go according to plan, with certain developments catching the Earth Goat by surprise.

In his work, in particular, considerable change could take place. In recent years the Earth Goat will have gained much useful experience as well as impressed those around him and he will be excellently placed to make greater progress. However, this may not always be in the way he had envisaged. Some of those more senior to him may feel he should now widen his experience and learn about other aspects of his work and as a result he could find himself being transferred to a new post or recommended for a particular type of job. In some cases the change could be considerable and even involve moving to a new area. However, by making the most of what is offered or has been recommended for him, the Earth Goat will not only find he is able to add to his experience but also that what he achieves will be another important step in his overall career development.

The positive aspects also extend to those Earth Goats seeking work as well as those who may feel their present role has limited prospects. By looking for positions which they feel offer the chance to develop their skills in new directions, many will be successful in gaining what can be an exciting and significant opportunity. Not only will such a position allow these Earth Goats to broaden their skills but they could also find they have a real forte for their new role and can build upon it in future years.

For work opportunities, April, May, September and November are particularly favourable, but interesting possibilities could strike at almost any moment, such is the nature of the Monkey year.

The progress that the Earth Goat makes in his work will also lead to a welcome increase in income. Some Earth Goats may be able to supplement their usual earnings with freelance work, possibly by writing, giving tuition or putting a skill to additional use. The Earth Goat's earning abilities will certainly be strong, and for the enterprising, additional opportunities will emerge. But while money will flow into the Earth Goat's accounts, it will flow out too, and with his obligations as well as the plans he wants to carry out, he does need to manage his finances well. If he succumbs to too many impulsive purchases, he could find it becomes more difficult to proceed with some of his more ambitious undertakings. In 2004 the Earth Goat would be wise to control his finances and set funds aside for specific purposes. The more self-discipline he has, the more he will find he can ultimately afford.

Domestically, this will be a busy year, with others often looking to the Earth Goat for support and advice. Those Earth Goats with babies and young children will give much time to encouraging their development. The year will certainly bring its joys and moments that the Earth Goat will treasure for many years. In addition he will enjoy time spent with his partner, sharing interests as well as planning and carrying out projects to add to the comfort and style of their home. The Earth Goat's creative input will be especially appreciated.

The Earth Goat will also do much to assist more senior relations over the year and again his support will count for a great deal. However, while the Earth Goat will do so much to help others and give his time so generously, he should not neglect his own well-being. Although he may drive himself hard, he must make sure he has sufficient rest, does not skimp on exercise and pays sufficient attention to his diet. To keep himself on good form he *does* need to give himself some time and consideration. Also, he should not hesitate to ask others for help or advice if certain household tasks are falling behind or he has matters concerning him.

During the year the Earth Goat will get much value from his social life, again enjoying the opportunities he gets to go out. For Earth Goats who may desire more companionship or have had some recent personal difficulties, this is a year which offers happier times. In some cases new friendships and romance can really transform the Earth Goat's life, again underlining the significant nature of the Monkey year. For socializing and meeting others, April, June, August and December are especially favourable.

Overall, the Monkey year does hold much potential for the Earth Goat and while he will need to adapt and make the most of the situations that arise, he will make important progress as well as enjoy a rewarding personal life and some of the very special times the year will bring.

TIP FOR THE YEAR
Look positively on the changes that occur. They can be a significant step forward.

FAMOUS GOATS

Pamela Anderson, W. H. Auden, Jane Austen, Anne Bancroft, Cilla Black, Lord Byron, Leslie Caron, John le Carré, Coco Chanel, Mary Higgins Clark, Nat 'King' Cole, Catherine Deneuve, John Denver, Charles Dickens, Ken Dodd, Sir Arthur Conan Doyle, Umberto Eco, Douglas Fairbanks, Dame Margot Fonteyn, Noel Gallagher, Bill Gates, Mel Gibson, Whoopi Goldberg, Mikhail Gorbachev, John Grisham, Larry Hagman, Oscar Hammerstein,

George Harrison, Sir Edmund Hillary, John Humphrys, Billy Idol, Julio Iglesias, Sir Mick Jagger, Norah Jones, Ulrika Jonsson, Nicole Kidman, Sir Ben Kingsley, Doris Lessing, Franz Liszt, John Major, Daphne du Maurier, Michelangelo, Joni Mitchell, Rupert Murdoch, Mussolini, Randy Newman, Robert de Niro, Des O'Connor, Sinead O'Connor, Michael Owen, Michael Palin, Eva Peron, Marcel Proust, Keith Richards, Julia Roberts, William Shatner, Gary Sinise, Jerry Springer, Lana Turner, Mark Twain, Rudolph Valentino, Vangelis, Barbara Walters, John Wayne, Fay Weldon, Bruce Willis.

---

2 FEBRUARY 1908 〜 21 JANUARY 1909   *Earth Monkey*

20 FEBRUARY 1920 〜 7 FEBRUARY 1921   *Metal Monkey*

6 FEBRUARY 1932 〜 25 JANUARY 1933   *Water Monkey*

25 JANUARY 1944 〜 12 FEBRUARY 1945   *Wood Monkey*

12 FEBRUARY 1956 〜 30 JANUARY 1957   *Fire Monkey*

30 JANUARY 1968 〜 16 FEBRUARY 1969   *Earth Monkey*

16 FEBRUARY 1980 〜 4 FEBRUARY 1981   *Metal Monkey*

4 FEBRUARY 1992 〜 22 JANUARY 1993   *Water Monkey*

22 JANUARY 2004 〜 8 FEBRUARY 2005   *Wood Monkey*

THE
MONKEY

THE PERSONALITY OF THE MONKEY

If opportunity doesn't knock, build a door.

Milton Berle, a Monkey

The Monkey is born under the sign of fantasy. He is imaginative, inquisitive and loves to keep an eye on everything that is going on around him. He is never backward in offering advice or trying to sort out the problems of others. He likes to be helpful and his advice is invariably sensible and reliable.

The Monkey is intelligent, well read and always eager to learn. He has an extremely good memory and there are many Monkeys who have made particularly good linguists. The Monkey is also a convincing talker and enjoys taking part in discussions and debates. His friendly, self-assured manner can be very persuasive and he usually has little trouble in winning people round to his way of thinking. It is for this reason that the Monkey often excels in politics and public speaking. He is also particularly adept in PR work, teaching and any job which involves selling.

The Monkey can, however, be crafty, cunning and occasionally dishonest, and he will seize on any opportunity to make a quick gain or outsmart his opponents. He has so much charm and guile that people often don't realize what he is up to until it is too late. But despite his resourceful nature, the Monkey does run the risk of outsmarting even himself. He has so much confidence in his abilities that he rarely listens to advice or is prepared to accept help from anyone. He likes to help others but prefers to rely on his own judgement when dealing with his own affairs.

Another characteristic of the Monkey is that he is extremely good at solving problems and has a happy knack of extricating himself (and others) from the most hopeless of positions. He is the master of self-preservation.

With so many diverse talents the Monkey is able to make considerable sums of money, but he does like to enjoy life and will think nothing of spending his money on some exotic holiday or luxury which he has had his eye on. He can, however, become very envious if someone else has what he wants.

The Monkey is an original thinker and despite his love of company, he cherishes his independence. He has to have the freedom to act as he wants and any Monkey who feels hemmed in or bound by too many restrictions can soon become unhappy. Likewise, if anything becomes too boring or monotonous, the Monkey soon loses interest and turns his attention to something else. He lacks persistence and this can often hamper his progress. He is also easily distracted, a tendency which all Monkeys should try to overcome. The Monkey should concentrate on one thing at a time and by doing so will almost certainly achieve more in the long run.

The Monkey is a good organizer and even though he may behave slightly erratically at times, he will invariably have some plan at the back of his mind. On the odd occasion when his plans do not work out, he is usually quite happy to shrug his shoulders and put it down to experience. He will rarely make the same mistake twice and throughout his life he will try his hand at many things.

The Monkey likes to impress and is rarely without followers or admirers. Many are attracted to him by his good looks, his sense of humour, or simply because he instils so much confidence.

Monkeys usually marry young and for it to be a success their partner must allow them time to pursue their many interests and indulge their love of travel. The Monkey has to have variety in his life and is especially well suited to those born under the sociable and outgoing signs of the Rat, Dragon, Pig and Goat. The Ox, Rabbit, Snake and Dog will also be enchanted by the Monkey's resourceful and outgoing nature, but he is likely to exasperate the Rooster and Horse, and the Tiger will have little patience with his tricks. A relationship between two Monkeys will work well – they will understand each other and be able to assist each other in their various enterprises.

The female Monkey is intelligent, extremely observant and a shrewd judge of character. Her opinions are often highly valued and, having such a persuasive nature, she invariably gets her own way. She has many interests and involves herself in a wide variety of activities. She pays great attention to her appearance, is an elegant dresser and likes to take particular care over her hair. She can be a doting parent and will have many good and loyal friends.

Provided the Monkey can curb his desire to take part in everything that is going on around him and concentrate on one thing at a time, he can usually achieve what he wants in life. Should he suffer any disappointments, he is bound to bounce back. The Monkey is a survivor and his life is usually both colourful and eventful.

THE FIVE DIFFERENT TYPES OF MONKEY

In addition to the 12 signs of the Chinese zodiac there are five elements, and these have a strengthening or moderating influence on the sign. The effects of the five elements on the Monkey are described below, together with the years in which the elements were exercising their influence. Therefore all Monkeys born in 1920 and 1980 are Metal Monkeys, those born in 1932 and 1992 are Water Monkeys, and so on.

Metal Monkey: 1920, 1980
The Metal Monkey is very strong-willed. He sets about everything he does with a dogged determination and often prefers to work independently rather than with others. He is ambitious, wise and confident, and is certainly not afraid of hard work. He is very astute in financial matters and usually chooses his investments well. Despite his somewhat independent nature, the Metal Monkey enjoys attending parties and social occasions and is particularly warm and caring towards his loved ones.

Water Monkey: 1932, 1992
The Water Monkey is versatile, determined and perceptive. He also has more discipline than some of the other Monkeys and is prepared to work towards a certain goal

rather than be distracted by something else. He is not always open about his true intentions and when questioned can be particularly evasive. He can be sensitive to criticism but also very persuasive and usually has little trouble in getting others to fall in with his plans. He has a very good understanding of human nature and relates well to others.

Wood Monkey: 1944, 2004

This Monkey is efficient, methodical and extremely conscientious. He is also highly imaginative and is always trying to capitalize on new ideas or learn new skills. Occasionally his enthusiasm can get the better of him and he can get very agitated when things do not quite work out as he had hoped. He does, however, have a very adventurous streak and is not afraid of taking risks. He also loves travel. He is usually held in great esteem by his friends and colleagues.

Fire Monkey: 1956

The Fire Monkey is intelligent, full of vitality and has no trouble in commanding the respect of others. He is imaginative and has wide interests, although sometimes these can distract him from more useful and profitable work. He is very competitive and always likes to be involved in everything that is going on. He can be stubborn if he does not get his own way and he sometimes tries to indoctrinate those who are less strong-willed than himself. He is a lively character, attractive to others and most loyal to his partner.

Earth Monkey: 1908, 1968

The Earth Monkey tends to be studious and well read, and can become quite distinguished in his chosen line of work. He is less outgoing than some of the other types of Monkey and prefers quieter and more solid pursuits. He has high principles, a very caring nature and can be most generous to those less fortunate than himself. He is usually successful in handling financial matters and can become very wealthy in old age. He has a calming influence on those around him and is respected and well liked by those he meets. He is, however, especially careful about whom he lets into his confidence.

PROSPECTS FOR THE MONKEY IN 2004

The Chinese New Year starts on 22 January 2004. Until then, the old year, the Year of the Goat, is still making its presence felt.

The Year of the Goat (1 February 2003 to 21 January 2004) will have been a reasonable one for the Monkey, with the closing months seeing much activity. In his work the Monkey can look forward to making pleasing progress, although his best results will come from concentrating on what he knows. This is not a time for spreading his energies too widely or involving himself in activities in which he is not so experienced. However, with his prospects looking so promising in his own year, any training or additional experience he can get will be to his advantage.

With the closing months of the year being an expensive time, where possible the Monkey should try to allow for this in advance. For most of the year, money will have flowed into his accounts but also flowed out fairly regularly, and come the last quarter of the year his outgoings could be quite substantial. However, despite his high spending, he will enjoy himself at this time and perhaps take advantage of any travel opportunities that come his way.

As far as the Monkey's relations with others are concerned, the Goat year does call for extra consideration. Although the Monkey is usually a master at this, he must make sure he consults others over any plans he has in mind and listens to their views. If not, misunderstandings could result. Providing he heeds this advice, the Monkey can look forward to some pleasing times with both family and friends as the year draws to a close.

The Year of the Monkey starts on 22 January and holds many possibilities for its own sign. With his drive, personality and experience, the Monkey has much in his favour and this year he will be able to draw on his strengths and make excellent progress. And in so much of what he does, luck will be on his side.

In his work the Monkey can look forward to making substantial headway. With his earnest approach and faith in his own abilities, he knows he has much to offer and he should resolve to make the most of himself in 2004.

Over the year, some Monkeys will find their experience, contacts and in-house knowledge will place them in an excellent position for promotion and for greater responsibilities. By making known their desire to further themselves and pursuing openings that interest them, many will find themselves being rewarded with a better and more responsible role. As the Monkey realizes, the initiative often rests with him, but once he takes action, events can move quite swiftly and in his favour.

Monkeys who are seeking work or a change of employment will also find that if they follow up any openings that interest them they can be offered an exciting opportunity to use their skills in a more fulfilling way. Work-wise, the Monkey year is a time of opportunity and progress, with the first quarter and July and November holding particularly encouraging prospects.

With his enterprising nature the Monkey should also make the most of his ideas during the year. He could find some of his proposals starting an interesting chain of events. In addition, any Monkey who has considered starting his own business or has entrepreneurial ambitions would find this a good year to take this further. With commitment, enthusiasm and backing, he could score some notable successes.

The progress that the Monkey makes in his work will also have a positive effect on his finances, with many Monkeys enjoying a noticeable increase in income over the year. However, with his active lifestyle, the Monkey's spending levels will often be high and it would be worth him keeping an eye on his general situation as well as budgeting in advance for known expenses. By monitoring his position he can do much to prevent problems and possible shortfalls from arising. In addition, if he is able to use this financial upturn to reduce his borrowings and make some provision for his future he would find it to his advantage. Also, while the Monkey will feel positive about his position, he should be wary about becoming involved in any risky situations or taking on new commitments without checking all the details. Even for the Monkey himself, the year can spring traps.

With his sociable nature, the Monkey attaches great importance to his relations with others and these are excellently aspected. In his home life, he can look forward to many rewarding times planning and carrying out home projects with his loved ones and sharing interests and activities. He will, as always, follow the progress of those close to him with fond interest and his support and guidance will mean a great deal.

The Monkey will also be grateful for the support he is given and while he may have a tendency to keep his thoughts to himself, by being forthcoming he will find others are able to assist in more ways than he may have anticipated. His loved ones are important to him and, by letting them share in his hopes and ideas, he will benefit from their input as well as maintain the rapport he so values.

The Monkey year is also favourably aspected on a social level. Not only will the Monkey find his work bringing him into contact with others and leading to some pleasant social occasions, but he will also have various invitations and opportunities to go out. Over the year his social circle is set to grow quite considerably, and for the unattached, the prospects for romance and marriage are excellent. In some cases a chance meeting can swiftly transform the Monkey's life and certainly Cupid will be shooting some arrows in his direction over the year! For any Monkey who may have had some personal difficulty or sadness of late, this year can be a turning-point and usher in a new and brighter chapter. March, April, June and August will see much social activity and will be especially good times for meeting others.

In so many respects, 2004 holds great potential and by making the most of the chances that arise, the Monkey can make good headway and enjoy some pleasing successes. On a personal level, too, this will be a fine year, with the Monkey's family, friends and, for some, a new romance helping to make his own year all the more special.

The Metal Monkey

As far as the different types of Monkey are concerned, this will be an excellent year for the Metal Monkey, enabling him to make satisfying progress as well as lead a full and rewarding personal life.

In recent years the Metal Monkey will have gained much useful experience in his work, not only dealing with a wide range of duties but also discovering where his real strengths lie. His efforts and diligence will be rewarded this year, with almost all Metal Monkeys being able to make pleasing headway. The Metal Monkey knows he is capable of going far and that to achieve his aims he needs to put himself forward, and he will feel better able to do this in the Monkey year.

As the year starts the Metal Monkey should give some thought to how he would like his career to develop. Some Metal Monkeys may decide to remain in their present area of work but apply for greater responsibilities, while others will choose to develop their skills in other directions. By considering his next move, the Metal Monkey will become more aware of the possibilities available to him as well as better prepared for when opportunities arise. Over the year he can find events moving in fortuitous ways. A chance remark to a senior colleague could lead to some useful information or he could perhaps spot an ideal job vacancy in a paper he does not usually read. Work-wise, he will enjoy several strokes of good fortune and by making the most of them, he will be able to make important progress.

This also applies to those Metal Monkeys who are seeking work. With persistence, many will be successful in securing a position which not only suits their talents but also offers scope for the future. The Monkey year will certainly present some fine work opportunities. In addition, if the Metal Monkey's work allows him to draw on his ideas and creative talents, he should make the most of them. With the year favouring enterprise, he could find himself scoring some impressive triumphs.

The progress the Metal Monkey makes in his work will lead to an increase in his income over the year and he could also benefit from a gift or bonus or payment for work completed previously. However, while this is an encouraging year for finance, the Metal Monkey should manage his resources well. With many commitments and travel and accommodation expenses, he will have some sizeable outgoings and he should make sure he allows for these in his budget. By handling his finances prudently, he will not only be able to ease some of the financial pressures he may have been under recently but will also enjoy planning and choosing his purchases all the more.

The Metal Monkey's personal life also holds some good prospects. Those Metal Monkeys with a partner will enjoy sharing interests and planning activities they can tackle together, including some home improvements. There will be times of fun and laughter and many rewarding moments. Metal Monkeys with babies and young children will also follow their development with much delight. Domestically, the year will certainly contain many memorable times.

However while so much will go well, there will be times when the Metal Monkey will feel tired, particularly if his sleep patterns are being disturbed or he has a particularly heavy workload. At such times, he should be willing to take up any offers of help or talk over his feelings with his partner or good friends. At busy and tiring times the Metal Monkey really can gain a lot by being forthcoming.

The Metal Monkey can also look forward to a rewarding social life over the year. In particular he will be grateful for the supportive nature of his close band of friends and will often appreciate their advice, help and camaraderie. In addition to meeting up with existing friends, he will also enjoy going to various social events that appeal to him. In the process, he will not only find his social circle widening but will also forge some important friendships. Romance, too, will figure prominently for the unattached Metal Monkey, either with an existing relationship taking on greater significance or a chance meeting suddenly becoming very special. Some Metal Monkeys will decide to marry. This can be an especially auspicious year where the affairs of the heart are concerned.

Overall, this is a highly favourable year for the Metal Monkey and by making the most of the opportunities that arise, he will make considerable progress as well as enjoy a rewarding personal life and the many special moments the year will bring.

TIP FOR THE YEAR
You have many great personal qualities and talents. Make the most of them. Enjoy yourself and look to advance.

The Water Monkey
This is a year of opportunity for the Water Monkey and one he will greatly enjoy.

Those Water Monkeys born in 1992 can look forward to making good headway. Encouraged by the support of others and friendship of many, the young Water Monkey will find himself growing in confidence and taking pleasure in his achievements. In his schoolwork he can make some impressive strides and will find himself becoming more involved in many of the subjects he has to study. The Water Monkey will also enjoy some of his additional activities, perhaps learning an instrument, advancing his sporting skills or becoming involved in an after-school club. By taking advantage of the opportunities that are available to him, he will enjoy himself and make progress.

In most of what he does the Water Monkey will be well supported, but should he have any problems with his schoolwork or any matters worrying him, he should not hesitate to tell others. They will often be able to advise and reassure, but to benefit the Water Monkey does need to be forthcoming.

Similarly, if he has any ideas he wants to try out or interests he is keen to take up, he should let these be known. He will often find others more amenable than he originally thought and his proposals more likely to come about.

This will also be a satisfying year for those Water Monkeys born in 1932. As always, the more senior Water Monkey will find much to do over the year and he will particularly enjoy furthering one of his existing interests or taking up a new one. This will sometimes have hidden benefits as well. In some cases the Water Monkey will be able to meet fellow enthusiasts or, if what he does is in any way creative or can be enjoyed by others, it can bring a heartening response. The Water Monkey will also be encouraged by the support given by his loved ones, and by involving them in plans, he will find they can help in a great many ways.

In addition to his own personal interests, the Water Monkey will enjoy activities he can share with others, whether choosing new items for his home or garden, going to social events or sharing mutual interests. The Monkey year will certainly contain many agreeable occasions.

As well as enjoying activities with those around him, the Water Monkey will take a fond interest in the progress of family members and there will be occasions which will make him truly proud. While he may not wish to appear interfering, any offers of support or advice he feels able to make (particularly to younger relations who may be under pressure) will be appreciated.

The Monkey year is also a fine one for travel and the Water Monkey should aim to go away at some time. A holiday, a break he decides to take on the spur of the moment or an invitation to visit friends and family can all lead to some pleasurable times away.

The Water Monkey will also appreciate his social life over the year and will value the chances to talk with his close friends. Any Water Monkey who may desire more companionship will find that joining a local group or even offering to help in the community in some way, perhaps with charity work, can lead to meeting others, some of whom will quickly become friends. Socially, this can be a rewarding and pleasing year.

This will also be a positive year for financial matters, with many Water Monkeys seeing an improvement in their situation, sometimes resulting from the fruition of a policy, a gift or even a competition win. However, the Water Monkey should not be too hasty in spending anything extra and will often find it more satisfying to plan carefully what he wants to do with this upturn in fortune. Also, he needs to be careful with any financial paperwork he receives. Without sufficient care he could find he is disadvantaged in some way. He does need to be thorough when completing financial forms and to keep receipts and guarantees safely.

Overall, the Monkey year holds much promise for the Water Monkey and whether born in 1932 or 1992, by setting about his activities in earnest and making the most of the opportunities the year will bring, he will find this a gratifying and rewarding time.

TIP FOR THE YEAR
Be forthcoming with your ideas and plans. You can gain a lot by involving others.

The Wood Monkey

This will be a significant year for the Wood Monkey, not only marking his sixtieth birthday but also allowing him greater opportunity to carry through some of his plans and ideas.

Some Wood Monkeys will decide to retire this year and those who do will often have given much thought to how to fill the extra time available to them. Now they will set about their plans with relish. Travel will figure on the agenda for many and can lead to some very pleasurable and memorable times. In addition to any planned holidays or breaks, some Wood Monkeys will take the chance to go away at short notice and the spontaneity of such trips will greatly appeal to them. The Wood Monkey should also follow up any invitations to visit family or friends who may live some distance away. These can also lead to some agreeable times. Generally, travel is so well aspected that the Wood Monkey will find that trips of any kind will make his sixtieth year all the more special.

The Wood Monkey will also be keen to develop his own personal interests and by setting himself some projects, he will often take much satisfaction in what he does. In particular, those who like writing, art, photography, craft-work or something similarly creative will find that extending and experimenting with their interest can add to the pleasure it brings. And if the Wood Monkey sees a new subject or even course that appeals to him, he should find out more.

The Wood Monkey will also enjoy some of his more practical activities. Whether he is planning modifications to his home or spending time in his garden, he will be pleased with how his plans unfold. The Wood Monkey has always been a doer and in 2004 he will certainly do a great deal!

In the course of his many activities, he will be grateful for the support he receives, and by talking over his ideas, he will find others are able to assist in more ways than he may have originally thought. Sometimes, as the Wood Monkey will find, offers of help or suggestions about how to tackle a certain activity can make a real difference.

In addition to carrying out activities with family members, the Wood Monkey will follow their news and progress with fond interest and will often be glad to help and advise any who may be busy or under pressure. He will enjoy some of the family occasions that take place, including his own sixtieth birthday, and will also be happy to celebrate the successes of those who mean so much to him. Domestically, 2004 is favourably aspected and will bring the Wood Monkey considerable contentment.

He will also value his social life, including the chances to meet up with friends and the various events he goes to. Any Wood Monkey who may desire more companionship or who has had some recent personal difficulty will find that if he becomes involved in different activities and gets to meet others, the year can usher in a brighter chapter. The Monkey year is very supportive to its own sign. For socializing and meeting others, March, April, June and August hold good prospects.

As far as work is concerned, those Wood Monkeys who do not retire will have some excellent opportunities to use their skills and experience, and by drawing on their often extensive knowledge, they will chalk up some impressive achievements. In addition, with the year so favouring enterprise, some ideas the Wood Monkey has could work out well. Even for those Wood Monkeys who retire or opt to reduce their working hours, there will often be interesting opportunities to put their strengths and knowledge to good use. As the Wood Monkey will find, his talents will be in demand and appreciated over the year.

This will also be a positive year for financial matters, with many Wood Monkeys receiving a bonus or additional sum of money. In view of some of the activities he would like to carry out, the Wood Monkey should consider setting some money aside for them in advance. The better he can manage his finances, the more he will find he is able to do. One word of warning that does need to be sounded in this otherwise favourable year is to avoid taking risks or entering into agreements without checking *all* the implications. Money matters do need careful handling and if the Wood Monkey becomes complacent or pushes his luck too far, he could suffer as a result. Wood Monkeys, take note.

Overall, though, this is a splendidly aspected year for the Wood Monkey and with the love and support of family and friends and the chance to follow through so many of his ideas, he can make his sixtieth year a very special one.

TIP FOR THE YEAR
Take up something new. This can be a personal interest, a new project or a subject that intrigues you, but by doing something different you will enjoy the challenge and benefit in the process.

The Fire Monkey

The Fire Monkey will make much of 2004. With his keen and enterprising ways and willingness to be involved in so much, he will be able to make good progress as well as draw satisfaction from most of what takes place. The Monkey year offers considerable potential and, almost as it starts, interesting opportunities will start to arise.

In his work the Fire Monkey will find his experience serving him well and others looking to him to take on further responsibilities or become involved in more specialist areas. Change and promotion will certainly beckon and the Fire Monkey, ever keen to put his skills to greater use, will relish the challenge. The months from January to mid April could see some particularly interesting chances for him to improve his position. However, change will not necessarily stop there, as further possibilities could result from any new role that he takes on. Colleagues moving on, new schemes being introduced or other openings falling available will provide further opportunities, and by indicating his interest, the Fire Monkey can often benefit from the situations that unfold. As he will discover, this *is* a year of opportunity.

Although many Fire Monkeys will make progress in their current line of work, some will consider the time is now right to do something different. These Fire Monkeys, as well as those looking for work, will find that by deciding what it is they want to do and following up suitable openings, they may well be able to set their career off on a new track. Not only will their new duties give them a welcome new incentive and challenge, but they could also open up other possibilities for the future. As far as the Fire

Monkey's work prospects are concerned, this can be an exciting year.

The Fire Monkey will also enjoy spending time on his personal interests over the year and whether these are purely recreational or allow him to use his creative and practical skills in some way, they will not only do him good but also bring him much personal satisfaction. Any Fire Monkey who, perhaps because of work or other commitments, has let his interests lapse should address this early in the year by setting time aside to do something *he* wants. These Fire Monkeys will find their interests can help bring an important balance to their life.

The Monkey year also favours travel and the Fire Monkey should aim to take a holiday at some time during 2004. He will benefit from the change of scene and rest this brings as well as the chance to visit what could be some interesting destinations.

Also, if he does not get much exercise during the day, he would benefit from considering how he can make up for this. Medical guidance will help him decide the best way to proceed. But whatever he does, by paying attention to his own well-being he will soon feel the benefit.

The progress that the Fire Monkey makes in his work will have a positive effect on his income and generally the year will bring an improvement in his financial situation. However, rather than letting this tempt him into too many spending sprees, he should see whether he can reduce some of his borrowings and plan his more major purchases. By managing his money, he will often find himself able to do more. Quite a few Fire Monkeys will also have considerable family expenses over the year, including helping younger relations with education costs or a possible wedding, and the more the Fire Monkey can plan for this in advance, the better he will fare.

Domestically, this will be a busy year with the Fire Monkey doing much to support others, including both younger and more senior relations. His care and advice will be greatly appreciated. In addition he could find himself organizing a great deal during the year, including some family celebrations and get-togethers.

However, while the Fire Monkey will be keen to be involved in so much, he should not hesitate to draw on the assistance of those around him. If certain household chores are mounting up or he has other pressures to deal with, he should avail himself of the help others can give. And, in addition to the generally active lifestyle he and those in his household may lead, he should aim to set time aside for shared activities and occasional family treats, as these can give rise to some particularly rewarding occasions. Busy though the year may be, it can be pleasant too.

The Fire Monkey will also value meeting up with his friends as well as the various social occasions he goes to. Again, with his wide interests, he will want to be involved in a great many things, and his social life will often be active and rewarding. Fire Monkeys who may be lonely and would welcome more companionship will find that by going out more and perhaps joining a local group, their social life can improve a lot within a short time. And for the unattached, the Monkey year can bring the gift of an important new friendship and, for some, true love.

Overall, this is a year of great potential for the Fire Monkey and by making the most of his talents, ideas and opportunities, he will prosper. A good year indeed.

TIP FOR THE YEAR
Make the most of your ideas and experience. These are real strengths and can lead to success in this auspicious year.

The Earth Monkey

This will be a positive year for the Earth Monkey, allowing him to make important progress as well as enjoy himself.

In his work the aspects are especially promising. With the experience he has behind him, he may find himself well placed to put in for greater responsibilities or follow up vacancies which offer better prospects. By putting himself forward, he can make substantial headway. And once he is given new responsibilities, by mastering his new duties and being willing to undertake any training required, he will quickly impress others and do his prospects much good.

There will also be some Earth Monkeys who decide to move away from the type of work they have been doing and try something different. Although such a change will demand much from the Earth Monkey, by making the most of any opportunity he is given, he will find himself rising to the challenge before him and feeling more motivated than he has for some time. Work-wise, this *is* a significant time, with positive and far-reaching developments. For opportunities, the first quarter of the year and July and November are especially favourable.

In so much of what he does, the Earth Monkey's commitment and ability to learn quickly will prove a great asset, but he should also advance any ideas he has, as some of his proposals could be welcomed. Earth Monkeys who are self-employed or considering setting up business on their own will find that by furthering their ideas and obtaining appropriate advice their plans will develop well. With this being a year which favours enterprise, the aspects are certainly on their side.

The progress that the Earth Monkey makes in his work will also lead to a welcome increase in income over the year. Some Earth Monkeys may even be able to supplement this with freelance work or receiving something extra by way of a gift or bonus. Financially, this will be a much improved year and as a result, the Earth Monkey will often be tempted to make certain acquisitions for his home as well as spend money on travel. By planning his purchases carefully, he will be pleased with how his ideas work out. If he is able, he should also consider making some savings for the longer term. In time, these could grow into a useful asset.

However, while this may be a positive year financially, the Earth Monkey should still be wary of taking risks. Important forms and agreements do need careful checking and if he has any doubts over any transaction or venture he may be considering, he does need to get these resolved and, if appropriate, seek professional guidance.

Domestically, the Earth Monkey will see much activity. With his own busy lifestyle as well as the activities of those around him, there will often be much to think about or arrange. Although, as with any year, strains and differences of opinion may sometimes arise, by showing understanding and addressing any problems, the Earth Monkey will find they can often be quickly defused. To help with this, he should try to ensure that time is set aside for joint activities rather than remaining too preoccupied with his own concerns. By maintaining and encouraging shared interests and projects, socializing and arranging occasional family treats and holidays, he will be able to enjoy a fine rapport with those around him as well as some memorable occasions.

Over the year the Earth Monkey will also do much to help a younger relation who may be facing important tests and academic work. His understanding and encouragement will be particularly appreciated. And even though sometimes a gap in years may lead to some differences of opinion, his supportive manner will mean a great deal.

The Earth Monkey's social life and personal interests will also be important over the year. Both can give him a break from his usual concerns and bring him a great deal of pleasure, and despite the many demands on his time, he should make sure he does not neglect them. Also, in this well-aspected year, any Earth Monkey who may feel lonely or who has had some recent personal difficulty could find a new friendship or romance suddenly transforming the year and indeed his life.

Overall, 2004 holds excellent prospects for the Earth Monkey, enabling him to make good headway and more effective use of his skills and ideas. On a personal level, too, he will find this a pleasing and encouraging year.

TIP FOR THE YEAR

Although this is a highly promising year, do aim to lead a balanced lifestyle. As well as looking to progress in your work, give time to your family, friends, interests and recreational pursuits. These *are* valuable treasures.

FAMOUS MONKEYS

Christina Aguilera, Gillian Anderson, Jennifer Aniston, Francesca Annis, Michael Aspel, J. M. Barrie, Johnny Cash, Jacques Chirac, Joe Cocker, Colette, John Constable, Alistair Cooke, David Copperfield, Patricia Cornwell, Joan Crawford, Timothy Dalton, Roger Daltry, Bette Davis, Danny De Vito, Celine Dion, Michael Douglas, Mia Farrow, Carrie Fisher, F. Scott Fitzgerald, Ian Fleming, Dick Francis, Fiona Fullerton, Paul Gauguin, Jerry Hall, Tom Hanks, Martina Hingis, Harry Houdini, P. D. James, Pope John Paul II, Lyndon B. Johnson, Julius Caesar, Buster Keaton, Edward Kennedy, Alicia Keys, Don King, Gladys Knight, Bob Marley, Walter Matthau, Kylie Minogue, V. S. Naipaul, Peter O'Toole, Anthony Perkins, Lisa Marie Presley, Lou Reed, Debbie Reynolds, Sir Tim Rice, Little Richard, Anne Robinson, Mary Robinson, Mickey Rooney, Diana Ross, Donald Rumsfeld, Boz Scaggs, Gerhard Schröder, Michael Schumacher, Tom Selleck, Omar Sharif, Wilbur Smith, Rod Stewart, Jacques Tati, Elizabeth Taylor, Dame Kiri Te Kanawa, Justin Timberlake, Harry Truman, Leonardo da Vinci, Venus Williams.

22 JANUARY 1909 ～ 9 FEBRUARY 1910   *Earth Rooster*

8 FEBRUARY 1921 ～ 27 JANUARY 1922   *Metal Rooster*

26 JANUARY 1933 ～ 13 FEBRUARY 1934   *Water Rooster*

13 FEBRUARY 1945 ～ 1 FEBRUARY 1946   *Wood Rooster*

31 JANUARY 1957 ～ 17 FEBRUARY 1958   *Fire Rooster*

17 FEBRUARY 1969 ～ 5 FEBRUARY 1970   *Earth Rooster*

5 FEBRUARY 1981 ～ 24 JANUARY 1982   *Metal Rooster*

23 JANUARY 1993 ～ 9 FEBRUARY 1994   *Water Rooster*

THE
ROOSTER

THE PERSONALITY OF
THE ROOSTER

If I were to wish for anything, I should not wish for wealth and power, but for the passionate sense of the potential, for the eye which, ever young and ardent, sees the possible ... what wine is so sparkling, so fragrant, so intoxicating, as possibility!

Søren Kierkegaard, a Rooster

The Rooster is born under the sign of candour. He has a flamboyant and colourful personality and is meticulous in all that he does. He is an excellent organizer and wherever possible likes to plan his various activities well in advance.

The Rooster is highly intelligent and usually very well read. He has a good sense of humour and is an effective and persuasive speaker. He loves discussion and enjoys taking part in any sort of debate. He has no hesitation in speaking his mind and is forthright in his views. He does, however, lack tact and can easily damage his reputation or cause offence by some thoughtless remark or action. The Rooster has a very volatile nature and should always try to avoid acting on the spur of the moment.

The Rooster is usually very dignified in his manner and conducts himself with an air of confidence and authority. He is adept at handling financial matters and organizes his financial affairs with considerable skill. He chooses his investments well and is capable of achieving great wealth. Most Roosters save or use their money wisely, but there are a few who are the reverse and are notorious spend-thrifts. Fortunately, the Rooster has great earning capacity and is rarely without sufficient funds to tide himself over.

Another characteristic of the Rooster is that he invariably carries a notebook or scraps of paper around with him. He is constantly writing himself reminders or noting down important facts lest he forgets – the Rooster cannot abide inefficiency and conducts all his activities in an orderly, precise and methodical manner.

The Rooster is usually very ambitious, but can be unrealistic in some of what he hopes to achieve. He occasionally lets his imagination run away with him and while he does not like any interference from others, it would be in his own interests to listen to their views a little more often. He also does not like criticism, and if he feels anybody is doubting his judgement or prying too closely into his affairs, he is certain to let his feelings be known. He can also be rather self-centred and stubborn over relatively trivial matters, but to compensate for this he is reliable, honest and trustworthy, and this is appreciated by all who come into contact with him.

Roosters born between the hours of five and seven, both at dawn and sundown, tend to be the most extrovert of their sign, but all Roosters like to lead an active social life and enjoy attending parties and big functions. The Rooster usually has a wide circle of friends and is able to build up influential contacts with remarkable ease. He often belongs to several clubs and societies and involves himself in a variety of different activities. He is particularly interested in the environment, humanitarian affairs and anything affecting the welfare of others. He has a very caring nature and will do much to help those less fortunate than himself.

He also gets much pleasure from gardening and while he may not always spend as much time in the garden as he would like, his garden is invariably well kept and productive.

The Rooster is generally very distinguished in his appearance and if his job permits he will wear an official uniform with great pride and dignity. He is not averse to publicity and takes great delight in being the centre of attention. He often does well at PR work or any job which brings him into contact with the media. He also makes a very good teacher.

The female Rooster leads a varied and interesting life. She involves herself in many different activities and there are some who wonder how she can achieve so much. She often holds strong views and, like her male counterpart, has no hesitation in speaking her mind or telling others how she thinks things should be done. She is supremely efficient and well organized and her home is usually very neat and tidy. She has good taste in clothes and usually wears smart but very practical outfits.

The Rooster usually has a large family and takes a particularly active interest in the education of his children. He is very loyal to his partner and will find that he is especially well suited to those born under the signs of the Snake, Horse, Ox and Dragon. Provided they do not interfere too much in the Rooster's various activities, the Rat, Tiger, Goat and Pig can also establish a good relationship with him, but two Roosters together are likely to squabble and irritate each other. The rather sensitive Rabbit will find the Rooster a bit too blunt for his liking, and the Rooster will quickly become exasperated by the ever-inquisitive and artful Monkey. He will also find it difficult to get on with the anxious Dog.

If the Rooster can overcome his volatile nature and exercise more tact, he will go far in life. He is capable and talented and will make a lasting – and usually favourable – impression almost everywhere he goes.

THE FIVE DIFFERENT TYPES OF ROOSTER

In addition to the 12 signs of the Chinese zodiac there are five elements, and these have a strengthening or moderating influence on the sign. The effects of the five elements on the Rooster are described below, together with the years in which the elements were exercising their influence. Therefore all Roosters born in 1921 and 1981 are Metal Roosters, those born in 1933 and 1993 are Water Roosters, and so on.

Metal Rooster: 1921, 1981
The Metal Rooster is a hard and conscientious worker. He knows exactly what he wants in life and sets about everything in a positive and determined manner. He can at times appear abrasive and he would almost certainly do better if he were more willing to reach a compromise with others rather than hold so rigidly to his beliefs. He is very articulate and most astute when dealing with financial matters.

He is loyal to his friends and often devotes much energy to working for the common good.

Water Rooster: 1933, 1993

This Rooster has a very persuasive manner and can easily gain the co-operation of others. He is intelligent, well read and enjoys taking part in discussions and debates. He has a seemingly inexhaustible amount of energy and is prepared to work long hours in order to secure what he wants. He can, however, waste a lot of valuable time worrying over minor and inconsequential details. He is approachable, has a good sense of humour and is highly regarded by others.

Wood Rooster: 1945

The Wood Rooster is honest, reliable and often sets himself high standards. He is ambitious, but he is also more prepared to work in a team than some of the other types of Rooster. He usually succeeds in life but does have a tendency to get caught up in bureaucratic matters and attempt too many things at the same time. He has wide interests, likes to travel and is very caring and considerate towards his family and friends.

Fire Rooster: 1957

This Rooster is extremely strong-willed. He has many leadership qualities, is an excellent organizer and is most efficient in his work. Through sheer force of character he often secures his objectives, but he does have a tendency to be very forthright and not always consider the feelings of others. If the Fire Rooster can learn to be more tactful he can often succeed beyond his wildest dreams.

Earth Rooster: 1909, 1969

This Rooster has a deep and penetrating mind. He is efficient, perceptive and particularly astute in business and financial matters. He is also persistent and once he has set himself an objective, he will rarely allow himself to be deflected from achieving his aim. The Earth Rooster works hard and is held in great esteem by his friends and colleagues. He usually enjoys the arts and takes a keen interest in the activities of the various members of his family.

PROSPECTS FOR THE ROOSTER IN 2004

The Chinese New Year starts on 22 January 2004. Until then, the old year, the Year of the Goat, is still making its presence felt.

The Year of the Goat (1 February 2003 to 21 January 2004) is a generally encouraging one for the Rooster, with the closing months being favourably aspected. The Rooster likes order and careful planning and his approach will serve him well in the Goat year. By maintaining his high standards and being his methodical self, he is set to enhance his reputation, and interesting opportunities to further his career could arise in September and November 2003. The Goat year will certainly give the Rooster the chance to develop his skills.

The closing stages of the year will, though, be an expensive time and while the Rooster will not begrudge his spending and the pleasure it brings, there could be occasions when he should think carefully about certain purchases. Sometimes more consideration could lead him to choose something more appropriate or even to save some money! Expensive purchases and transactions should not be rushed.

The Rooster can look forward to an active domestic and social life as the year draws to a close. Being the keen organizer that he is, he will often play a leading role in many of the arrangements that need to be made. Whether social occasions with family, friends and colleagues, family treats or trips out, a lot is likely to happen at this time and the Rooster will enjoy himself. For the unattached and those who may be seeking more companionship, there are particularly good prospects from September onwards, with many able to add to their social circle at this time.

Overall, the Goat year is a favourable one for the Rooster and by making the most of his talents and the opportunities the year will bring, he will find this a satisfying and rewarding time.

The Year of the Monkey starts on 22 January and will be a variable one for the Rooster. The Monkey year is often characterized by activity and while the Rooster is not averse to this, he does like to plan and be in control of his situation. In the Monkey year he will not always be comfortable with the speed with which events take place or decisions have to be made. There will be trying moments for him, but the year will not be without its more positive side too.

In his work the Rooster can look forward to building on his recent progress and making headway. However, throughout the year, he *will* need to tread warily. Changes are likely to be afoot in his place of work. New procedures could suddenly be introduced or the Rooster could be asked to take on other responsibilities. Although he may have misgivings about some of these, he should be prepared to show some flexibility. If not, he could undermine his position and lose out on possible opportunities.

Also, the Rooster will find some of the opportunities or proposals put to him will arise with little warning and while he may appreciate more time to reflect on his position, he should not be dilatory in making a response. To do so could again lessen his prospects. Similarly, if he sees an opening which particularly appeals to him, he should act quickly. This especially applies to those Roosters seeking work or eager to move on from their present position. As the Rooster will discover, things happen quickly in the Monkey year, and he must accept this.

The months of March, May, September and October in particular could see change and opportunity, but throughout 2004 the Rooster should remain alert to all that is happening at work as well as be aware of proposals that are under consideration.

Another important aspect of the year will be the way it allows the Rooster to extend his experience. This includes learning new skills through carrying out his duties as well as through any training he goes on. In many cases, what he learns now will help his prospects in the future. Roosters who may have been seeking work for some time should also take advantage of any training they are eligible for, as they could find a new skill opening up other possibilities for them.

As far as financial matters are concerned, this will be a reasonable year for the Rooster. However, with his many obligations, he does need to proceed carefully and would find it helpful to set funds aside for known expenses as well as saving towards holidays and other items he has in mind. By controlling his finances he will find he is able to cope better, often do more and sometimes avoid frittering money away needlessly. There are, after all, some Roosters who are notorious spendthrifts and a certain discipline would not come amiss!

Another area which requires care concerns the Rooster's relations with others. Although both his domestic and social life promise some splendid times, certain incidents could cause problems. Often these may start in a relatively minor way, but unless they are handled tactfully, there is a risk that they could escalate and lead to some awkward situations. If the Rooster does detect tensions brewing, he should try to address these as quickly as he can and, if necessary, show a greater flexibility in certain matters. A factor which may not always help is the busy lifestyle the Rooster may lead. Tiredness could quickly lead to him becoming tetchy and irritable, and if at any time he does feel tired or has concerns, he should talk to others about how he feels. Not only will they be more aware of his situation, but they could also help more as a result, perhaps by doing extra tasks around the home. In 2004 the Rooster should not forget that those around him are willing to help, but he does need to be forthcoming.

However, despite the tricky aspects, there will be much in the Rooster's domestic life which will bring him pleasure. This includes carrying out projects to enhance the home or garden, pursuing shared interests and arranging family occasions everyone can enjoy. The Rooster's ability to come up with ideas for activities will be appreciated, and spending quality time with those dear to him will mean a lot to everyone.

Although the Rooster will have a lot to keep him busy, it is also important he does not neglect either his social life or personal interests. As well as enjoying himself, he will benefit from the chance to relax and unwind. And for the unattached and those who may be desiring more company, the Monkey year can mark the start of a significant new relationship. May, July, November and December could all see much social activity.

Although the Year of the Monkey will contain its tricky moments and require the Rooster to show some flexibility in approach, it will not be without its pleasures or successes. Both the Rooster's family and his social life will bring some rewarding times, while work-wise the progress he makes will prove important and stand him in excellent stead for his own year that follows.

The Metal Rooster

As far as the different types of Rooster are concerned, the Monkey year will be a significant one for the Metal

Rooster and while it will not be without its more challenging moments, it will give him the chance to discover more about his own special qualities and strengths.

In his work this will be a year of interesting developments. Although the Metal Rooster may have ideas on how he would like his career to develop, the Monkey year could cause him to think again. During the year many Metal Roosters will find themselves being offered the chance to take on greater responsibilities, but often in an area they have not considered before. However, the opportunity will not only offer more remuneration but also be an excellent chance for the Metal Rooster to extend his skills and move his career forward. Work-wise, the year is capable of springing some surprises and the Metal Rooster should make the most of the opportunities he is given or situations in which he finds himself, even though they may not always fit in with his current aims. He should also remember that he is still in the early stages of his career and that the more experience he can get now, the more it can help his prospects later.

The Monkey year can also bring interesting developments for those Metal Roosters seeking work or feeling frustrated in their current position. Over the year they should remain alert for positions which they feel would give them more scope to develop, even if they are quite unlike anything they have done before. The Monkey year is a good one in which to experiment. And for quite a few Metal Roosters, a position they obtain this year can start their career off in a completely new direction as well as allow them to discover talents they can make much of in the future. March, May, September and October could see interesting chances arising, but generally this is a year when opportunities could occur at almost any time and often quickly.

The Metal Rooster should also make the most of any training he is offered. By furthering his skills he will not only benefit from what he learns but also indicate his keenness to progress. And this, together with his methodical approach, will do much to help his standing in the eyes of his employer. The Metal Rooster has a good future ahead of him and what he does now will be another stepping-stone on the road to success.

Although the Metal Rooster's income is set to increase in 2004, he will need to be careful when dealing with money matters. Over the year many Metal Roosters will face some heavy expenses. If the Metal Rooster has to borrow or enter into any agreement, he should compare the terms being offered by various companies as well as check the obligations he is taking on. Money-wise, this *is* a year in which he must be thorough, especially over agreements that are likely to run for many years. Also, he would find it helpful to set funds aside for future activities and purchases. Savings made early, whether for a holiday, a personal event (with some Metal Roosters marrying in 2004) or a deposit on a home, can help ease some of the pressures later on.

As far as the Metal Rooster's relations with others are concerned, the Monkey year promises some interesting times. For many Metal Roosters, romance will lead to many happy and memorable occasions. There could also be good cause for a personal celebration, with some Metal Roosters marrying or seeing an addition to their family, while for the unattached, the prospects for meeting someone who will become special are excellent.

However, while the Monkey year is well aspected for personal matters, it does also require some care. Over the year the Metal Rooster needs to remain mindful of others and be accommodating in certain situations. He may hold strong views and like to hold sway, but there will be times when it would be wise for him to tread carefully if he does not want to endanger his good relations with those around him.

Although the Metal Rooster's work and other commitments may sometimes prevent him from going out as regularly as he would like, he will nevertheless appreciate meeting up with his friends over the year as well as enjoying the social events he does go to. Changes in his work will often lead to him meeting others and, in the process, making new friends as well as useful contacts for the future.

Overall, the Monkey year will be an important one for the Metal Rooster and by adapting to the situations that arise, he will do well, learn much and considerably enhance his prospects. And on a personal level, love will mean a great deal to him.

TIP FOR THE YEAR
Be mindful of others. You may have set ideas and particular plans, but do listen to any advice as well as to the views of those around you. This is not a year for going it alone or being too inflexible in attitude.

The Water Rooster

The Water Rooster has wide interests and likes to be involved in a great deal, and the active nature of the Monkey year will suit him well. Over the year he will be able to do much to further himself and his interests. However while this will be a satisfying year, it will not be free from its pressures or more challenging moments.

For Water Roosters born in 1993 this will be an important year, as many will move to a new school and start new subjects. While the young Water Rooster will be anxious about some of what he faces, he will soon get into his stride. Not only will he be keen to make an impression and try hard, but his ability to adjust will serve him well. He will also be helped by the friendship and camaraderie of others and the realization that many share his thoughts and concerns. Some of the year will be demanding, but the Water Rooster will acquit himself well.

In addition the Water Rooster will be well supported, and if he has any worries, he should tell others. Often those around him, whether his family at home or his tutors at school, can help put his mind at ease. If he encounters any problems in his schoolwork, some extra guidance can often resolve his uncertainties. Throughout the Monkey year it is important that the Water Rooster makes use of the help that is available.

Young Water Roosters will also enjoy furthering their interests and again should take advantage of the opportunities open to them. For sporting enthusiasts, joining an after-school club or a local group can do much to improve their skills as well as lead to some fun occasions. Similarly, those keen on music, drama, dance or any other creative activities should aim to develop their interest further. However, to benefit, they need to make the most of what is available.

As far as the Water Rooster's personal development is concerned, the Monkey year is one which offers great opportunities, but a warning does need to be sounded. Despite his many fine abilities, the young Water Rooster can at times be stubborn and if he decides to close his mind to a certain subject or activity, he could create difficulties for himself and sour an otherwise positive time. The year will require a certain flexibility in attitude and a willingness to try and experiment. Fortunately, many Water Roosters do possess an adventurous spirit, but for those who dig their heels in, problems could loom. Water Roosters, take note.

This also applies to the Water Rooster's home life. Although he will be grateful for the support he is given as well as enjoy some of the family activities that take place, he should listen carefully to advice he is given as well as be aware of the attitudes of those around him. Sometimes not all his ideas or plans may meet with the response or approval he was hoping for and he should accept this rather than let certain matters get out of proportion or spoil the rapport he has with those around him.

The more senior Water Rooster, born in 1933, also places great value on his home life and can look forward to some enjoyable times with his loved ones and in carrying out activities both he and others can appreciate. For the many Water Roosters who enjoy being out of doors and are keen gardeners, projects in their garden will prove especially satisfying. The Water Rooster's personal interests will bring him much pleasure and he will certainly set himself some interesting projects to do over the year.

With travel well aspected, the Water Rooster will also enjoy going away for any breaks and holidays as well as visiting family and friends who live some distance away.

However, while so much can go well, no year is completely free from its problems and the Monkey year will be no exception. Sometimes a matter will arise which leads to a disagreement, and if this happens, rather than let it linger or escalate, the Water Rooster should use his skills to resolve it. Here his ability to listen as well as communicate his own views so effectively will be helpful. As he will find, dialogue can do much to ease awkward situations.

Another area which could cause problems is bureaucracy. The Water Rooster should deal with any important forms and paperwork he receives carefully and promptly, especially if relating to tax, pension, benefits or insurance. If he has any uncertainties, he should seek advice rather than make assumptions or take risks. Extra vigilance can prevent problems arising. Water Roosters, take note.

Overall, this will be a generally positive year for the Water Rooster, with both the younger and more senior Water Rooster taking a great deal of pleasure from their interests and making good use of their time and skills. The opportunities will be there, the Water Rooster will be supported in much of what he does, and it rests with him to make the most of his ideas and take advantage of the many chances that are available. The more willing he is, the more he will get out of the year – and the more he will enjoy himself too!

TIP FOR THE YEAR

Listen to others. Those around you are keen to offer support and have your best interests at heart. Be aware of this and be forthcoming.

The Wood Rooster

This will be a year of interesting developments for the Wood Rooster and, by making the most of the chances that arise, he will emerge from it with much to his credit.

In his work, in particular, this will be a significant time. Although many Wood Roosters will be content to remain in their present position, change will be in the offing. In some cases, colleagues leaving or being transferred will lead to the Wood Rooster being offered greater responsibilities or promotion. This may involve him leaving a position he likes to take on what could be a far more demanding role. However, by rising to the challenge, the Wood Rooster will find his career will be given an unexpected boost and he will have the chance to develop his skills in new areas. The months from March to May and September could see much activity, and when opportunities arise the Wood Rooster should look positively on them and follow them through.

For those Wood Roosters who are seeking work, again the Monkey year can bring some positive developments. By pursuing openings that appeal to them, many will be successful in securing a position which will give them a good opportunity to use and extend their skills.

There will also be some Wood Roosters who decide to take early retirement over the year or switch to positions involving fewer hours. These Wood Roosters should give careful thought to how they would like to spend their additional time and discuss their ideas with those around them. These plans could involve travel, taking up new interests or projects in the home or garden, but whatever they are, it is important that the Wood Rooster is forthcoming about what he has in mind and listens carefully to the views of his loved ones. That way he will find his plans more likely to develop in the way he wants. This is not a year for independent-mindedness!

One area which could be especially rewarding is the Wood Rooster's own personal interests and if he is able to join fellow enthusiasts, perhaps through a society or by going to events, he will find this can give his interests a fillip as well as lead to some enjoyable occasions. Often the Wood Rooster's interests will involve his love of the outdoors, but with his enquiring mind, he will also take pleasure in some of the reading and research he carries out over the year. Some Wood Roosters may also decide to set themselves a project to do or skill to learn. By doing something that appeals and satisfies, all Wood Roosters can find this another rewarding aspect of the year.

Although the Wood Rooster often keeps himself active, those who are sedentary for much of the day or feel they lack exercise should also consider remedying this during the year. By seeking medical guidance on the best way to proceed and following the advice given, they can do much to improve their fitness levels. Again, this is a good year for personal development.

The Wood Rooster's home life can also give rise to some pleasing times, with shared interests and domestic projects as well as some agreeable family occasions all meaning much. The Wood Rooster will also delight in the progress of those dear to him and be glad to assist relations who may be under pressure, including those with young families. However, while so much will go well, he does need to consult others over his plans and ideas and be mindful of their views. Also, if any matter gives rise to a difference of opinion, the Wood Rooster should try to resolve it quickly rather than run the risk of it escalating unnecessarily. Domestically, this can be a fine year, but it is one in which the Wood Rooster will need to tread carefully and considerately.

The Wood Rooster's social life will also bring him pleasure over the year. He will enjoy spending time with friends as well as going to a variety of events. Any Wood Rooster who may be feeling lonely or who, perhaps because of work commitments, has let his social life lapse will find the Monkey year can bring a welcome opportunity to build up his social circle. In many cases the Wood Rooster's own interests can help with this through bringing him into contact with other enthusiasts, and some good friendships can be formed as a result.

As far as financial matters are concerned, the Wood Rooster will fare well over the year, with many Wood Roosters receiving a bonus in addition to their usual earnings. With some of the plans the Wood Rooster will have in mind, this will certainly be welcome. However, he would still do well to keep track of his outgoings and plan his major purchases rather than proceed too hastily. Without care, some expensive mistakes and misjudgements could arise. Similarly, the Wood Rooster needs to be his vigilant self when dealing with important forms, especially any relating to tax or benefits.

Although the Monkey year will demand much of the Wood Rooster, by making the most of the situations that arise, particularly the changes in his work, he will be generally content with what he achieves. His personal life and interests can bring him much satisfaction.

TIP FOR THE YEAR
Be prepared to adapt. Although certain plans or ideas may not work out as you had hoped, interesting and sometimes better possibilities could emerge in their wake.

The Fire Rooster
The Fire Rooster can do well in the Monkey year, but in order to benefit he will need to show a certain flexibility in his outlook.

In his work the Fire Rooster will be able to make much of his skills and experience and will often find himself in a strong position when new openings or promotion opportunities arise. However, he could be forced to make some tricky decisions. Sometimes the offers made to him or the chances that arise will be different from those he was envisaging or in areas in which he is not so familiar. However, by looking positively at what occurs, the Fire Rooster will be able to widen his experience and, in the process, open up other possibilities for the future. He should also remember that there are many routes to the top and the events of the Monkey year will give him the chance to develop and impress in another capacity.

The Monkey year can also present some interesting opportunities for those Fire Roosters seeking work. By pursuing positions that interest them as well as being flexible in what they are prepared to consider, many will secure a position which will add to their skills as well as offer scope for future development. Work-wise, the Monkey year can be a significant time, but to benefit the Fire Rooster must be adaptable in his outlook. March, May, September and October can bring some interesting developments.

With the progress he makes in his work, the Fire Rooster can look forward to a rise in income over the year, but money matters do need careful handling. Many Fire Roosters will be particularly keen to make sizeable purchases for their accommodation, including replacing furnishings and making other improvements, but before proceeding with an expensive purchase, the Fire Rooster does need to take the time to compare ranges and prices as well as thoroughly check any obligations he may be taking on. This can prevent problems later. The Fire Rooster would also find it helpful to budget for forthcoming expenses. The more control he has over his finances, the more he will find he can ultimately do. He should also aim to set some money aside for a holiday over the year. With his generally busy lifestyle he does need (and deserve) a proper break, and a change of scene will do him good.

The Fire Rooster will also see much activity in his home life and here his ability to organize will be a great asset, particularly with some of the family occasions that take place. These could include celebrating a wedding or birth of a grandchild. The Monkey year will certainly bring its moments of joy. However, while the Fire Rooster will play such a full and valued role in family life, he does need to liaise with others and be mindful of their views. He may have his own ideas, but discussion and a certain flexibility in attitude can do much to prevent possible differences of opinion or misunderstandings from arising. Also, despite the many calls on his time, it is important that he sets time aside to spend with those close to him. If he becomes too preoccupied with his own concerns, tensions could arise. Fire Roosters, take careful note.

The Fire Rooster should also make sure his social life and personal interests do not get squeezed out over the year, as they can provide an important balance to his lifestyle. By going to events that appeal to him as well as meeting friends and spending time on activities he enjoys, he will find both his social life and personal interests doing him good. Any Fire Rooster who may feel lonely or who, perhaps because of work commitments, has let his personal life suffer should make an effort to address this in the Monkey year. By balancing his activities and going out more, he could find his life becoming much more mean-ingful. For some, the Monkey year can bring the gift of significant romance.

The Monkey year does offer fine prospects for the Fire Rooster, but to benefit he does need to be flexible in his outlook and be prepared to make the most of the opportu-nities and situations that arise. With the right attitude, though, this can be a successful and significant year.

TIP FOR THE YEAR

Go with the enterprising spirit of the year and be prepared to adapt and to progress. What is achieved now can have far-reaching benefits. Also, do aim for a balanced lifestyle.

The Earth Rooster

The Monkey year will be a time of opportunity for the Earth Rooster, although to benefit he will need to be flexible in his attitude and willing to make the most of the situations that arise. Sometimes these may not always be ideal, but by rising to the challenge the Earth Rooster will not only be furthering his experience but also preparing the way for his future progress. The long-term effects of what he achieves or sets in motion can be significant.

As a result of the Earth Rooster's experience and standing, he will often find himself well placed over the year to put in for promotion and further responsibilities. Sometimes these may be slightly different from what he wanted, but by showing enthusiasm and commitment, he will quickly make an impact. Also, he could find that any new duties he takes on or changes to his role can open up possibilities for the future, sometimes in unexpected ways. For work opportunities, March, May, September and October are especially favourable.

The Monkey year also holds interesting prospects for those Earth Roosters wanting to move away from their present type of work and for those seeking work. Competition will be considerable and they could face disappointments in their quest, but by remaining persistent (a good Earth Rooster trait) and adaptable in outlook, many will make the breakthrough they want. And again, once given a chance, these Earth Roosters will rise to the challenge and quickly make their mark.

The Earth Rooster should also make the most of any training opportunities available to him. By keeping his skills up to date as well as learning new ones, he will enhance his prospects. And if there is a subject or interest he would like to discover more about, he should consider enrolling on a course or setting time aside for private reading and study. With his enquiring mind, he can make this a satisfying and beneficial aspect of the year.

While the Earth Rooster will have many demands on his time, it is also important that he balances his activities and allows time for recreational pursuits. These will not only bring him pleasure but also be a good way for him to relax and unwind. The Earth Rooster may be conscientious and busy himself with a great many things, but in the Monkey year he *must* give some time to himself rather than feel he has to be continually active. He will also benefit from any holiday or short breaks he takes as well as from activities which provide him with additional exercise.

As far as financial matters are concerned, this will be a year for care. While the Earth Rooster's income may increase, he has many obligations and plans, and should manage his money carefully, allowing for his obligations and budgeting for forthcoming expenses. Without such control, he could find his outgoings start to creep up and become far greater than he anticipated. Succumbing to too many temptations or impulsive purchases will not help.

This need for care also applies to the Earth Rooster's relations with others. Although the Monkey year will bring many happy and meaningful occasions, certain differences of opinion could arise which will require tactful handling. Sometimes, where younger relations are concerned, there could be differences in outlook or the Earth Rooster could have misgivings about ideas and plans put forward by others in his household. However, by being willing to talk over such matters and addressing them in an open and fair-minded way, the Earth Rooster can do much to defuse any difficulties and prevent them from undermining the good rapport he has with those around him. And while he will have much to keep him occupied over the year, by ensuring he spends time with those who are important to him and encouraging activities and interests everyone can enjoy, he can help to make his home life rewarding for everyone.

The Earth Rooster should also make sure his social life does not suffer due to the other demands on his time, as it will bring him pleasure as well as do him good. For those Earth Roosters who may be lonely or desire more companionship, a chance encounter with someone who shares similar interests could quickly become important.

Overall, the Monkey year can be a significant one for the Earth Rooster and by making the most of the opportunities that arise and being willing to adapt, he will not only make satisfying progress but also pave the way for his future progress, with next year being especially well aspected.

TIP FOR THE YEAR
Make the most of the opportunities that arise, whether they involve learning new skills or taking on new duties or

a new role. By showing willing and gaining further experience you will be doing your future prospects a lot of good.

FAMOUS ROOSTERS

Francis Bacon, Dame Janet Baker, Enid Blyton, Barbara Taylor Bradford, Sir Michael Caine, Enrico Caruso, Christopher Cazenove, Jean Chrétien, Eric Clapton, Joan Collins, Rita Coolidge, Craig David, Daniel Day Lewis, Sasha Distel, the Duke of Edinburgh, Gloria Estefan, Mohamed al Fayed, Bryan Ferry, Errol Flynn, Benjamin Franklin, Dawn French, Stephen Fry, Steffi Graf, Melanie Griffith, Deborah Harry, Goldie Hawn, Katherine Hepburn, Lleyton Hewitt, Quincy Jones, Diane Keaton, Anna Kournikova, D. H. Lawrence, David Livingstone, Ken Livingstone, Jayne Mansfield, Steve Martin, James Mason, W. Somerset Maugham, Paul Merton, Bette Midler, Van Morrison, Willie Nelson, Kim Novak, Yoko Ono, Dolly Parton, Michelle Pfeiffer, Priscilla Presley, Mary Quant, Nancy Reagan, Joan Rivers, Paul Scofield, Jenny Seagrove, George Segal, Carly Simon, Britney Spears, Johann Strauss, Sir Peter Ustinov, Richard Wagner, Serena Williams, Neil Young, Catherine Zeta-Jones.

10 FEBRUARY 1910 ⁓ 29 JANUARY 1911	*Metal Dog*
28 JANUARY 1922 ⁓ 15 FEBRUARY 1923	*Water Dog*
14 FEBRUARY 1934 ⁓ 3 FEBRUARY 1935	*Wood Dog*
2 FEBRUARY 1946 ⁓ 21 JANUARY 1947	*Fire Dog*
18 FEBRUARY 1958 ⁓ 7 FEBRUARY 1959	*Earth Dog*
6 FEBRUARY 1970 ⁓ 26 JANUARY 1971	*Metal Dog*
25 JANUARY 1982 ⁓ 12 FEBRUARY 1983	*Water Dog*
10 FEBRUARY 1994 ⁓ 30 JANUARY 1995	*Wood Dog*

THE
DOG

THE PERSONALITY OF THE DOG

Firmness of purpose is one of the most necessary sinews
of character, and one of the best instruments of success.
The Earl of Chesterfield, a Dog

The Dog is born under the signs of loyalty and anxiety. He
usually holds very firm views and beliefs and is the cham-
pion of good causes. He hates any sort of injustice or unfair
treatment and will do all in his power to help those less
fortunate than himself. He has a strong sense of fair play
and will be honourable and open in all his dealings.

The Dog is very direct and straightforward. He is never
one to skirt round issues and speaks frankly and to the
point. He can be stubborn, but he is more than prepared to
listen to the views of others and will try to be as fair as
possible in coming to his decisions. He will readily give
advice where it is needed and will be the first to offer assistance when things go wrong.

The Dog instils confidence wherever he goes and there
are many who admire him for his integrity and resolute
manner. He is a very good judge of character and he can
often form an accurate impression of someone very shortly
after meeting them. He is also very intuitive and can
frequently sense how things are going to work out long in
advance.

Despite his friendly and amiable manner, the Dog is not
a big socializer. He dislikes having to attend large functions
or parties and much prefers a quiet meal with friends or a
chat by the fire. He is an excellent conversationalist and is

often a marvellous raconteur of amusing stories and anec-
dotes. He is also quick-witted and his mind is always alert.

The Dog can keep calm in a crisis and although he does
have a temper, his outbursts tend to be short-lived. He is
loyal and trustworthy, but if he ever feels badly let down
or rejected by someone, he will rarely forgive or forget.

The Dog usually has very set interests. He prefers to
specialize and become an expert in a chosen area rather
than dabble in a variety of different activities. He usually
does well in jobs where he feels that he is being of service
to others and is often suited to careers in the social services,
the medical and legal professions and teaching. He does,
however, need to feel motivated in his work. He has to
have a sense of purpose and if ever this is lacking he can
quite often drift through life without ever achieving very
much. Once he has the motivation, however, very little can
prevent him from securing his objective.

Another characteristic of the Dog is his tendency to
worry and to view things rather pessimistically. Quite
often his worries are totally unnecessary and are of his
own making. Although it may be difficult, worrying is a
habit which the Dog should try to overcome.

The Dog is not materialistic or particularly bothered
about accumulating great wealth. As long as he has the
necessary money to support his family and to spend on the
occasional luxury, he is more than happy. However, when
he does have any spare money he tends to be rather a
spendthrift and does not always put his money to its best
use. He is also not a very good speculator and would be
advised to get professional advice before entering into any
major long-term investment.

The Dog will rarely be short of admirers, but he is not an easy person to live with. His moods are changeable and his standards high, but he will be loyal and protective to his partner and will do all in his power to provide a good and comfortable home. He can get on extremely well with those born under the signs of the Horse, Pig, Tiger and Monkey, and can also establish a sound and stable relationship with the Rat, Ox, Rabbit, Snake and another Dog, but will find the Dragon a bit too flamboyant for his liking. He will also find it difficult to understand the imaginative Goat and is likely to be highly irritated by the candid Rooster.

The female Dog is renowned for her beauty. She has a warm and caring nature, although until she knows someone well she can be both secretive and very guarded. She is highly intelligent and despite her calm and tranquil appearance she can be most ambitious. She enjoys sport and other outdoor activities and has a happy knack of finding bargains in the most unlikely of places. She can also get rather impatient when things do not work out as she would like.

The Dog usually has a very good way with children and can be a doting parent. He will rarely be happier than when he is helping someone or doing something that will benefit others. Providing he can cure himself of his tendency to worry, he will lead a very full and active life – and in that life he will make many friends and do a tremendous amount of good.

THE FIVE DIFFERENT TYPES OF DOG

In addition to the 12 signs of the Chinese zodiac there are five elements, and these have a strengthening or moderating influence on the sign. The effects of the five elements on the Dog are described below, together with the years in which the elements were exercising their influence. Therefore all Dogs born in 1910 and 1970 are Metal Dogs, those born in 1922 and 1982 are Water Dogs, and so on.

Metal Dog: 1910, 1970
The Metal Dog is bold, confident and forthright and sets about everything he does in a resolute and determined manner. He has a great belief in his abilities and has no hesitation about speaking his mind or devoting himself to some just cause. He can be rather serious at times and can become anxious and irritable when things are not going according to plan. He tends to have very specific interests and it would certainly help him if he were to broaden his outlook and become more involved in group activities. He is extremely loyal and faithful to his friends.

Water Dog: 1922, 1982
The Water Dog has a very direct and outgoing personality. He is an excellent communicator and has little trouble in persuading others to fall in with his plans. He does, however, have a somewhat carefree nature and is not as disciplined or as thorough as he should be in certain

matters. Neither does he keep as much control over his finances as he should, but he can be most generous to his family and friends and will make sure that they want for nothing. The Water Dog is usually very good with children and has a wide circle of friends.

Wood Dog: 1934, 1994

This Dog is a hard and conscientious worker and will usually make a favourable impression wherever he goes. He is less independent than some of the other types of Dog and prefers to work in a group rather than on his own. He is popular, has a good sense of humour and takes a keen interest in the activities of the various members of his family. He is often attracted to the finer things in life and can obtain much pleasure from collecting stamps, coins, pictures or antiques. He prefers to live in the country rather than the town.

Fire Dog: 1946

This Dog has a lively, outgoing personality and is able to establish friendships with remarkable ease. He is an honest and conscientious worker and likes to take an active part in all that is going on around him. He also likes to explore new ideas and providing he can get the necessary support and advice, he can often succeed where others have failed. He does, however, have a tendency to be stubborn. Providing he can overcome this, he can often achieve considerable fame and fortune.

Earth Dog: 1958

The Earth Dog is very talented and astute. He is method-ical and efficient and is capable of going far in his chosen profession. He tends to be rather quiet and reserved but has a very persuasive manner and usually secures his objectives without too much opposition. He is generous and kind and is always ready to lend a helping hand when it is needed. He is also held in very high esteem by his friends and colleagues and is usually most dignified in his appearance.

PROSPECTS FOR THE DOG IN 2004

The Chinese New Year starts on 22 January 2004. Until then, the old year, the Year of the Goat, is still making its presence felt.

The Year of the Goat (1 February 2003 to 21 January 2004) will have been a demanding one for the Dog and while it will have brought its achievements, it will also have had its frustrations and pressures. However, as it draws to a close, the Dog will find events moving more in his favour.

The Dog can make particularly useful progress in his work at this time, and for those seeking a position or wanting to make further headway, October and November 2003 will hold some interesting opportunities. In general, the closing months of the Goat year will give the Dog an excellent chance to use his skills in a more satisfying way.

The last quarter of the year will, though, be an expen-sive time and as far as possible the Dog should try to spread some of his seasonal purchases out as well as make early provision for end of year expenses. If there are any particularly expensive purchases he wants to make, he could save himself considerable outlay by waiting for more favourable buying opportunities rather than being too hasty.

On both a domestic and social level the Dog will find himself in demand at this time. However, with so much to do, he will need to stay well organized and keep his diary up to date. If there are any plans he wants to carry out or any matters concerning him, he should talk to those around him. Throughout the Goat year it is better for the Dog to be open rather than keep his thoughts to himself, especially as he does have a tendency to worry. In most cases he will find that others will be helpful and supportive and can put his mind to rest.

Although the Goat year will have brought its pressures, the Dog will still have accomplished and learned a great deal and he will be able to draw on this in the more positive Monkey year that follows.

The Year of the Monkey starts on 22 January and will be a rewarding one for the Dog. In his work he will be able to build on his more recent achievements and make good progress, while on a personal level, the Monkey year promises a busy and often exciting time.

As the Monkey year starts, the Dog should regard it as a time of opportunity. He does, after all, have much experience behind him and many hold him in high regard, and he should make the most of this. The onus to progress does rest with him and, as the year starts, he should resolve to make more of himself *and* his position.

Many Dogs will be able to successfully draw on the knowledge and contacts they have in their current work and will be ideal candidates for promotion. Accordingly, whenever openings occur, the Dog should put himself forward. Sometimes some of the vacancies that arise will be in areas different from what he is used to, but by indicating his interest, he will often be successful.

Some Dogs may, though, feel there are better prospects elsewhere. Over the year these Dogs, together with those seeking work, should widen the scope of positions they are prepared to consider. Once they do secure a post, they will often find their new duties a welcome contrast to their previous work and this will give them an added incentive to do well. For work opportunities, April to July is a well-aspected period, but this is very much a year when the Dog should seize the initiative and look to advance.

In addition, the Monkey year will provide the Dog with some excellent learning opportunities. Sometimes he can cover for absent colleagues and learn additional skills, or take advantage of training courses. By making the most of such opportunities, he can make his work more satisfying and enhance his prospects as well.

However, while there will be good opportunities for the Dog over the year, his commitment will often mean that he will work long hours and he should be careful this does not make too many incursions into other areas of his life. In the Monkey year he must ensure he has a balanced lifestyle.

To help with this, the Dog should make sure his interests and recreational pursuits are not squeezed out through lack of time or other commitments. Ideally, he should set a regular time aside for activities he enjoys and which help him relax and unwind. Also, he should make sure he looks after himself, taking regular exercise as well as eating a balanced diet. To make the most of himself and the fine opportunities the year will bring, he does need to keep in good form.

Over the year accommodation matters could also keep the Dog busy. He will often be keen to carry out improvements as well as buy comforts for his home. However, such projects do need careful planning and time to carry out. The Dog should keep his zealous nature in check and tackle household projects one at a time rather than start too many all at once.

There will also be quite a few Dogs who decide to move in 2004 and again this will involve considerable time and effort. Any Dog who does have the intention of moving would do well to prepare early with any sorting and packing he can do in advance helping to reduce the tasks that need to be done later. Moving will certainly bring its pressures, but once settled in his new home, the Dog will feel satisfied with what he has achieved.

The Dog will also be helped in much of what he does by the support of others and domestically this will be a fine year. Everyone in the Dog's household can gain from being open, giving advice and assisting each other with projects and interests. Also, by setting time aside for activities everyone can enjoy, including meals, trips out or other treats, the Dog will find his home life especially rewarding. In addition, many Dogs will have excellent cause for celebration – perhaps a wedding, a birth in the family, a house-warming, the Dog's own success or that of a close relation. The Monkey year certainly has a celebratory feel to it!

Although the Dog will have much to do over the year, he should also make sure his social life is not neglected, as it is an important aspect of his life. He will benefit from meeting up with friends and going to social events that appeal to him. Any Dogs who would like more companionship will find that by going out and meeting others, perhaps at a local or special interest group, they can soon build up some strong friendships. Again, the Monkey year *is* supportive of the Dog, but it does require him to take the initiative. For meeting others and socializing, the period from April to June and December are especially favourable times.

Another positively aspected area is finance and the Dog will not only see a rise in income over the year but could also enjoy some strokes of luck. However, to benefit, he should plan his purchases as well as make provision for forthcoming expenses, especially if he intends to move. The one thing he should avoid is squandering any additional money as he soon as he receives it rather than considering how it can best be used.

Overall, the Monkey year holds fine prospects for the Dog, but it does call on him to take action and to make the most of himself and the often very favourable opportunities.

The Metal Dog

As far as the different types of Dog are concerned, this will be a rewarding year for the Metal Dog. With Metal as his element, giving him determination, and his conscientious Dog nature, he will be keen to accomplish a great deal over the year and, as a result, will make good headway.

YOUR CHINESE HOROSCOPE 2004

Although the Metal Dog will have achieved much in the last few years, many Metal Dogs will still feel they are not making the most of their skills and potential and early in the year will consider how they can improve on their position. Although the Metal Dog will have ideas of his own, he should discuss them with those close to him as well as colleagues who can give him informed advice. He will find himself benefiting from what he is told as well as being encouraged in what he is hoping to do. Also, by giving thought to the direction of his career, he will find himself becoming more focused in his efforts as well as better able to identify suitable opportunities. Over the year, there will certainly be some excellent chances for the Metal Dog to progress in the direction he wants.

This also applies to those Metal Dogs seeking work. By deciding on the type of position they now want and following up suitable openings, many will be successful in their quest. The message for all Metal Dogs is to seize the initiative. With determination, this can be a year in which they can advance their career and give their prospects an encouraging boost.

All Metal Dogs, regardless of their present position, should also make full use of any training that may be available. Not only will this be helpful for their current situation, but in some cases learning or becoming more proficient in a particular skill could also open up new possibilities.

The progress the Metal Dog makes in his work will lead to a welcome increase in his income over the year and this again will tempt him to go ahead with some of his ideas. These could include a holiday to a place he has long wanted to visit as well as some comforts for his home. Some Metal Dogs will even decide to move. Whatever the Metal Dog decides to do, by giving careful consideration to his plans and purchases he will be pleased with the outcome.

With the Monkey year holding such encouraging aspects, the Metal Dog should further his interests too and perhaps follow up something that may have been intriguing him for some time. He can find his personal interests another rewarding and beneficial aspect of the year.

This will also be a busy year domestically. With the Metal Dog's own activities as well as those of others in his household, there will often be several different schedules to organize and reconcile. However, with a spirit of co-operation the Metal Dog will be content with how his home life develops. While some weeks will turn out especially busy, especially in March and November, there will also be many pleasurable times, including family holidays and treats. The Metal Dog will enjoy shared interests and activities as well as do much to support his loved ones. Those Metal Dogs with children in education will find that the encouragement they can offer will count for a great deal. As with all years, there will be times when views may clash or tiredness gives rise to irritability, but with understanding and a willingness to talk and help out, these will not mar an otherwise fine year.

Although his life will be busy, it is also important that the Metal Dog gives himself the time to go out and socialize. Social events offer him a good chance to unwind as well as provide a welcome break from other activities. Also, he could find his interests or work bringing him into contact with others with whom he can get on particularly well and he will forge some important new friendships as a result.

Overall, the Monkey year holds considerable potential for the Metal Dog and by making the most of his talents and ideas, he will find his efforts and determined approach well rewarded.

TIP FOR THE YEAR
Plan. Decide what you want and then set about making it happen. By being focused as well as making the most of the opportunities that arise, you can achieve a great deal and make good progress.

The Water Dog

This will be an exciting year for the Water Dog, bringing both change and opportunity. Also, he will enjoy a fair amount of luck, as the aspects are firmly on his side.

The Water Dog's personal life is especially well aspected and over the year he will have every cause for celebration. Some Water Dogs will get engaged or married, see an addition to their family or celebrate a splendid personal achievement. Also, the Water Dog will be greatly encouraged by the love of another and this support will give an added lift to the year. For Water Dogs who are unattached, the prospects for romance are excellent. For socializing, late March to July is a favourably aspected time, but such is a promising nature of the year that romance and key personal developments could occur at almost any time.

The Water Dog will enjoy his social life over the year and he will rarely find himself at a loss for things to do or places to go. Also, he could find his interests have a good social element to them. Whether he follows sport, enjoys music or dancing or has other interests, he will find them leading to some pleasing occasions and sometimes new friendships too. The Water Dog will also be pleased with the way he is able to further his interests and by adding to his knowledge, meeting other enthusiasts and setting himself stimulating projects, he will take much satisfaction from what he is able to do over the year.

This also applies to his own personal development, particularly vocationally. During the Monkey year the Water Dog would do well to add to his skills and, if possible, his qualifications too. Some Water Dogs may already be on academic courses and the effort they make as they prepare for examinations will be well rewarded. With their working life ahead of them and the ambitions they have, these Water Dogs know this time of preparation and learning will be particularly important.

This emphasis on learning also applies to those Water Dogs in work. By showing a willingness to master the various aspects of his job as well as taking advantage of any training opportunities, the Water Dog will quickly mark himself out as one keen to advance and could, as the year progresses, be offered the chance to take on greater responsibilities. As he will find, that extra effort can pay sizeable dividends.

For those Water Dogs who are seeking work or who are dissatisfied in their present position, the Monkey year will also bring some good opportunities, but to benefit the

Water Dog *must* take the initiative and put himself forward. That is the nature of the year. However, by making enquiries, following up possible openings and remaining persistent, many Water Dogs will be given what can be an excellent chance to add to their experience and enhance their prospects. For work opportunities, the months from April to early August are well aspected.

The Monkey year also has an enterprising spirit to it and those Water Dogs whose work involves an element of creativity should make the most of their talents and ideas. With luck on their side, the support of others and their often innovative approach, some could find their ideas developing in an encouraging manner. Again, this is a year to be bold and forthcoming.

As far as finance is concerned, the Water Dog will see an increase in his income over the year, but he will have a great many obligations as well as many plans. However, with careful management, he will be generally pleased with what he is able to do as well as some of the bargains and special opportunities he spots. Also, quite a few Water Dogs will be tempted to travel over the year and could find it helpful to save up for their trips in advance. Generally, the Water Dog's resourcefulness will serve him well in 2004.

If, though, at any time he does have any concerns or uncertainties over decisions he has to make, he should remember there are many – including more senior relations – who will be keen to help and advise him, should he ask.

Overall, the Monkey year can be an important one for the Water Dog, but it does rest with him to make the most of his opportunities. On a personal level, he will find himself much in demand, with love and romance and some great personal events helping to make this a special year.

TIP FOR THE YEAR
Be bold and put yourself forward. As a Water Dog you have great personal qualities and strengths. Make the most of these in 2004 and you will be well rewarded.

The Wood Dog

This will be a satisfying year for the Wood Dog, with many of his activities developing well and bringing him pleasure.

For the Wood Dog born in 1994 the Monkey year is especially well aspected. The young Wood Dog will make good progress as well as further his interests and skills. However, to benefit from the favourable aspects, he does need to put in some effort and make the most of the chances available to him. By applying himself to his school-work in particular, he will find himself building an excellent base for when he moves on to more advanced work.

This will also be an excellent year for the young Wood Dog to further his skills and interests. Those keen on sport, drama, learning an instrument or some other activity should take advantage of any clubs or classes either at school or near where they live. And if the Wood Dog does not have a particular activity to do in his spare time and sees something that appeals to him, he should mention it and see what can be arranged.

The young Wood Dog will also value his close group of friends and he could find his social circle widening as he involves himself in more out-of-school activities and has the chance to meet others.

There will also be many aspects of his home life that he will enjoy, including the chance to help more with some household activities. He will appreciate the support and interest shown by those around him and by being forthcoming about what he is doing or would like to do, he will gain from the encouragement and advice others are able to give. Also, should he have any worries or problems, he will be helped by talking these over rather than keeping them to himself.

For those Wood Dogs born in 1934, this will also be a promising year. However, as it starts, these more senior Wood Dogs would do well to give some thought to what they would like to do over the year. Their plans can concern their accommodation, travel or furthering particular interests, but by having some aims and talking them over with others, the Wood Dog will find his ideas often developing in an encouraging manner.

Many Wood Dogs will decide to spend time on their accommodation and garden over the year, adding features, tidying up certain areas and carrying out other projects. By planning these activities with family members, the Wood Dog will take great satisfaction in what he accomplishes. However, where practical activities are concerned, he does need to allow plenty of time as well as be careful if undertaking anything strenuous or hazardous.

The more senior Wood Dogs will also enjoy spending time on their interests, with those that have a practical and creative element being especially pleasurable. If the Wood Dog is able to join fellow enthusiasts or set himself some interesting projects, he will often find himself becoming more inspired and knowledgeable about what he does as a result. Some Wood Dogs may also enjoy activities that involve writing and research, perhaps recounting their own experiences, studying family or local history or passing on specialist knowledge. By doing something they enjoy and feel has purpose, they will find their interests a very satisfying aspect of the year.

The Monkey year will also bring some excellent travel opportunities and all Wood Dogs should take advantage of invitations they receive to visit family and friends who may live some distance away, as well as follow up some of their own travel ideas. The travelling the Wood Dog does undertake can often bring him much pleasure.

The more senior Wood Dog will also value the support given by those around him and if at any time he does have any matters concerning him, he should not hesitate to raise them, or if applicable, contact those who can give him informed advice. By being forthcoming, rather than keeping his concerns to himself, he will find others are better able to assist and advise. At all times he should remember that help *is* available should he need it.

He will also be blessed with a certain amount of luck over the year, and if he sees a competition which interests him, he would do well to enter it. He could also be fortunate in some of the purchases he makes, including spotting certain items he may have been wanting at a very favourable price. His eye for a good buy will certainly serve him well in 2004.

Overall, the Monkey year will be a favourable one for the Wood Dog and, whether born in 1934 or 1994, he should make good use of his ideas and the opportunities that arise. His interests will bring him especial pleasure and he will also be grateful for the support of his loved ones and his good friends.

TIP FOR THE YEAR
Be open with your ideas and plans. By seeking support and advice you will find what you want will have a far greater chance of being realized.

The Fire Dog

The Monkey year holds fine prospects for the Fire Dog and will give him a good chance to use his talents and make the most of his ideas. In addition his home and social life, although busy, will bring him great pleasure.

The Fire Dog has always been a doer and his desire for action will bring him some substantial rewards over the year. In his work, in particular, he will find his approach and extensive experience will enable him to make important progress. Many Fire Dogs will take on greater responsibilities as the year develops. While these could sometimes involve a considerable change in duties, the Fire Dog will revel in the chance to tackle something new. The year will also allow him to further some of his ideas and he could find these are well received. The Monkey year is certainly a year for enterprise, and the Fire Dog, with his commitment and experience, can be a major beneficiary of the prevailing trends.

While many Fire Dogs will remain with their present employer and will benefit from the knowledge and contacts they already have, some will feel the time is right for change. By following through their ideas and looking for positions which allow them to use their skills in other ways, many will be successful in securing a position which will suit them better. In some cases, their new position could also have other benefits, including less commuting or better working conditions. Certainly these Fire Dogs will feel that the change represents a fresh opportunity and a chance to further themselves.

Similarly, Fire Dogs seeking work will find that by following up openings which appeal to them they will often be successful in their quest. Although sometimes there will be heavy competition for the positions they are applying for, by finding out more about the company and job itself, their informed comments can tip the balance in their favour. Late March to July could see some of the best work opportunities, but generally the Monkey year is a time to seize the initiative and to follow through ideas.

The year is also favourably aspected for the Fire Dog's personal interests and despite the pressure on his time, he should make sure he does not neglect these. Any Fire Dogs who may have let their interests lapse, perhaps due to work or other commitments, should address this over the year and make sure they give themselves time to spend in the way *they* want. The Fire Dog's interests and recreational pursuits can have great benefits for him as well as bringing a balance to his life.

The Monkey year will also see much activity in the Fire Dog's personal and social life. At home the Fire Dog's practical nature will often get the better of him and he will be keen to embark on improvements, including altering the décor of certain rooms and adding new comforts to his home. However, while he may be eager to set his ideas in motion, he does need to discuss them fully with others as well as consider the choices available. In some cases, too much haste could lead to less satisfactory results. Fire Dogs, take note and do allow plenty of time for practical activities.

The Fire Dog will also do much to help and encourage those around him over the year and others will set great store by his views. The support and advice he can offer younger relations will be especially valued. His general input into family life will also be appreciated and while there will often be much domestic activity, with various family members leading busy lifestyles, the Fire Dog's ability to draw everything together and come up with ideas everyone can enjoy will be highly valued. The Fire Dog will do a lot to help others and if he is under any pressure or has concerns of his own, he too should be forthcoming and ask for advice or assistance. He will be grateful for the help he is given and those around him will often be glad to reciprocate his kindnesses.

The Fire Dog's social life is favourably aspected, particularly with regard to the widening of his social circle. Whether this is due to changes in his work, his interests bringing him into contact with others or simply the decision to go out more, the Monkey year can mark a substantial upturn in the Fire Dog's social life. Any Fire Dogs who would welcome more companionship will find the Monkey year can give them the chance to move their life forward and forge some important friendships. Again, the Monkey year *is* an encouraging one for the Fire Dog.

As far as his finances are concerned, the Monkey year is also capable of springing some surprises. This could include a bonus payment or the fruition of a policy the Fire Dog may not have been expecting. The Fire Dog can certainly look forward to receiving some extra money over the year. To benefit, though, he should think carefully about what to do with anything extra rather than be too hasty in spending it. The better he manages his resources, the more satisfied he will be.

Overall, the Monkey year holds good prospects for the Fire Dog and by taking advantage of the opportunities it will bring, he will find it a fulfilling time.

TIP FOR THE YEAR
Spend time on personal interests. These can be beneficial and enjoyable as well as provide an important balance to your life. In some cases they could also lead to new friend-ships.

The Earth Dog
The Earth Dog is set to do well in the Monkey year. Both his personal life and work prospects look encouraging, and by making the most of himself and his talents, he can make this a most rewarding year.

Over the last year many Earth Dogs will have seen changes in the nature of their work and in the Monkey year they will be able to build on recent developments and make further headway. With the Earth Dog's experience and contacts, this will be a time to advance. In addition, the Earth Dog will be blessed with a fair amount of luck.

Sometimes he could find himself in the right place to benefit from opportunities or become involved in a project which has a great deal of potential. By remaining alert and taking action when opportunities arise, he can certainly make good progress, with late March to July being a particularly favourable time.

The Earth Dog should also take advantage of any training opportunities. Keeping himself informed of the latest developments and learning new techniques and skills will be helpful both for what he does now and for new possibilities later on. Training and personal development really can be of great benefit to him over the year.

With his experience and practical nature, the Earth Dog will also often find himself coming up with thoughts on how certain things could be improved or ideas he feels could be developed. Instead of keeping these to himself and risk them coming to nothing, he should put them forward and see where they lead. With the Monkey year favouring enterprise, he could find his ideas and contributions much appreciated and, in some instances, having important implications.

For those Earth Dogs who are seeking work or who feel the time is now right for change, again the Monkey year will hold some fine opportunities. Admittedly, they may sometimes face much competition and have to overcome some rejections in their quest, but by keeping faith with their abilities and stressing their experience and what they have to offer, these Earth Dogs can secure a good position with fine prospects for the future.

This will also be a positive year for money matters, with the Earth Dog not only seeing an increase in his income but in many cases also receiving an additional payment or bonus. However, despite the favourable aspects, the Earth Dog does need to manage his resources carefully if he is to benefit. This includes setting funds aside for known requirements, adding, if he can, to his savings and reducing some of his borrowings. The more care and control he has over his finances, the better he will find his position will be. Also, rather than being in too great a hurry to spend anything extra he receives, he should consider any large purchases carefully. That way he will find them all the more satisfying and may sometimes be able to buy them on more favourable terms too.

The Monkey year will also be a pleasing one for personal matters. Although family life will be busy, the Earth Dog will value the many rewarding times it will bring. These will include occasions everyone can enjoy, any domestic projects the Earth Dog and others decide to tackle, and interests and other activities that can be shared. The Monkey year will also bring some memorable occasions, including a fine family holiday, as well as good cause for a celebration. And throughout the year the Earth Dog will be encouraged by the support and love of those who are important to him.

As far as his social life is concerned, he may be more selective in the times he goes out, but he will find the social events he does attend are a good way for him to unwind and enjoy himself as well as meet others. For some Earth Dogs, the Monkey year can bring the gift of a wonderful new friendship. For socializing, the period from April to June and the month of December are especially favourable times.

Although the Earth Dog will have much to occupy him over the year, it is important that his personal interests are not squeezed out, and to prevent this, he should set a regular time aside for activities he enjoys. He will not only take a great deal of satisfaction from most of what he does, especially more creative projects and those that take him out of doors, but he will also find that his interests provide an important balance to all his other activities.

Overall, the Monkey year holds excellent prospects for the Earth Dog and by making the most of himself and the opportunities that arise, he can look forward to making some good and well-deserved progress. His professional interests are well aspected and his home life and relations with others will also bring him pleasure and mean a great deal to him.

TIP FOR THE YEAR
Take action. This is a year for enterprise, for following up ideas and making the most of your talents. You have much to offer and the Monkey year can reward you well.

FAMOUS DOGS

André Agassi, King Albert II of Belgium, Elizabeth Arden, Jane Asher, Brigitte Bardot, Gary Barlow, Candice Bergman, David Bowie, Bertolt Brecht, George W. Bush, Kate Bush, Laura Bush, Max Bygraves, Naomi Campbell, Mariah Carey, King Carl XVI Gustaf of Sweden, José Carreras, Paul Cézanne, Cher, Sir Winston Churchill, Petula Clark, Bill Clinton, Leonard Cohen, Jamie Lee

Curtis, Charles Dance, Claude Debussy, Dame Judi Dench, Blake Edwards, Sally Field, Joseph Fiennes, Robert Frost, Ava Gardner, Judy Garland, George Gerschwin, Barry Gibb, Lenny Henry, O. Henry, Victor Hugo, Barry Humphries, Holly Hunter, Michael Jackson, Al Jolson, Felicity Kendal, Jennifer Lopez, Sophia Loren, Joanna Lumley, Shirley MacLaine, Madonna, Norman Mailer, Barry Manilow, Freddie Mercury, Liza Minelli, Samantha Mumba, David Niven, Gary Numan, Sydney Pollack, Elvis Presley, Lord George Robertson, Paul Robeson, Linda Ronstadt, Gabriela Sabatini, Susan Sarandon, Jennifer Saunders, Claudia Schiffer, Dr Albert Schweitzer, Sylvester Stallone, Robert Louis Stevenson, Sharon Stone, Jack Straw, David Suchet, Donald Sutherland, Chris Tarrant, Mother Teresa, Uma Thurman, Donald Trump, Voltaire, Prince William, Shelley Winters.

30 JANUARY 1911 ～ 17 FEBRUARY 1912		*Metal Pig*
16 FEBRUARY 1923 ～ 4 FEBRUARY 1924		*Water Pig*
4 FEBRUARY 1935 ～ 23 JANUARY 1936		*Wood Pig*
22 JANUARY 1947 ～ 9 FEBRUARY 1948		*Fire Pig*
8 FEBRUARY 1959 ～ 27 JANUARY 1960		*Earth Pig*
27 JANUARY 1971 ～ 14 FEBRUARY 1972		*Metal Pig*
13 FEBRUARY 1983 ～ 1 FEBRUARY 1984		*Water Pig*
31 JANUARY 1995 ～ 18 FEBRUARY 1996		*Wood Pig*

THE
PIG

THE PERSONALITY OF THE PIG

For the resolute and determined there is time and opportunity.

Ralph Waldo Emerson, a Pig

The Pig is born under the sign of honesty. He has a kind and understanding nature and is well known for his abilities as a peacemaker. He hates any sort of discord or unpleasantness and will do everything in his power to sort out differences of opinion or bring opposing factions together.

He is also an excellent conversationalist and speaks truthfully and to the point. He dislikes any form of falsehood or hypocrisy and is a firm believer in justice and the maintenance of law and order. In spite of these beliefs, however, the Pig is reasonably tolerant and often prepared to forgive others for their wrongs. He rarely harbours grudges and is never vindictive.

The Pig is usually very popular. He enjoys other people's company and likes to be involved in joint or group activities. He will be a loyal member of any club or society and can be relied upon to lend a helping hand at functions. He is also an excellent fundraiser for charities and is often a great supporter of humanitarian causes.

The Pig is a hard and conscientious worker and is particularly respected for his reliability and integrity. In his early years he will try his hand at several different jobs, but he is usually happiest where he feels that he is being of service to others. He will unselfishly give up his time for the common good and is highly valued by his colleagues and employers.

The Pig has a good sense of humour and invariably has a smile, joke or some whimsical remark at the ready. He loves to entertain and to please others, and there are many Pigs who have been attracted to careers in show business or who enjoy following the careers of famous stars and personalities.

There are, unfortunately, some who take advantage of the Pig's good nature and impose upon his generosity. The Pig has great difficulty in saying 'no' and, although he may dislike being firm, it would be in his own interests to say occasionally, 'Enough is enough.' The Pig can also be rather naïve and gullible; however, if at any stage in his life he feels that he has been badly let down, he will make sure that it will never happen again and will try to become self-reliant. There are many Pigs who have become entrepreneurs or forged a successful career on their own after some early disappointment in life. Although the Pig tends to spend his money quite freely, he is usually very astute in financial matters and there are many Pigs who have become wealthy.

Another characteristic of the Pig is his ability to recover from setbacks reasonably quickly. His faith and his strength of character keep him going. If he thinks that there is a job he can do or he has something that he wants to achieve, he will pursue it with a dogged determination. He can also be stubborn and, no matter how many may plead with him, once he has made his mind up he will rarely change his views.

Although the Pig may work hard, he also knows how to enjoy himself. He is a great pleasure-seeker and will quite happily spend his hard-earned money on a lavish holiday or an expensive meal – for the Pig is a connoisseur of good food and wine – or taking part in a variety of recreational activities. He also enjoys small social gatherings and if he is in company he likes he can very easily become the life and soul of the party. He does, however, tend to become rather withdrawn at larger functions or when among strangers.

The Pig is a creature of comfort and his home will usually be fitted with all the latest in luxury appliances. Where possible, he will prefer to live in the country rather than the town and will opt to have a big garden, for the Pig is usually a keen and successful gardener.

The Pig is very popular with others and will often have numerous romances before he settles down. Once settled, however, he will be loyal to his partner and he will find that he is especially well suited to those born under the signs of the Goat, Rabbit, Dog and Tiger and also to another Pig. Due to his affable and easy-going nature he can also establish a satisfactory relationship with all the remaining signs of the Chinese zodiac, with the exception of the Snake. The Snake tends to be wily, secretive and very guarded, and this can be intensely irritating to the honest and open-hearted Pig.

The female Pig will devote all her energies to the needs of her children and her partner. She tries to ensure that they want for nothing and their pleasure is very much her pleasure. She can be a caring and conscientious parent and has very good taste in clothes. Her home will either be very clean and orderly or hopelessly untidy. Strangely, there seems to be no in between with Pigs – they either love housework or detest it! The female Pig does, however, have considerable talents as an organizer and this, combined with her friendly and open manner, enables her to secure many of her objectives.

The Pig is usually lucky in life and will rarely want for anything. Provided he does not let others take advantage of his good nature and is not afraid of asserting himself, he will go through life making friends, helping others and winning the admiration of many.

THE FIVE DIFFERENT TYPES OF PIG

In addition to the 12 signs of the Chinese zodiac there are five elements, and these have a strengthening or moderating influence on the sign. The effects of the five elements on the Pig are described below, together with the years in which the elements were exercising their influence. Therefore all Pigs born in 1911 and 1971 are Metal Pigs, those born in 1923 and 1983 are Water Pigs, and so on.

Metal Pig: 1911, 1971
The Metal Pig is more ambitious and determined than some of the other types of Pig. He is strong, energetic and likes to be involved in a wide variety of different activities. He is very open and forthright in his views, although he can be a little too trusting at times and has a tendency to accept things at face value. He has a good sense of humour and loves to attend parties and other social gatherings. He has a warm, outgoing nature and usually has a large circle of friends.

Water Pig: 1923, 1983

The Water Pig has a heart of gold. He is generous and loyal and tries to remain on good terms with everyone. He will do his utmost to help others, but sadly there are some who will take advantage of his kind nature and he should, in his own interests, be a little more discriminating and be prepared to stand firm against anything that he does not like. Although he prefers the quieter things in life, he has a wide range of interests. He particularly enjoys outdoor pursuits and attending parties and social occasions. He is a hard and conscientious worker and invariably does well in his chosen profession. He is also gifted in the art of communication.

Wood Pig: 1935, 1995

This Pig has a friendly, persuasive manner and is easily able to gain the confidence of others. He likes to be involved in all that is going on around him but can sometimes take on more responsibility than he can properly handle. He is loyal to his family and friends and derives much pleasure from helping those less fortunate than himself. The Wood Pig is usually an optimist and leads a very full, enjoyable and satisfying life. He also has a good sense of humour.

Fire Pig: 1947

The Fire Pig is both energetic and adventurous and he sets about everything he does in a confident and resolute manner. He is very forthright in his views and does not mind taking risks in order to achieve his objectives. He can, however, get carried away by the excitement of the moment and ought to exercise more caution in some of the enterprises in which he gets involved. The Fire Pig is usually lucky in money matters and is well known for his generosity. He is also very caring towards the members of his family.

Earth Pig: 1959

This Pig has a kindly nature. He is sensible and realistic and will go to great lengths in order to please his employers and to secure his aims and ambitions. He is an excellent organizer and is particularly astute in business and financial matters. He has a good sense of humour and a wide circle of friends. He also likes to lead an active social life, although he does sometimes have a tendency to eat and drink more than is good for him.

PROSPECTS FOR THE PIG IN 2004

The Chinese New Year starts on 22 January 2004. Until then, the old year, the Year of the Goat, is still making its presence felt.

The Year of the Goat (1 February 2003 to 21 January 2004) offers considerable scope for the Pig, with the closing months being favourably aspected. With his sociable nature, the Pig will have found himself in demand over the Goat year and will often have enjoyed himself. Both his domestic and social life will have seen considerable activity and this will gather momentum as the year draws to a close. August, November and December 2003 will be particularly busy. And for those Pigs who may have had some recent personal difficulty or are seeking friendship or perhaps romance, the last quarter can bring the chance to meet someone who could become important.

The Pig should also give consideration to his well-being at this time. As he likes to live life so much to the full, there will be times when he could be tempted to skimp on sleep or become over-reliant on convenience foods, and without care he could find himself lacking his usual energy and sparkle. Pigs, take note and do look after yourselves!

As far as the Pig's work is concerned, the Goat year will have given him a good chance to add to his experience and while opportunities may not have been plentiful, he will have been able to make steady progress. For those looking to advance or seeking work, November could bring some interesting openings.

The closing months will, though, be an expensive time and in view of this, if the Pig is able to save towards end of year expenses and spread out some of his more seasonal purchases he should do so.

The Year of the Monkey starts on 22 January and will be an interesting one for the Pig. Although not all his activities may go as well as he would like, by rising to the challenges and opportunities that the year will bring, he can make good progress. His personal life holds much promise, with affairs of the heart being especially well aspected.

At work the Monkey year will not be without its chances or successes but the Pig will need to work hard for them. Also, there are certain points he needs to bear in mind. Perhaps most importantly, this is *not* a year when he can be too independent in attitude or act without support. Fortunately, the Pig is usually adept at forging good relationships and liaising with others, but in 2004 he cannot afford to neglect this if he wishes to make progress. The more support he has, the better he will fare.

Also, although the Pig usually sets about his activities in determined style, there could be certain tasks which he considers unnecessary or burdensome. However, in many cases these still need to be done and if the Pig appears too dilatory or less than thorough, he could be storing up problems for himself. In 2004 he needs to remain his efficient *and* thorough self!

However, provided the Pig remains aware of the trickier aspects and makes an extra effort both in carrying out his duties and in maintaining good relations with colleagues, then he will find the year does provide some good opportunities. In some cases his experience will lead to him being given further responsibilities and possible promotion, while those Pigs who want a change or who are seeking work will find the Monkey year bringing interesting developments. Although their quest may not be easy and there will be disappointments when certain applications do not go their way, by remaining persistent, these Pigs will often secure a position which will not only be an improvement on what they have been doing but also bring with it an exciting new personal challenge. And, as has been shown so many times, challenge does bring out the best in the Pig.

For work opportunities, March to June and October are favourable times. The Pig will need to work hard to progress, but with his determination and fine personal qualities, he has it within him to make important headway.

As far as financial matters are concerned, the Monkey year calls for care and restraint. There will be many temptations to spend and, without some watchfulness, the Pig could find his outgoings becoming far greater than he anticipated or allowed for. Also, if he wants to make a major purchase, he could find it better to consider his choices carefully and wait for more favourable buying opportunities rather than be too hasty. If he does find his borrowings are mounting up, he could find it helpful to look at his financial position and see whether any modifications can be made. By managing his resources and watching his spending, he can do much to avoid problems and prevent shortfalls from arising. This is, though, a year for care.

More positively, the Pig's personal life is splendidly aspected. For the unattached or those newly in love, the year will hold some wonderful times. Existing romances, including those formed in the last quarter of the Goat year, will often blossom, while for the unattached or lonely there will be many chances to meet others, including someone who could become very special. Many Pigs, with their loving nature and genial disposition, will win the heart of another during the year. For meeting others, the months from April to June and August and September are well aspected and such is the nature of the year that many Pigs will get engaged or settle down with their partner. This is indeed a romantic and heady year for the Pig.

The Pig will also enjoy his domestic life. As he is aware, close relationships have to be nurtured and his willingness to spend time with those who are important to him is another reason why, on a personal level, the Monkey year can go so well. Pigs with families will find that their love and care for their children, as well as more senior relations, will also be valued and will help maintain the special bond the Pig considers so important.

However, no year is free from its more difficult moments and 2004 will be no exception. When problems or differences of opinion do arise the Pig should not, as some may be tempted to do, turn a blind eye, but talk over matters and see whether a solution or compromise can be found. Better a compromise than letting problems linger and sour an otherwise agreeable time.

With the aspects as they are, any Pig who starts the year at a low personal ebb should regard the Monkey year as heralding a new chapter in his life and should resolve to move forward. By going out more, taking up different interests and taking charge of his situation, he will find his outlook and prospects becoming much brighter. For personal matters, the Monkey year does hold much promise.

Overall, although the Pig will need to proceed carefully in the Monkey year and ensure he is both thorough and careful in work and financial matters, on a personal level the year will give rise to many treasured moments. And for many Pigs the love of another will make this a *very* special time.

The Metal Pig

As far as the different types of Pig are concerned, the Monkey year holds much promise for the Metal Pig. With his ambitious nature and ability to make the most of himself, he is set to make deserving progress over the year. In addition his personal life and interests will bring him a great deal of pleasure.

In his work the Metal Pig will quickly discover that this is no ordinary year. Changes are afoot and almost all Metal Pigs will see substantial alterations to their role. By remaining alert to proposals under consideration and acting quickly when opportunities arise, the Metal Pig can make progress. In many cases his experience will see him well placed for promotion or greater responsibilities. March to early June and October could be interesting months, but generally this is a year when events happen quickly.

Despite the encouraging aspects, however, the Monkey year does require care and vigilance. The Metal Pig does need to liaise well with colleagues, show himself a good team member and secure and maintain the support of others. Also, even though pressures may sometimes be great, he should not let his standards slip. To be less than thorough with certain duties or paperwork could cause problems.

For those Metal Pigs seeking work the Monkey year will provide some interesting chances. Again, they will need to remain persistent, but by deciding on the type of work they would like and stressing their experience and potential contribution, many will be successful in gaining a suitable position. Although this may demand a lot of them and sometimes involve learning new skills, by making the most of the opportunities they are given, these Metal Pigs will gain valuable experience and, in the process, do their prospects much good.

As far as financial matters are concerned, this is a year for care. In 2004 the Metal Pig will face many expenses, particularly relating to family activities and travel, and he does need to watch his spending. He could find it helpful to save towards some of his more sizeable purchases and outgoings. Also, while he has both a generous nature and enjoys reaping the fruits of his endeavours, if he succumbs to too many moments of extravagance or impulse buying his spending could quickly mount up and problems could arise. This is also not a year for risks or for committing money to undertakings without thorough investigation. The Monkey year can cost the unwary dear. Metal Pigs, take note and do control those purse strings.

More positively, the Metal Pig will greatly enjoy his interests and recreational pursuits over the year. Not only will many of these have a social element, allowing him to meet up with friends and enthusiasts, but they will also bring him much satisfaction. And whether his interests are creative, practical or involve the outdoors, the Metal Pig will often find them a welcome contrast to his other activities.

This is also a favourable year for personal matters, with the Metal Pig's domestic and social life seeing much activity. He will take a fond interest in the activities of those in his household and his organizational ability will prove a great asset. So too will his ability to empathize, and whenever anyone around him is under pressure or has concerns, his considerate nature will be much appreciated. Some more senior relatives will be especially grateful for the Metal Pig's attention and help. He will also enjoy many of the domestic activities that take place and the year could see some particularly pleasurable family events, including holidays, trips and get-togethers.

On a social level this will also be a busy year, with the Metal Pig regularly meeting up with friends, receiving invitations and going out to a variety of social functions. In true Metal Pig style, he will enjoy himself a great deal and often find his circle of friends and acquaintances growing as the year progresses. Metal Pigs who may have had some recent personal difficulties will find the Monkey year can mark the start of a much happier time, with many enjoying a new romance or finding an activity which they feel has real value.

Overall, the Monkey year holds good prospects for the Metal Pig and by making the most of his talents and the situations that arise *and* working hard, he can make rewarding headway, while, on a personal level, he will find this a positive and enjoyable year.

TIP FOR THE YEAR
Be vigilant and thorough. Give your best and maintain your high standards and you will be well rewarded.

The Water Pig

This will be an exciting year for the Water Pig and while it will not be without its pressures or more challenging moments, a lot *will* go in his favour.

Especially well aspected is the Water Pig's personal life. For those in love, the year will bring some wonderful times. There will be interests to share and, for some, the joy of setting up home together. Encouraged by the love of another, the Water Pig will grow in confidence and find himself taking more control of his life rather than just letting things happen. This increasing sense of responsibility will be one of the most important aspects of the Monkey year, helping the Water Pig to make more of himself and start to realize his true potential.

For those Water Pigs who are unattached or who may have found previous romances were not to be, the Monkey year holds excellent prospects, with many meeting their future partner and soul mate. Sometimes such a meeting could come about in a fortuitous way and within a short time these Water Pigs' lives can be transformed. For meeting others, the months of April, May, August and September are especially favourable, but personally, the Monkey year holds excellent prospects.

The Water Pig will also find himself in demand on a social level. There will be parties and plenty of other events to go to and rarely a week will go by without something to do or look forward to. Even for those Water Pigs who may be more selective in the times they go out, the Monkey year holds interesting prospects. Sometimes an interest they have will lead to a meeting with others or a change in circumstance will bring social invitations. The Monkey year *is* an encouraging and positive time for the Water Pig.

Another satisfying area concerns the Water Pig's personal development and he should make the most of any chance to add to his qualifications or skills. Those Water Pigs currently involved in study will find that by making an extra effort and keeping in mind the possible benefits their qualifications will bring, they can do well. Again, as far as his own development and skills are concerned, this will be an important year for the Water Pig, and one with long-term significance.

For those Water Pigs who are in work or who may be seeking work this will be a more challenging year. Although the Water Pig is keen to make the most of himself, he could find progress difficult. It may take those seeking work several attempts to be successful and the process will at times seem hard and disheartening. Sometimes those Water Pigs already in work may also feel disillusioned and consider that they could be making more of their skills or that it is proving hard to make the progress they would like. However, the Water Pig should remember he is still in the early stages of his career and what he is doing now will not only give him useful experience but also enable him to find out where his true strengths lie. For work opportunities the months from March to early July and October could see interesting developments.

One of the more awkwardly aspected areas of the year concerns finance. With many Water Pigs taking on new commitments, particularly accommodation-wise, as well as leading an active personal and social life, their resources will often be stretched. As a result, the Water Pig will need to keep a close watch on his spending and if he has to borrow, make sure he gets the most favourable terms. Money matters do need great care over the year and when taking on any new obligations, the Water Pig must check the details and implications carefully. This is not a year for risks.

The Water Pig will, though, find more senior family members particularly helpful over the year. While he may not always want to trouble them, he should tell them about any concerns he may have as well as letting them share in his successes. Family bonds are important to the Water Pig and he should remember he does have others to turn to should he need advice.

Generally, the Monkey year will be one of mixed fortunes for the Water Pig. On a personal and social level the aspects are excellent and he will also take a good deal of satisfaction from his interests and personal development. However, work-wise and financially, the Monkey year does require care. But, despite the demands and pressures he may face, the Water Pig will emerge from the Monkey year with more experience and often a clearer idea of how he would like his future to develop. And with so many Water Pigs enjoying the love of another, the future certainly looks promising.

TIP FOR THE YEAR
Look to others. You may have your own ideas and aspirations, but you do need support and advice. Be forthcoming and benefit from the help that those around are able to give.

The Wood Pig
The Monkey year holds much potential for the Wood Pig, allowing him to develop both himself and his ideas.

Wood Pigs born in 1935 will want to do a great deal over the year. Their ideas could range from alterations and additions to their home to interests they wish to pursue or places they would like to visit. When an idea strikes, the

Wood Pig should raise it with others. Sometimes he could be surprised to find that just mentioning his ideas starts a sequence of events that helps lead to their realization.

The Wood Pig will also be pleased with how supportive those around him are, and again, by asking for opinions – even, for example, when out shopping – he will be grateful for the advice that others can give. Similarly the assistance he receives with practical projects can make a real difference, and if he wants to carry out any major undertaking or strenuous activity, he should ask for help.

This need to be forthcoming also applies to any matters that may be concerning the Wood Pig. Whether these are personal, financial or other concerns, it is important that he seeks guidance from those qualified to advise. In some cases, helplines can assist him. In the Monkey year the Wood Pig will find much truth in the maxim 'A worry shared is a worry halved.' Whenever he is worried, he *should* seek advice.

Over the year the Wood Pig will follow the activities of family members with fond interest and often be willing to help those with young children or those who may be under particular pressure. He can also look forward to several pieces of pleasing family news, including one which will fill him with pride. Family bonds are important to the Wood Pig and they will mean a lot to him during the Monkey year.

The Wood Pig will also take considerable pleasure from his interests. Not only will he find them an often absorbing and satisfying use of his time, but sometimes, by joining other enthusiasts or enrolling on a course, he will enjoy the social element too.

Similarly, he will value his social life, appreciating chatting to friends and also the various social occasions that he goes to. For some Wood Pigs, new friendships can come from their interests and activities, and from a social point of view the Wood Pig will find this an active and rewarding year.

There will also be opportunities for him to travel and if there are places he would like to go to or offers which appeal to him, he should see what is possible. Again, this is a year to follow up ideas and make the most of the chances available.

The most awkward area of the year will involve financial matters and the Wood Pig will need to be careful in his undertakings and to make sure he gets sound advice on any major transaction or agreement he may be considering. Care and attention are also needed when completing any forms related to finance. This is not a year for risks. Wood Pigs, take note.

For the Wood Pig born in 1995, this will be an encouraging year. Not only will these younger Wood Pigs learn much over the year but they will also enjoy being able to further their interests and skills. However, to benefit from the opportunities and support that are available, the young Wood Pig does need to be forthcoming as well as be prepared to follow up ideas and activities that interest him. With initiative and good backing, this can be a satisfying year for him.

Overall, the Monkey year holds much potential for the Wood Pig and by making the most of his ideas and opportunities, he will find this a personally rewarding and positive time.

TIP FOR THE YEAR

Always remember that help and support are available and if you need advice or have ideas you want to take further, do be forthcoming.

The Fire Pig

This will be a year of positive developments for the Fire Pig and while it will not be without its pressures or more challenging moments, he will be content with most of what he manages to achieve.

In his work the Fire Pig will often face a heavy workload, particularly as many Fire Pigs will take on fresh responsibilities or have to deal with new schemes and working practices. However, by being willing to adapt and making the most of the situations that arise, the Fire Pig will make useful headway as well as do his standing and prospects much good. In view of the variable aspects, however, he must be careful not to jeopardize his position by appearing too set in his ways or distancing himself from others. This is a year for being a team player and being flexible in approach as well as playing an active role in all that goes on.

The Fire Pig also needs to stay well organized. With so much expected of him, he needs to be his efficient and productive self. Keeping his workplace tidy and knowing where everything is will help in a great many ways.

Many Fire Pigs will remain with their present employer this year and take advantage of internal opportunities, but for those wanting change or seeking work, the Monkey year will bring some interesting opportunities. By deciding on the type of work they would like to do and following up suitable openings, many Fire Pigs will secure a position which not only represents an interesting challenge but also offers the chance to use their skills in other ways. Admittedly, the first few weeks of any new job will be demanding, but this can be a great opportunity for the Fire Pig. For positive work developments, late March to June and October are especially favourable, but generally this is a year in which the Fire Pig should give his best, work closely with others and be adaptable.

The Fire Pig will also benefit from any training that is available or from following up subjects which he feels could be useful. Keeping his skills up to date will help his current situation and sometimes open up possibilities for later. The Fire Pig's self-development need not be restricted to his vocation, but can extend to his personal interests as well. If there is something which has been intriguing him and which he has been meaning to take up, he should follow it through, as it can be a satisfying and beneficial aspect of the year.

The Fire Pig will also enjoy some of the personal projects he sets himself. These could relate to his interests or his home or garden, but by giving himself an objective and carrying it through, he will be pleased with what he accomplishes. Again, however, the Fire Pig does need to talk to others and get support for what he has in mind, rather than act too independently.

The Fire Pig too needs to be careful when dealing with financial matters. His plans can involve considerable cost and whenever possible he should make provision for this in advance. Also, when making any purchases, he should ensure he is getting the most favourable terms and check any obligations he may be taking on. Large transactions should not be rushed and to prevent problems the Fire Pig does need to keep a check on his spending. Also, bearing in mind the trickier aspects of the year, he should avoid risky situations and if he has any uncertainties, obtain proper advice. Money matters *do* require care.

More favourably aspected, though, is the Fire Pig's personal life. Although his domestic life will often be busy, by helping out, being forthcoming and setting time aside for joint interests and family activities, the Fire Pig can look forward to a good rapport with his loved ones as well as to many fine occasions. He too will be pleased with the progress made by those dear to him and there could also be good cause for a family celebration over the year. By giving time to those who are important to him, the Fire Pig will find his family life both enjoyable and rewarding.

His social life is also favourably aspected. In addition to enjoying meeting up with friends, the Fire Pig will often be tempted to go out, and whether he is pursuing his interests or going to events that appeal to him, his social life will be enjoyable, do him good and lead to a widening of his circle.

In many respects this will be a satisfying year for the Fire Pig, particularly as it will allow him to further his skills and interests. However, throughout the year he does need to liaise with others and be prepared to adapt to changing situations. The Monkey year will require him to tread carefully, but his perceptive nature and talents will serve him well.

TIP FOR THE YEAR
Look to do something new. This could be a new role, interest, skill or project, but by giving yourself something to tackle which has an element of challenge about it, you will find the year all the more satisfying.

The Earth Pig

The Monkey year holds interesting prospects for the Earth Pig, but throughout he needs to remain aware of the traps it can suddenly spring. Sometimes everything seems to be going well, then problems and unexpected snags raise their head. Some parts of the Monkey year can be testing for the Earth Pig, but with his resourceful nature, he will still be able to make good headway as well as enjoy many aspects of the year.

In his work the Earth Pig will be able to build on his present position and put his strengths to good use. Many Earth Pigs, because of their experience and background, will be offered the chance to take on further responsibilities or will find themselves well placed for promotion. The Earth Pig should also make the most of his ideas. This is a year which favours both enterprise and creative endeavour, and some of the Earth Pig's suggestions could be well received. However, as with all Pigs in 2004, the Earth Pig does need to take careful note of the attitudes of colleagues and build up support. Also, he should remember that the Monkey year can contain its awkward moments and while he will often be ingenious in the way he deals with problems, again he should act closely with others rather than be too independent in approach.

While many Earth Pigs will decide to remain with their present employer, for those who feel they can better their prospects elsewhere or who are looking for work, the Monkey year will bring some splendid opportunities. To uncover these, though, the Earth Pig should actively follow up openings that interest him as well as approach companies or organizations which might have vacancies or be able to offer advice. In this way these Earth Pigs will often be able to secure a position which will be excellent for them. Late March to June and October could see some good opportunities, but by being his determined and enterprising self, the Earth Pig can make significant advances at any time of the year.

The Earth Pig does, though, need to be careful when dealing with financial matters. Here again the Monkey year's trickier aspects could raise their head and a mistake or risk could lead to problems. Similarly, when dealing with paperwork or forms related to finance, the Earth Pig needs to be vigilant and check all the details he may be required to submit. Although he is usually careful in such matters, an error or delay in replying could be to his detriment. Also, if there is a financial matter he does not understand or that is causing concern, he would do well to contact a helpline or seek professional advice. Financial paperwork and more general bureaucratic matters can, without care, prove troublesome this year. Earth Pigs, take note.

However, while vigilance is needed, the Earth Pig will be pleased with what he does with his money. He will be happy to spend it on his family and on useful acquisitions for his home – and here he could be fortunate in acquiring some bargains or ideal items in the most unusual of places

– as well as on more recreational activities, personal interests, trips out and forms of travel. With some thought and planning, the Earth Pig will find his spending brings both him and those close to him a good deal of pleasure.

Domestically, this will be a busy year, with the Earth Pig finding himself much in demand. His ability to organize and keep track of what everyone is doing will prove a real asset. His perceptive nature will also help, as he will be quick to realize when those in his household have problems or concerns. Here the Earth Pig's considerate nature and ability to relate so effectively will count for a great deal.

The Earth Pig will enjoy many of the family occasions and activities that take place, and again will often be instrumental in suggesting and arranging a great deal, including entertaining (the Earth Pig makes a superb host), practical home projects or activities and interests that can be shared. The Earth Pig will invariably make sure there is something happening or something to look forward to in his household.

His social life too will hold much promise, with the Earth Pig again enjoying meeting his friends and going to a variety of social events. He could also find his work and personal interests leading to a widening of his social circle. Any Earth Pigs who may have had some personal problems or who are seeking more companionship will find the Monkey year offering real hope. By going out more and being willing to move their lives forward, even though it may sometimes take a lot of effort, these Earth Pigs could soon find themselves meeting others and enjoying themselves that much more. For some, an important new romance or friendship could beckon. On a personal level, the Monkey year *is* favourably aspected. April, June, August and September are particularly good months for socializing and meeting others.

There will certainly be much for the Earth Pig to enjoy in the Monkey year, with his domestic and social life bringing many rewarding and pleasurable occasions. Work-wise, he will be able to make good use of his skills and make useful progress but he should remain aware that the year also has awkward aspects. In 2004 he needs to liaise with others, build up support for his ideas and activities and be careful when dealing with financial matters. If he heeds this advice, then he can do much to avoid some of the traps set by the Monkey year and reap *many* rewards.

TIP FOR THE YEAR
Make the most of your personal strengths. You really do relate well to others and during 2004 will gain by building up contacts as well as by talking to those around you. Your charm and ability to empathize are real assets and in this year when support is so essential, your talents will help you in a great many ways.

FAMOUS PIGS

Bryan Adams, Woody Allen, Julie Andrews, Marie Antoinette, Fred Astaire, Sir Richard Attenborough, Hector Berlioz, David Blunkett, Humphrey Bogart, James Cagney, Maria Callas, Richard Chamberlain, Hillary Rodham Clinton, Glenn Close, David Coulthard, Noël Coward, Oliver Cromwell, Billy Crystal, the Dalai Lama,

Ted Danson, Richard Dreyfuss, Ben Elton, Ralph Waldo Emerson, Sven-Goran Eriksson, Henry Ford, Emmylou Harris, Audley Harrison, William Randolph Hearst, Ernest Hemingway, Henry VIII, Conrad Hilton, Alfred Hitchcock, Sir Elton John, Tommy Lee Jones, Carl Gustav Jung, Boris Karloff, Charles Kennedy, Stephen King, Nastassja Kinski, Kevin Kline, Hugh Laurie, Nigella Lawson, David Letterman, Jerry Lee Lewis, Ewan McGregor, Marcel Marceau, Ricky Martin, Johnny Mathis, Meat Loaf, Wolfgang Amadeus Mozart, Camilla Parker Bowles, Michael Parkinson, Luciano Pavarotti, Iggy Pop, Prince Rainier of Monaco, Maurice Ravel, Ronald Reagan, Ginger Rogers, Salman Rushdie, Françoise Sagan, Pete Sampras, Carlos Santana, Arnold Schwarzenegger, Steven Spielberg, Holly Valance, Jules Verne, Michael Winner, the Duchess of York.

APPENDIX

---◆---

The relationship between the 12 animal signs, both on a personal level and business level, is an important aspect of Chinese horoscopes and in this appendix the compatibility between the signs is shown in the two tables that follow.

PERSONAL RELATIONSHIPS

KEY
1 Excellent. Great rapport.
2 A successful relationship. Many interests in common.
3 Mutual respect and understanding. A good relationship.
4 Fair. Needs care and some willingness to compromise in order for the relationship to work.
5 Awkward. Possible difficulties in communication with few interests in common.
6 A clash of personalities. Very difficult.

	Rat	Ox	Tiger	Rabbit	Dragon	Snake	Horse	Goat	Monkey	Rooster	Dog	Pig
Rat	1											
Ox	1	3										
Tiger	4	6	5									
Rabbit	5	2	3	2								
Dragon	1	5	4	3	2							
Snake	3	1	6	2	1	5						
Horse	6	5	1	5	3	4	2					
Goat	5	5	3	1	4	3	2	2				
Monkey	1	3	6	3	1	3	5	3	1			
Rooster	5	1	5	6	2	1	2	5	5	5		
Dog	3	4	1	2	6	3	1	5	3	5	2	
Pig	2	3	2	2	2	6	3	2	2	3	1	2

BUSINESS RELATIONSHIPS

KEY

1 Excellent. Marvellous understanding and rapport.
2 Very good. Complement each other well.
3 A good working relationship and understanding can be developed.
4 Fair, but compromise and a common objective are often needed to make this relationship work.
5 Awkward. Unlikely to work, either through lack of trust, understanding or the competitiveness of the signs.
6 Mistrust. Difficult. To be avoided.

	Rat	Ox	Tiger	Rabbit	Dragon	Snake	Horse	Goat	Monkey	Rooster	Dog	Pig
Rat	2											
Ox	1	3										
Tiger	3	6	5									
Rabbit	4	3	3	3								
Dragon	1	4	3	3	3							
Snake	3	2	6	4	1	5						
Horse	6	5	1	5	3	4	4					
Goat	5	5	3	1	4	3	3	2				
Monkey	2	3	4	5	1	5	4	4	3			
Rooster	5	1	5	5	2	1	2	5	5	6		
Dog	4	5	2	3	6	4	2	5	3	5	4	
Pig	3	3	3	2	3	5	4	2	3	4	3	1

YOUR ASCENDANT

The hours of the day are named after the 12 animal signs and the sign governing the time you were born is your ascendant.

The ascendant has a very strong influence on your personality and, together with the information already given about your sign and the effects of the element on your sign, it will help you gain an even greater insight into your true personality according to Chinese horoscopes.

To find your ascendant, look up the time of your birth on the table below, bearing in mind any local time differences in the place you were born.

11 p.m.	to	1 a.m.	The hours of the Rat
1 a.m.	to	3 a.m.	The hours of the Ox
3 a.m.	to	5 a.m.	The hours of the Tiger
5 a.m.	to	7 a.m.	The hours of the Rabbit
7 a.m.	to	9 a.m.	The hours of the Dragon
9 a.m.	to	11 a.m.	The hours of the Snake
11 a.m.	to	1 p.m.	The hours of the Horse
1 p.m.	to	3 p.m.	The hours of the Goat
3 p.m.	to	5 p.m.	The hours of the Monkey
5 p.m.	to	7 p.m.	The hours of the Rooster
7 p.m.	to	9 p.m.	The hours of the Dog
9 p.m.	to	11 p.m.	The hours of the Pig

RAT: The influence of the Rat as ascendant is likely to make the sign more outgoing, sociable and careful with money. A particularly beneficial influence for those born under the signs of the Rabbit, Horse, Monkey and Pig.

OX: The Ox as ascendant has a restraining, cautionary and steadying influence which many signs will benefit from. This ascendant also promotes self-confidence and will-power and is especially good for those born under the signs of the Tiger, Rabbit and Goat.

TIGER: This ascendant is a dynamic and stirring influence which makes the sign more outgoing, action-orientated and impulsive. A generally favourable ascendant for the Ox, Tiger, Snake and Horse.

RABBIT: The Rabbit as ascendant has a moderating influence, making the sign more reflective, serene and discreet. A particularly beneficial influence for the Rat, Dragon, Monkey and Rooster.

DRAGON: The Dragon as ascendant gives strength, determination and ambition to the sign. A favourable influence for those born under the signs of the Rabbit, Goat, Monkey and Dog.

SNAKE: The Snake as ascendant can make the sign more reflective, intuitive and self-reliant. A good influence for the Tiger, Goat and Pig.

HORSE: The influence of the Horse will make the sign more adventurous, daring and, on some occasions, fickle. Generally a beneficial influence for the Rabbit, Snake, Dog and Pig.

GOAT: This ascendant will make the sign more tolerant, easy-going and receptive. The Goat could also impart some creative and artistic qualities to the sign. An especially good influence for the Ox, Dragon, Snake and Rooster.

MONKEY: The Monkey as ascendant is likely to impart a delicious sense of humour and fun to the sign. This ascendant will make the sign more enterprising and outgoing – a particularly good influence for the Rat, Ox, Snake and Goat.

ROOSTER: The Rooster as ascendant helps to give the sign a lively, outgoing and very methodical manner. Its influence will increase efficiency and is good for the Ox, Tiger, Rabbit and Horse.

DOG: The Dog as ascendant makes the sign more reasonable and fair-minded as well as giving an added sense of loyalty. A very good ascendant for the Tiger, Dragon and Goat.

PIG: The influence of the Pig can make the sign more sociable, content and self-indulgent. It is also a caring influence and one which can make the sign want to help others. A good ascendant for the Dragon and Monkey.

HOW TO GET THE BEST FROM YOUR CHINESE SIGN AND THE YEAR

To supplement the earlier chapters on the personality and horoscope of the signs, I have included in this appendix a guide on how you can get the best out of your sign and the year.

Each of the 12 Chinese signs possesses its own unique strengths and by identifying them you can use them to your advantage. Similarly, by becoming aware of possible weaknesses you can do much to rectify them and in this respect I hope the following sections will be useful. Also included are some tips on how you can get the best from the Year of the Monkey. The areas covered are general prospects, career prospects, finance and relations with others.

THE RAT

The Rat is blessed with many fine talents, but his undoubted strength lies in his ability to get on with others. He is sociable, charming and a good judge of character. He also possesses a shrewd mind and is good at spotting opportunities.

However, to make the most of himself and his abilities, the Rat does need to impose some discipline upon himself. He should resist the temptation (sometimes very great!) of getting involved in too many activities all at the same time and decide upon his priorities and objectives. By concentrating his energies on specific matters he will fare much better as a result. Also, given his personable manner, he should seek out positions where he can use his personal relations skills to good effect. For a career, sales and marketing could prove ideal.

The Rat is also astute in dealing with finance, but while often thrifty, he can sometimes give way to moments of indulgence. Although he deserves to enjoy the money he has so carefully earned, it may sometimes be in his interests to exercise more restraint when tempted to satisfy too many expensive whims!

The Rat's family and friends are important to him and while he is loyal and protective towards them, he does tend to keep his worries and concerns to himself. He would be helped if he were more willing to discuss his anxieties. Others think highly of him and are prepared to do much to help him, but for them to do this he does need to be less secretive and guarded.

With his sharp mind, keen imagination and sociable manner the Rat does, however, have much in his favour. First, though, he should decide what he wants to achieve and then concentrate upon his chosen objectives. When he has commitment, the Rat can be irrepressible and, given his considerable charm, often be irresistible as well! Provided he channels his energies wisely, he can make much of his life.

Advice for the Rat's Year Ahead

GENERAL PROSPECTS

This will be a highly favourable year for the Rat and by taking action to secure what he wants and improve his situation, he will make good headway. His actions will bring him a greater level of satisfaction and often have long-term benefits.

CAREER PROSPECTS

With his skills and ability to get on well with most people, the Rat will find himself well placed to progress and make more of his talents. This is a time to seize the initiative and be bold.

FINANCE

The Rat's earning abilities will be in good form, with many Rats increasing their income and some being able to supplement it with other work. However, the Rat should still manage his resources carefully and, if possible, make provision for the future. Good management *will* be rewarded.

RELATIONS WITH OTHERS

The Rat can look forward to a rewarding personal life and will find himself in demand. This is an excellent year for romance, with many unattached Rats meeting someone who will become special. So favourable are the aspects that many will marry during the year. For those who have had some recent unhappiness, this is a year in which they should try to move their lives forward, perhaps by taking up new interests and meeting others. So many can benefit from the kindly and supportive nature of the Monkey year.

THE OX

Strong-willed, determined and resolute, the Ox certainly has a mind of his own! He is persistent and sets about achieving his objectives with a dogged determination. In addition he is reliable and tenacious and is often a source of inspiration to others. The Ox is a doer and an achiever and he often accomplishes a great deal. However, for him to really excel, he would do well to try and correct some of his weaknesses.

Being so resolute and having such a strong sense of purpose, the Ox can be inflexible and narrow-minded. He can be resistant to change and prefers to set about his activities in his own way rather than be too dependent on others. He should aim to be more outgoing and adventurous in his outlook. His dislike of change can sometimes be to his detriment and if he were prepared to be more adaptable he could find his progress easier.

The Ox would also be helped if he were to broaden his range of interests and become more relaxed in his approach. At times he can be so preoccupied with his own activities that he is not always as mindful of others as he should be and his demeanour can sometimes be studious and serious. There are times when he would benefit from a lighter touch.

However, the Ox is true to his word and loyal to his family and friends. He is admired and respected by others and his tremendous willpower usually enables him to achieve much in life.

Advice for the Ox's Year Ahead

GENERAL PROSPECTS
A pleasing year. Events may sometimes move swiftly, but by taking advantage of the opportunities that become available and following up his ideas, the Ox can do himself a lot of good.

CAREER PROSPECTS
A year of opportunity which will allow the Ox to use his strengths well. There will be some excellent chances for him to advance his position, but he will need to act quickly and be prepared to seize the initiative. This is a year to be bold and swift.

FINANCE
The Ox's earning abilities will be in good form and by managing his situation well and planning major purchases, he will be pleased with how he fares. If possible, he would find it helpful to reduce his borrowings and add to his savings.

RELATIONS WITH OTHERS
A personally rewarding year. By spending time with those who are important to him, the Ox can look forward to many agreeable occasions as well as benefit from the

support and advice he receives. On a social level his prospects are especially encouraging, with excellent opportunities for establishing new friendships and for romance.

THE TIGER

Lively, innovative and enterprising, the Tiger enjoys an active lifestyle. He has a wide range of interests, an alert mind and a genuine liking of others. He likes to live life to the full. However, despite his enthusiastic and well-meaning ways, he does not always make the most of his considerable potential.

By being so versatile, the Tiger does have a tendency to jump from one activity to another or dissipate his energies by trying to do too much at the same time. To make the most of himself he should try to exercise a certain amount of self-discipline. Ideally, he should decide how best he can use his abilities, give himself some objectives and stick to them. If he can overcome his restless tendencies, he will find he will accomplish much more.

Also, in spite of his sociable manner, the Tiger likes to retain a certain independence in his actions, and while few begrudge him this, he would sometimes find life easier if he were more prepared to work in conjunction with others. His reliance upon his own judgement does sometimes mean that he excludes the views and advice of those around him, and this can be to his detriment. The Tiger may possess an independent spirit, but he must not let it go too far!

The Tiger does, however, have much in his favour. He is bold, original and quick-witted. If he can keep his restless nature in check, he can enjoy considerable success. In addition, with his engaging personality, he is much admired and well liked.

Advice for the Tiger's Year Ahead

GENERAL PROSPECTS
There will be good chances for the Tiger to make much of his talents and ideas this year, but he does need to be thorough and careful in all he does. A year for progress, but at the same time not a year for throwing caution to the wind!

CAREER PROSPECTS
There will be excellent chances to move to a more rewarding position and by taking on new challenges many Tigers will discover new strengths. With the year favouring enterprise, the Tiger could find some of his ideas well received.

FINANCE
A good year, but there will be many temptations to spend and some control of the purse strings would be wise. With travel well aspected, it would be worth setting money aside for holidays and breaks.

RELATIONS WITH OTHERS
The Tiger can look forward to some happy and rewarding times in both his domestic and social life. However he does need to be mindful of the views of others. Dialogue will be important as well as helpful in maintaining rapport. Shared

activities and interests should be encouraged and will lead to some agreeable occasions.

THE RABBIT

The Rabbit is certainly one who appreciates the finer things in life. With his good taste, companionable nature and wide range of interests, he knows how to live well – and usually does!

However, for all his finesse and style, the Rabbit does possess traits he would do well to watch. His desire for a settled lifestyle makes him err on the side of caution. He dislikes change and as a consequence can miss out on opportunities. Also, there are many Rabbits who will go to great lengths to avoid difficult and fraught situations, and again, while few may relish these, sometimes in life it is necessary to take risks or stand your ground. At times it would certainly be in the Rabbit's interests to be bolder and more assertive in going after what he desires.

The Rabbit also attaches great importance to his relations with others and while he has a happy knack of getting on with most people, he can be sensitive to criticism. Difficult though it may be, he should really try to develop a thicker skin and recognize that criticism can provide valuable learning opportunities, as can some of the problems he strives so hard to avoid.

However, with his agreeable manner, keen intellect and shrewd judgement, the Rabbit does have a lot in his favour and invariably makes much of his life – and usually enjoys it too!

Advice for the Rabbit's Year Ahead

GENERAL PROSPECTS
A reasonable year ahead, although the Rabbit will need to pay close attention to all that is going on as well as be prepared to consult others and listen closely to their views. This is not a time to be too independent in his actions. A good year to develop personal interests.

CAREER PROSPECTS
The best results will come from making the most of existing strengths and developing skills. Opportunities will arise, but the Rabbit will need to be on his mettle and prepared to give his best. Yet what is achieved now will often have long-term significance.

FINANCE
The Rabbit will need to be his prudent and careful self. This is not a year for risks or for being less than thorough when handling money matters or dealing with important paperwork. Mistakes and delays could prove costly.

RELATIONS WITH OTHERS
This year holds great promise, with excellent prospects for romance and building new friendships. In addition to enjoying the company of others, the Rabbit will benefit by being forthcoming and sharing ideas, plans and activities with those close to him.

THE DRAGON

Enthusiastic, enterprising and honourable, the Dragon possesses many admirable qualities and his life is often full and varied. He always gives his best and even though not all his endeavours may meet with success, he is nonetheless resilient and hardy, and is much admired and respected.

However, for all his many qualities, the Dragon can be blunt and forthright and, through sheer strength of character, sometimes domineering. It would certainly be in his interests to listen more closely to others rather than be so self-reliant. Also, his enthusiasm can sometimes get the better of him and he can be impulsive. To make the most of his abilities, he should set himself priorities and set about his activities in a disciplined and systematic way. More tact and diplomacy might not go amiss either!

However, with his lively and outgoing manner, the Dragon is popular and well liked. With good fortune on his side (and the Dragon is often lucky), his life is almost certain to be eventful and fulfilling. He has many talents and if he uses them wisely he will enjoy much success.

Advice for the Dragon's Year Ahead

GENERAL PROSPECTS
The Monkey year favours action and enterprise, and the Dragon, with his flair, is set to do particularly well. This is a year for seizing the initiative and making the most of his experience and ideas. Fortune will favour the brave.

CAREER PROSPECTS

In 2004 the Dragon will often find himself in the right place at the right time and will make good progress. This is a year for putting himself forward and looking to advance.

FINANCE

An expensive year and the Dragon should budget carefully and be thorough when taking on any new commitments. This is not a year for risks or proceeding in too ad hoc a manner.

RELATIONS WITH OTHERS

The Dragon enjoys company and he will certainly be in demand over the year. He will gain a great deal by consulting others and in certain instances should consider a more accommodating approach rather than hold so rigidly to his views. An excellent year for romance and making new friends.

THE SNAKE

The Snake is blessed with a keen intellect. He has wide interests, an enquiring mind and good judgement. He tends to be quiet and thoughtful and plans his activities with considerable care. With his fine abilities he often does well in life, but he does possess traits which can undermine his progress.

The Snake is often guarded in his actions and sometimes loses out to those who are more action-oriented and assertive. He can also be a loner and likes to retain a certain independence in his actions, and this too can hamper his progress. It would be in his interests to be more forthcoming and involve others more readily in his plans. The Snake has many talents and possesses a warm and rich personality, but there is a danger that this can remain concealed behind his often quiet and reserved manner. He would fare better by being more outgoing and showing others his true worth.

However, the Snake is very much his own master. He invariably knows what he wants in life and is often prepared to journey long and hard to achieve his objectives. He does, though, have it in his power to make that journey easier. Lose some of that reticence, Snake, be more open and assertive, and do not be afraid of the occasional risk!

Advice for the Snake's Year Ahead

GENERAL PROSPECTS
To do well in the Monkey year the Snake must conquer his independent tendencies, seek support for his ideas, be forthcoming and liaise with others. Although he may like to determine his own course, by being prepared to adapt to changing situations he can do his prospects much good.

CAREER PROSPECTS
Although the year will bring challenges and some pressures, it will give the Snake an excellent chance to draw on his experience and show some of his best qualities. This is a year when effort will be rewarded and there will be good opportunities for those seeking work or hoping to move on.

FINANCE

The Snake's earning abilities will be in good form. However, the Monkey year will bring many temptations to spend and he must watch his outgoings. If possible, he should aim to add to his savings.

RELATIONS WITH OTHERS

The Snake values the love and support of those around him and even in this busy year should always set aside time for them. For the unattached, romance is particularly well favoured, while the lonely Snake should resolve to go out more and meet others. Family and social activities can bring much happiness.

THE HORSE

Versatile, hard-working and sociable, the Horse makes his mark wherever he goes. He has an eloquent and engaging manner and makes friends with ease. He is quick-witted, has an alert mind and is certainly not averse to taking risks or experimenting with new ideas.

The Horse possesses a strong and likeable personality, but he does also have his weaknesses. With his wide interests he does not always finish everything he starts and he would do well to be more persevering. He has it within him to achieve considerable success, but when he has made his plans he should stick with them. To make the most of his talents he does need to overcome his restless tendencies.

The Horse loves company and values both his family and friends. However, there will have been many a time when he has lost his temper or spoken in haste and regretted his words. Throughout his life, he needs to keep his temper in check and be diplomatic in tense situations. If not, he could risk jeopardizing the respect and good relations he so values.

However, the Horse has a multitude of talents and a lively and outgoing personality. If he can overcome his restless and volatile nature, he can lead a rich and highly fulfilling life.

Advice for the Horse's Year Ahead

GENERAL PROSPECTS
The Horse is a doer and he will be greatly encouraged by the activity and opportunities that the Monkey year will bring. By making the most of his opportunities and getting support for his activities, he will find this an auspicious year. It is a time to be bold, seize the initiative and forge ahead with plans and ideas.

CAREER PROSPECTS
A year of opportunity. With his experience and fine repu-tation, the Horse will find himself well placed to go after some of the openings that arise, and by acting quickly and decisively, he can do much to improve his position. His new duties will enable him to develop his skills and he will feel more inspired than for some time.

FINANCE
An improved income plus the possibility of funds from another source will lift the Horse's financial position.

However, he does still need to watch his spending as well as be careful with any important financial matters or agreements he enters into. This is not a year for risks.

RELATIONS WITH OTHERS
The Horse will be in good form and will enjoy an active social life. The aspects are good for making new friends and for romance. The Horse is also likely to devote much time and energy to his home, perhaps even move house. However, while he will be eager to go ahead with his plans, sometimes more thought and consultation and less haste would be to his advantage.

THE GOAT

The Goat has a warm, friendly and understanding manner and gets on well with most people. He is generally easy-going, has a fond appreciation of the finer things in life and possesses a rich imagination. He is often artistic and enjoys the creative arts and outdoor activities.

However, despite his engaging manner, there lurks beneath his skin a sometimes tense and pessimistic nature. The Goat can be a worrier and without the support and encouragement of others can feel insecure and be hesitant in his actions.

To make the most of himself the Goat should aim to become more assertive and decisive as well as more at ease with himself. He has much in his favour, but he really does need to promote himself more and be bolder in his actions. He would also be helped if he were to sort out his priorities and set about his activities in an organized and disciplined manner. There are some Goats who tend to be haphazard in the way they go about things and this can hamper their progress.

Although the Goat will always value the support of others, it would also be in his interests to become more independent and not be so reticent about striking out on his own. He does, after all, possess many talents, as well as a sincere and likeable personality, and by always giving his best he can make his life rich, rewarding and enjoyable.

Advice for the Goat's Year Ahead

GENERAL PROSPECTS

The Goat could feel uneasy with the activity and pressures the Monkey year will bring, but this is a time to adapt and make the most of changing situations. With a willing attitude, important advances can be made.

CAREER PROSPECTS

This will be a year of change with many Goats taking on new responsibilities or having to adjust their role in some way. Although some of the Goat's new tasks and duties will seem challenging, they will enable him to widen his experience and often discover new strengths.

FINANCE

A positive year, but to benefit the Goat needs to manage his money well. He will need to keep a tight control over his purse strings and avoid succumbing to too many impulsive buys.

RELATIONS WITH OTHERS

The Goat will be in fine form and will be greatly encouraged by the support he receives. This is a year for joining with others, carrying out joint interests and projects and engaging in dialogue. Both domestically and socially this will be a good year, and Goats seeking more company and perhaps love will find the Monkey year particularly supportive.

THE MONKEY

Lively, enterprising and innovative, the Monkey certainly knows how to impress. He has wide interests, a good sense of fun and relates well to others. He also possesses a shrewd mind and often has a happy knack of turning events to his advantage.

However, despite his versatility and considerable gifts, the Monkey does have his weaknesses. He often lacks persistence, can get distracted easily and also places tremendous reliance upon his own judgement. While his belief in himself is a commendable asset, it would certainly be in his interests to be more mindful of the views of others. Also, while he likes to keep tabs on all that is going on around him, he can be evasive and secretive with regard to his own feelings and activities, and again a more forth-coming attitude would be to his advantage.

In his desire to succeed the Monkey can also be tempted to cut corners or be crafty and he should recognize that such actions can rebound on him!

However, the Monkey is resourceful and his sheer strength of character will ensure he has an interesting and varied life. If he can channel his considerable energies wisely and overcome his sometimes restless tendencies, his life can be crowned with success and achievement. Added to which, with his amiable personality, he will enjoy the friendship of many.

Advice for the Monkey's Year Ahead

GENERAL PROSPECTS

An excellent year ahead, but to benefit the Monkey will need to take action. With clear ideas and determination, he will be able to accomplish a great deal and often enjoy himself in the process. This is, though, a year that calls for purposeful action.

CAREER PROSPECTS

With his experience, contacts and knowledge, the Monkey will find he is well placed to take advantage of the opportunities that become available. He should make the most of his ideas and will find his resourceful and innovative approach an often winning combination. This is a year to advance.

FINANCE

The Monkey will enjoy an improvement in his financial situation, but rather than be tempted to spend too readily, should give careful consideration to his purchases and his other plans.

RELATIONS WITH OTHERS

The Monkey will be in great form and can look forward to an active domestic and social life. By being forthcoming with his ideas, he will welcome the support he receives as well as enjoy many fine occasions. The prospects are excellent for making new friends and for romance.

THE ROOSTER

With his considerable bearing and incisive and resolute manner, the Rooster cuts an impressive figure. He has a sharp mind, is well informed on many matters and expresses himself clearly and convincingly. He is meticulous and efficient in his undertakings and commands much respect. He also has a genuine and caring interest in others.

The Rooster has much in his favour, but there are some aspects of his character that can tell against him. He can be candid in his views and sometimes over-zealous in his actions, and without forethought he can say or do things he later regrets. His high standards also make him fussy, even pedantic, and he can get diverted into relatively minor matters when in truth he could be occupying his time more profitably. This is something all Roosters would do well to watch. Also, while the Rooster is a great planner, he can sometimes be unrealistic in his expectations. In making plans – in most of his activities – he would do well to consult others. By doing so, he will greatly benefit from their input.

The Rooster has considerable talents as well as a commendable drive and commitment, but to make the most of himself he does need to channel his energies wisely and watch his candid and sometimes volatile nature. With care, however, he can make a success of his life, and with his wide interests and outgoing personality, he will enjoy the friendship and respect of many.

Advice for the Rooster's Year Ahead

GENERAL PROSPECTS
The Rooster likes to follow set patterns and procedures, but the Monkey year could have different ideas. Sudden changes could upset the Rooster's plans, but by being willing to adapt and make the most of situations, important gains can be made. The Rooster should not be too rigid in his approach, but go with the flow.

CAREER PROSPECTS
The Rooster can advance his position over the year as well as further his skills and experience, but to benefit fully he will need to make the most of the chances that arise, even though they may be different from what he may have been hoping for.

FINANCE
The Rooster needs to manage his money well, setting funds aside for specific requirements and purchases. Without some control, he could find his spending creeping up and his money not always being put to its best use.

RELATIONS WITH OTHERS
The Rooster can enjoy both his domestic and social life and, for some, love, romance and marriage can make the year all the more special. However, the Rooster does need to be mindful of others and be accommodating in his attitude.

Too many candid remarks or insisting on having his own way could endanger an otherwise positive year. Roosters, you mean so well, but do take care!

THE DOG

Loyal, dependable and with a good understanding of human nature, the Dog is well placed to win the respect and admiration of many. He is a no-nonsense sort of person and hates any sort of hypocrisy and falsehood. With the Dog you know where you stand and, given his direct manner, where he stands on any issue. He also has a strong humanitarian nature and often champions good and just causes.

The Dog has many fine attributes, although there are certain traits that can prevent him from either enjoying or making the most of his life. He is a great worrier and can get anxious over all manner of things. Although it may not always be easy, he should try to rid himself of the 'worry habit'. Whenever he is tense or concerned, he should be prepared to speak to others rather than shoulder his worries all by himself. In some cases, they could even be of his own making! Also, the Dog has a tendency to look on the pessimistic side and he would certainly be helped if he were to view his undertakings more optimistically. He does, after all, possess many skills and should justifiably have faith in his abilities. Another weakness is his tendency to be stubborn over certain issues. If he is not careful, this could at times undermine his position.

If the Dog can reduce the worrying and pessimistic side of his nature, then he will not only enjoy life more but also find he is achieving more. He possesses a truly admirable character and his loyalty, reliability and sincerity are appreciated by all he meets. In his life he will do much good and befriend many – and he owes it to himself to enjoy life too. Sometimes it might help him to recall the words of another Dog, Sir Winston Churchill: 'When I look back on all these worries I remember the story of the old man who said on his deathbed that he had had a lot of trouble in his life, most of which never happened.'

Advice for the Dog's Year Ahead

GENERAL PROSPECTS

The Dog will enjoy the active nature of the Monkey year and by making the most of his ideas and following up the often good opportunities that come his way, he will make good progress. This is very much a year for action and will suit the Dog.

CAREER PROSPECTS

By drawing on his skills and experience and looking for opportunities to pursue, the Dog can make good headway. This is a year for action, enterprise and for the Dog to keep faith with his abilities. He has much to offer and this year his efforts will lead to some important advances.

FINANCE

A positive year, but resources do need to be managed well, particularly as many Dogs will move or make expensive purchases for their accommodation.

RELATIONS WITH OTHERS

A busy year, sometimes made all the busier by a change of residence. However, the Dog will welcome the support he is given by family and friends and there could also be celebrations in store, with some Dogs becoming engaged, marrying, seeing an addition to their family or having some other good cause for rejoicing. On a personal level, the Monkey year holds exciting prospects.

THE PIG

Genial, sincere and trusting, the Pig gets on well with most people. He has a kind and caring nature, a dislike of discord and often a good sense of humour. In addition, he has a fondness for socializing and enjoying the good life!

The Pig also possesses a shrewd mind, is particularly adept at dealing with business and financial matters, and has a robust and resilient nature. Although not all his plans may work out as he would like, he is tenacious and will often rise up and succeed after experiencing setbacks and difficulties. In his often active and varied life he can accomplish a great deal, although there are certain aspects of his character that can tell against him. If he can modify these or keep them in check then his life will certainly be easier and possibly even more successful.

In his activities the Pig can sometimes overcommit himself and while he does not want to disappoint, he would certainly be helped if he were to set about his activities in an organized and systematic manner and give himself priorities at busy times. He should not allow others to take advantage of his good nature and it would be in his interests to be more discerning. There will have been times when he has been gullible and naïve; fortunately, though, he quickly learns from his mistakes. He also possesses a stubborn streak and if new situations do not fit in with his line of thinking, he can be inflexible. Such an attitude may not always be to his advantage.

The Pig is a great pleasure-seeker and while he should enjoy the fruits of his labours, he can sometimes be self-indulgent and extravagant. This again is something he would do well to watch.

However, though the Pig may possess some faults, those who come into contact with him are invariably impressed by his integrity, amiable manner and intelligence. If he uses his talents wisely, his life can be crowned with considerable achievement and the good-hearted Pig will also be loved and respected by many.

Advice for the Pig's Year Ahead

GENERAL PROSPECTS

The Monkey year holds fine prospects, but to benefit the Pig must ensure he has support for his activities and liaises with others. His usually kind and sociable manner will help, but this is not a year for going it alone or being too independent in attitude.

CAREER PROSPECTS

There will certainly be chances for the Pig to make headway in 2004, but to do well he needs to work closely with colleagues and show himself a good team member. Also, he should not allow his often high standards to slip. This is a year for care, hard work and vigilance, but in return the Pig will be rewarded for his endeavours and will enhance his prospects.

FINANCE

Great care is needed and the Pig should watch his spending as well as check the details of any new commitment he takes on. This is not a year for risks.

RELATIONS WITH OTHERS

The Pig's family and social life will both mean a great deal and provide him with many rewarding and happy occasions. His input into family life will be especially appreciated. For the unattached, this can be a significant year, with the prospects of romance and, for some, marriage. All Pigs will see a widening of their social circle and will relish the opportunities to go out and enjoy themselves in fine style.

Make
www.thorsonselement.com
your online sanctuary

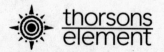